IMAGES
of America

COQUILLE

On the Cover: In 1903, the second *Dispatch* was built by Charles Trigg at Parkersburg and commissioned by the Coquille River Transportation Company. Please see page 24 for more information. (Courtesy of Robyn Greenlund.)

IMAGES
of America

COQUILLE

Bert Dunn, Andie E. Jensen, Yvonne-Cher Skye,
and the Coquille Valley Museum

ARCADIA
PUBLISHING

ISBN 978-1-4671-2949-7

Published by Arcadia Publishing
Charleston, South Carolina

Printed in the United States of America

Library of Congress Control Number: 2018960363

For all general information, please contact Arcadia Publishing:
Telephone 843-853-2070
Fax 843-853-0044
E-mail sales@arcadiapublishing.com
For customer service and orders:
Toll-Free 1-888-313-2665

Visit us on the Internet at www.arcadiapublishing.com

CONTENTS

ACKNOWLEDGMENTS

Authoring a book is not the work of one person. Many contributors have provided their knowledge and family photographs to make this book a reality. First and foremost, we must acknowledge the Coquille Valley Museum, Coos History Museum, Bandon Historical Society Museum, and Douglas County Museum. If not for their vast collections of photographs, an undertaking such as this would have been far more difficult to present. We thank executive director Susan Tisso, collections manager Debra Semrau, and volunteer Joan Grief of the Coos History Museum. We thank executive director Galye Nix and board president Jim Proehl of the Bandon Historical Society Museum. We thank director Jamie Davis and research librarian Karen Bratton of the Douglas County Museum. We give a very special thanks to Coquille Valley Museum volunteer Mary Barton for all her hours of photographic research and scanning.

The "Native People and Settlement" chapter could not have been completed without the knowledge and expertise of cultural anthropologist Denni Hockema and tribal historic preservation officer Kassandra Rippee of the Coquille Indian tribe.

Many more individuals have provided their family photographs and knowledge of the area to enhance the quality of this book. We give our thanks to the following people: Robyn Greenlund, Jay Farr, Bill Wells, Lance Nix, Ray Thurman, Cheri Walker, and Vonnie Major.

A photograph credit appears at the end of each caption. Abbreviations include CVM for Coquille Valley Museum, CHM for Coos History Museum, BM for Bandon Historical Society Museum, DCM for Douglas County Museum, CIT for Coquille Indian tribe, ODOT for Oregon Department of Transportation, RG for Robyn Greenlund, JF for Jay Farr, BW for Bill Wells, VM for Vonnie Major, and LN for Lance Nix.

Introduction

For thousands of years, Native Americans inhabited the Coquille Valley. Just prior to settlement by peoples of European descent, the area was occupied by the Upper Coquille native people. The Coquille River was likely the center of their world, as it provided essential food and a means of transportation. The climate was mild and moist, while the abundant forests provided critical building materials.

These attributes of the Coquille Valley proved to be important to the settlers of European descent who sought lands that could support farming and ranching. The valley had considerable bottomland compared to other coastal areas, including the Coos River. The surrounding hills offered vast quantities of virgin timber, gold, and coal deposits that attracted the settlers.

The Coquille Valley was first known to the early settlers as the Scoquel Country. As settlers moved into the region, the river and the people living nearby became known as the Coquell or Coquelle. When early government treaties were written about the area, the local tribespeople were called Coquille, and this spelling was printed on maps.

While a few explorers visited the area earlier, Evan Cunningham was the first to establish a home in the area that became Coquille. He arrived in 1855 and served as a soldier who reported to Fort Kitchen near Myrtle Point. As others settled in the area, he established the first school near Cunningham Creek. In 1871, Tillman Vowell and other settlers established the first store in the area that became downtown Coquille. This site was chosen because it is a small plateau high enough above the river to escape seasonal floodwaters.

With the initial establishment of stores in the new settlement, the first riverboats began to frequent the location. Hence, the waterfront development began. In 1880, a sawmill was built by Bunch, Bennett & Company on the waterfront. The output of this sawmill supported the construction of wood-framed homes and commercial buildings. The community grew and remained dependent on the river. Travel to communities up and down the river was relatively easy, but travel to Marshfield was difficult. In 1884, a wagon road was completed from Coquille to Marshfield, improving this situation. Commercial businesses such as a bank, a brewery, hotels, taverns, and stores were established along the Front Street waterfront. Unfortunately, in 1892, a major fire destroyed most of the downtown.

The city rebuilt quickly along Front Street, including the construction of the landmark Hotel Coquille. This activity was encouraged by the anticipated arrival of a railroad. The railroad was completed from Marshfield to Myrtle Point in 1893 with tracks laid on Front Street. Coquille was now connected to the rest of the county via river, wagon roads, and railroad. This ease of access and its central location led to the county seat being moved from Empire to Coquille. In 1898, an impressive courthouse was completed in Coquille. A growing population led to the construction of a significantly larger public school. During this period, several large homes were constructed near downtown. Both sides of Front Street were occupied with businesses for two blocks. In conjunction with the arrival of the railroad, river commerce and the waterfront continued to increase. As a result, newer and larger riverboats were built.

In 1900, electric power was introduced to the area by the Johnson Mill, which produced it until the mill was destroyed by fire in 1910. Thereafter, power was generated at two locations: the downtown sawmill and the Peart Brothers coal mine near where Jefferson School was later located.

In 1909–1910, three large brick buildings were constructed that remain today: the First National Bank Building, the Richmond-Barker Building (currently used by the Coquille Broiler), and the Laird Building.

When the first automobiles appeared in Coquille, the town had wood-planked roads, while wagon roads were unpaved, rough, and seasonally closed, making travel difficult beyond the city. This was an interesting period of transportation via horses, railroads, riverboats, and early autos.

In 1911, a second sawmill was built just west of downtown supported by local investors, including Joseph Collier and Louis Simpson. This mill would later become famous as the Sitka Spruce Mill in World War I. Three creameries were built in or near the city producing milk, butter, and cheese. By 1915, most of the city streets were paved. In 1918, another major fire engulfed Coquille. This time, the fire centered on First Street and destroyed several buildings.

In 1921, a paved highway was completed from Marshfield to Coquille. It was conceived as part of the Roosevelt Military Coast Highway, later to be named Highway 101. The concrete road surface was only 16 feet wide. The following year, the steel bridge over the river was completed. Thereafter, improved roads were built to Bandon and Myrtle Point. These road improvements promoted travel to and from Coquille and gave a major boost to commerce within the city. However, the riverboats that had plied the Coquille River for 50 years quickly fell into disuse.

About 1923, a third sawmill was built by the Oerding brothers. This mill was south of downtown, where the Georgia-Pacific mill was later located. They cut white cedar and myrtle wood. In 1924, a new three-story concrete Hotel Coquille was constructed after fire damaged the earlier wood-framed version. This impressive addition gave the downtown a more urban appearance.

In the late 1920s, the Oerding mill was sold. Smith-Wood Products was established on the same site with an emphasis on producing battery separators made from white cedar. George Ulett was a major contributor to this business. In the 1930s, he was instrumental in expanding the mill to produce plywood using Douglas fir logs. The mill was later sold to Coos Bay Lumber Company and then to Georgia-Pacific.

In 1952, George Ulett helped build the Coquille Plywood Mill at Cedar Point, about one mile north of downtown. The mill was later sold to Textron and then Roseburg Lumber Company.

In 1960, Highway 101, which had given Coquille such a boost earlier in its history, was rerouted to bypass Coquille. This resulted in a major setback for retail businesses. Although growth slowed, the town remained relatively healthy until the 1980s, when recession and new reduced harvesting of federal timber severely slowed the wood products industry.

Please note that references to streets in this book will be done using current street names. An exception to this is Front Street, which later became Main Street and Highway 42.

One

Native Peoples and Settlement

The Upper Coquille native peoples inhabited the Coquille Valley for centuries. The Upper Coquille spoke an Athabaskan dialect related to the languages of the Apache and Navaho people of the American Southwest, as well as some native peoples of Alaska. Lower Coquille peoples spoke a different language.

Most of the Upper Coquille villages were on the upper main stem, the South and Middle Forks of the Coquille River. The North Fork had seasonal camps, gathering areas, and fish camps. Seasonal villages or gathering areas tended to exist where food items or raw materials were available to be harvested or processed. In the past, there were 32 known villages for the Upper Coquille people on the Coquille River.

The Coquille Valley was known to early settlers as the Scoquel Country. This spelling appeared in the *Oregonian* on January 7, 1854, in an advertisement by Perry B. Marple, whose Coose Bay Company explored and exploited Coos Bay. *Scoquel* was defined as the Indian name for eel. Marple tried to preserve the name in his correspondences. As settlers moved into the region, the river and the people living near it became known as Coquell or Coquelle. When the area's first governmental treaties were written, Coquille became the name of the tribe. Coquille appeared in a map of 1855 by G.H. Goddard from explorations of Gov. Isaac Stevens.

Evan Cunningham was the first to establish a home in the area that would become Coquille City. He arrived in 1855 and served as a soldier reporting to Fort Kitchen near Myrtle Point. As others came to the area, he established the first school near Cunningham Creek. Titus B. Willard is credited with establishing the town.

During the 2010 US Census, Coquille's population was 3,868, of which less than two percent were Native Americans. The small town of Coquille continues to thrive and has made a noticeable mark in Coos County history.

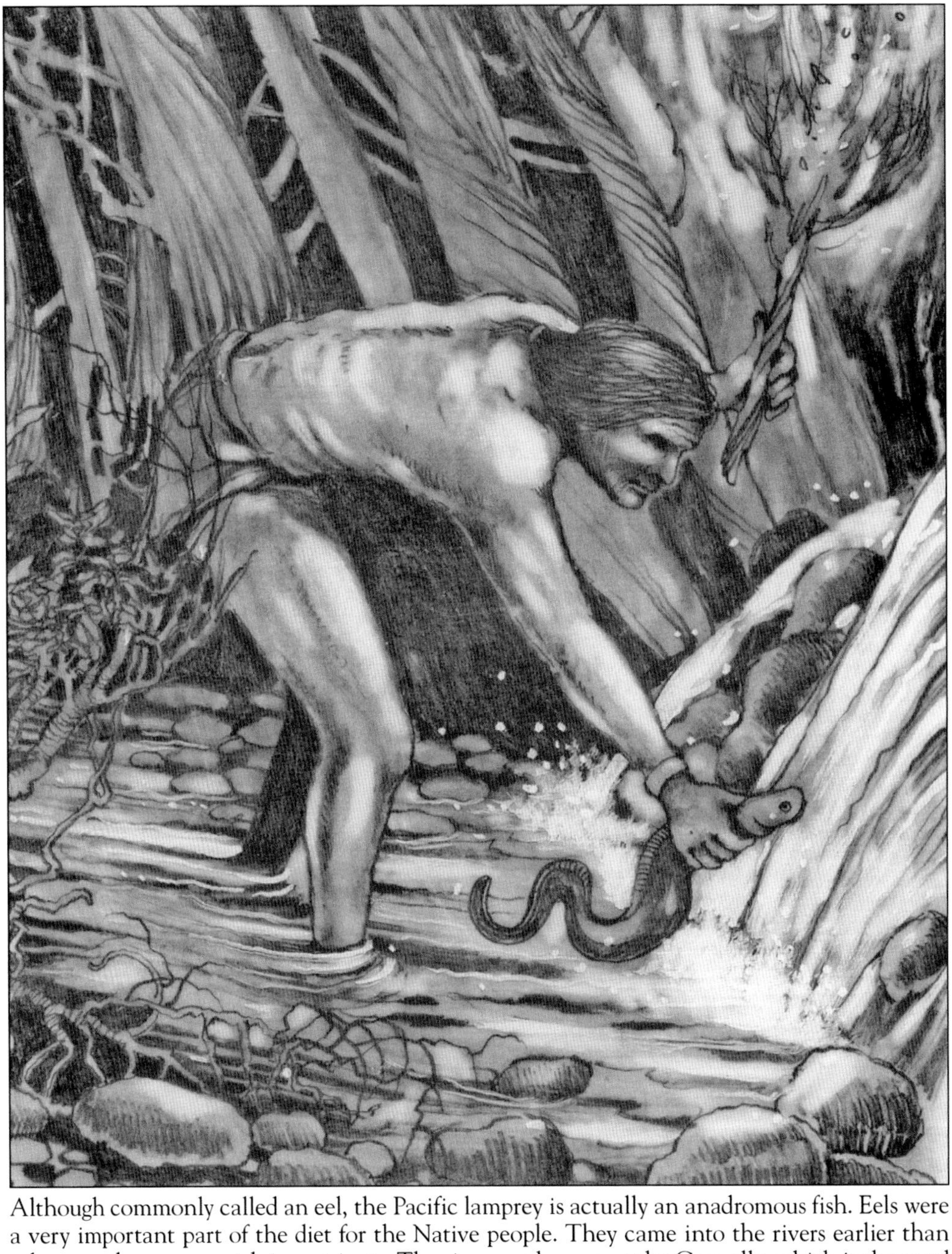

Although commonly called an eel, the Pacific lamprey is actually an anadromous fish. Eels were a very important part of the diet for the Native people. They came into the rivers earlier than salmon and were very rich in nutrients. The river was known as the Coquelle, which is the word for eel in Chinuk Wawa, and the town was known as Ko kwel. This pronunciation was used well into the 20th century. When discussing the tribe, the correct pronunciation is "ko-kwel." It is a way of honoring the traditions of the tribe and its elders. As early settlers moved into the region, the river and the people living near it became known as Coquell or Coquelle. Early treaties identified the tribe as Coquille, spelled like the French word for shell. Sometime after Coquille City was established, the pronunciation shifted from "ko-kwel" to "ko-keel." (CIT.)

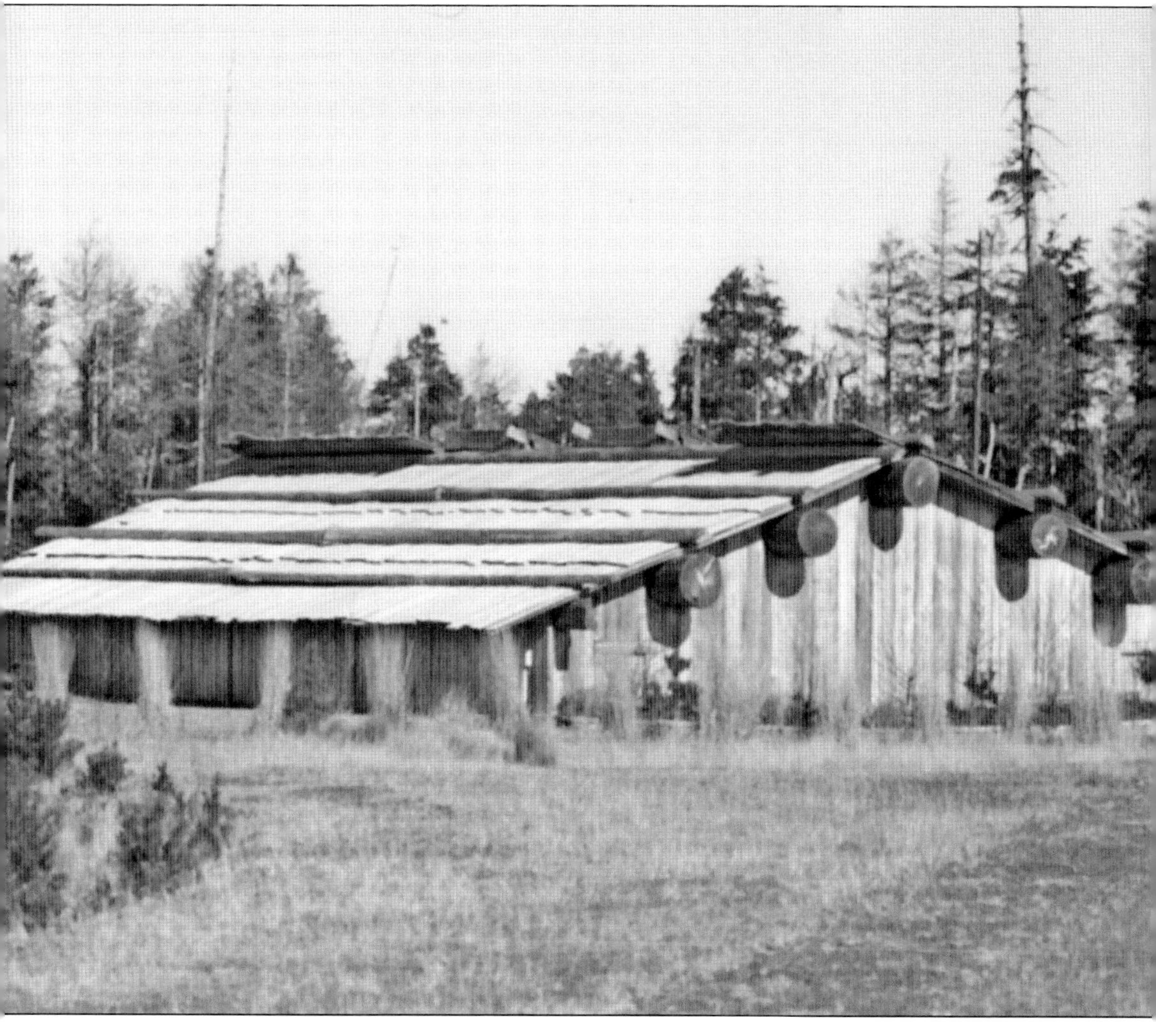

Village Lhanhashdan was three miles downstream from Coquille. There was also a village about two miles upstream. Both were year-round villages, and the Natives lived in plank houses similar to the one shown. The Coquille Community Plankhouse was built in 2005 by Coquille people using cedar and fir timber from the Coquille Forest. The cedar tree is sacred to the Coquille people and symbolizes the deep connection they have to the land. The purpose of the building is to host tribal events, such as weddings, funerals, and annual gatherings, so it was constructed much larger than a traditional plank house. The planks on the walls and the roof were hand split in the traditional manner; the floor is a rubber compound mixed with dirt to replicate a traditional clay floor. As tribal heritage dictates, the entry door is round and faces the water—in this case, the ocean and a lake. (CIT.)

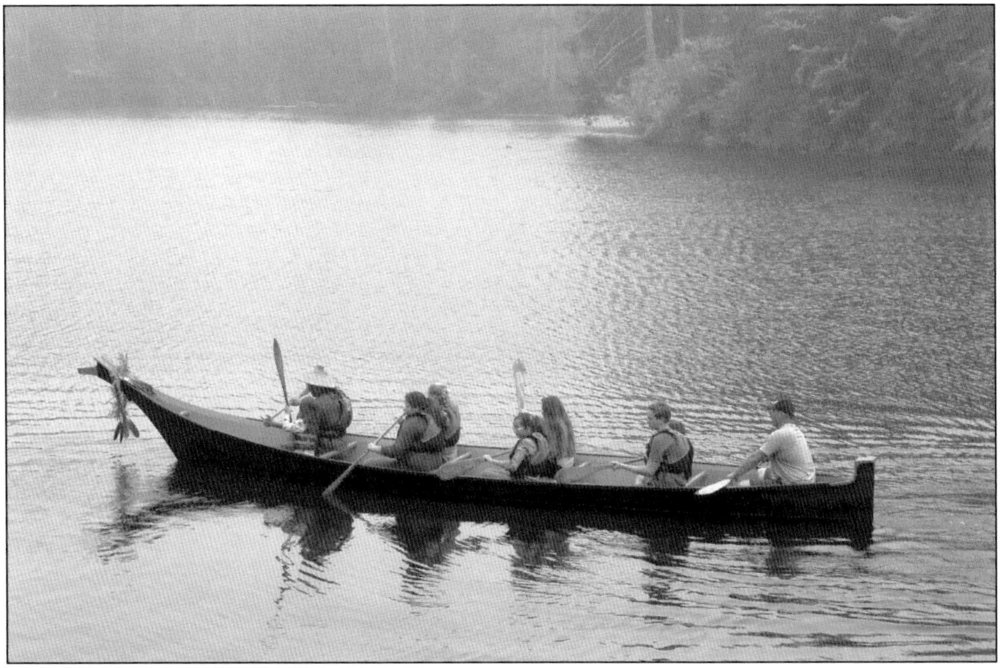

The canoe was the main source of transportation for the Coquille people for thousands of years. The tribe uses several different styles of canoes, which were used by youths and adults. Above are youths on the Coquille River in the Joyce Tanner Memorial Canoe, an example of the Alu'daq canoe. This canoe was built deep, with a high prow, usually maneuvered upriver by standing and using long poles. It could also go several miles into the ocean to troll for spring salmon. Below from left to right are Chief Ken Tanner, Chase Scott, Molly Hockema, and Tom Younker in a Ma'xmax canoe. This canoe was usually smaller, sturdier, wider, had rounded ends, and was difficult to tip over. This canoe was primarily used by women for short travel or daily chores, and it could be paddled while sitting or kneeling. (Both, CIT.)

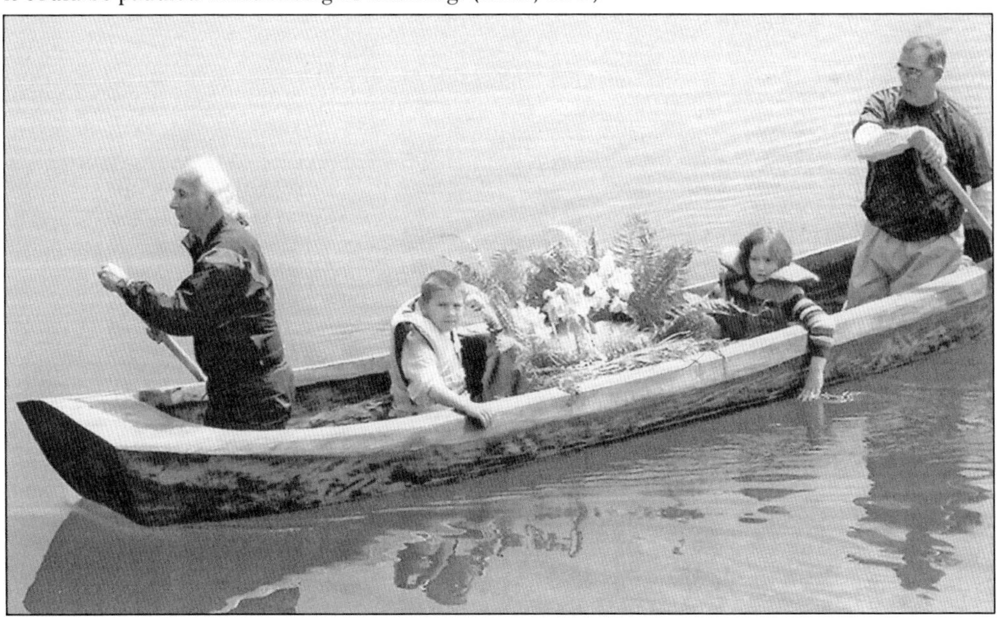

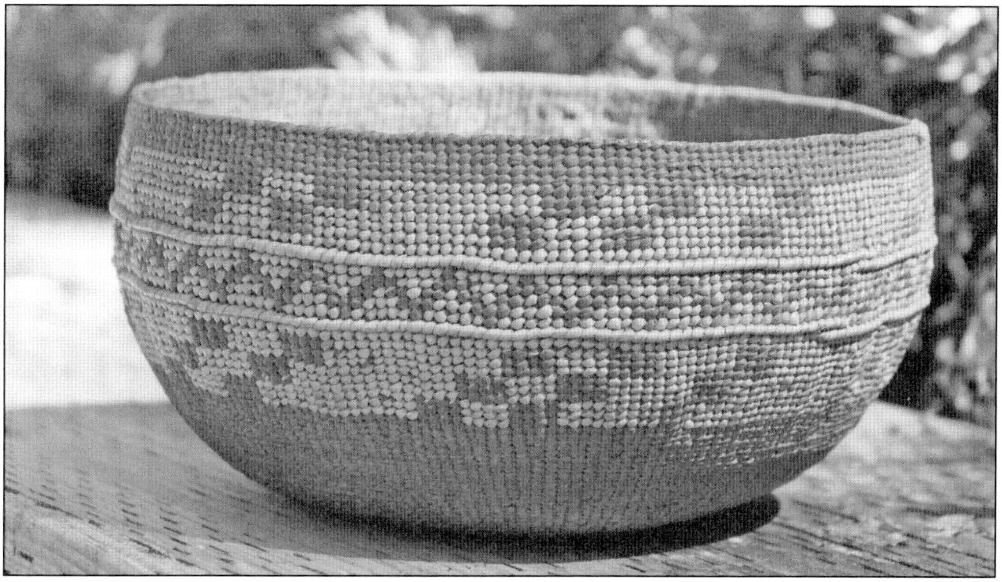

Coquille weavers traditionally were known for their twined basketry that combined artistry with utility. After the Coquilles were uprooted and dispersed in the 19th century, many traditional basket weavers died without passing down their skills. A good weaver was a valuable and necessary family member. Basketry was used for nearly everything from cooking to carrying wood. Above is a twined Coquille cooking basket made from willow sticks, spruce roots, and bear grass. It was water-tight after soaking; cooking was done with hot rocks while stirring constantly. Below is an open-weave burden basket. They are strong and made of spruce roots and willow or hazel sticks. A burden basket was carried on a person's back with a tumpline or strap over the forehead or shoulders. Burden baskets were used to carry anything. (Both, CIT.)

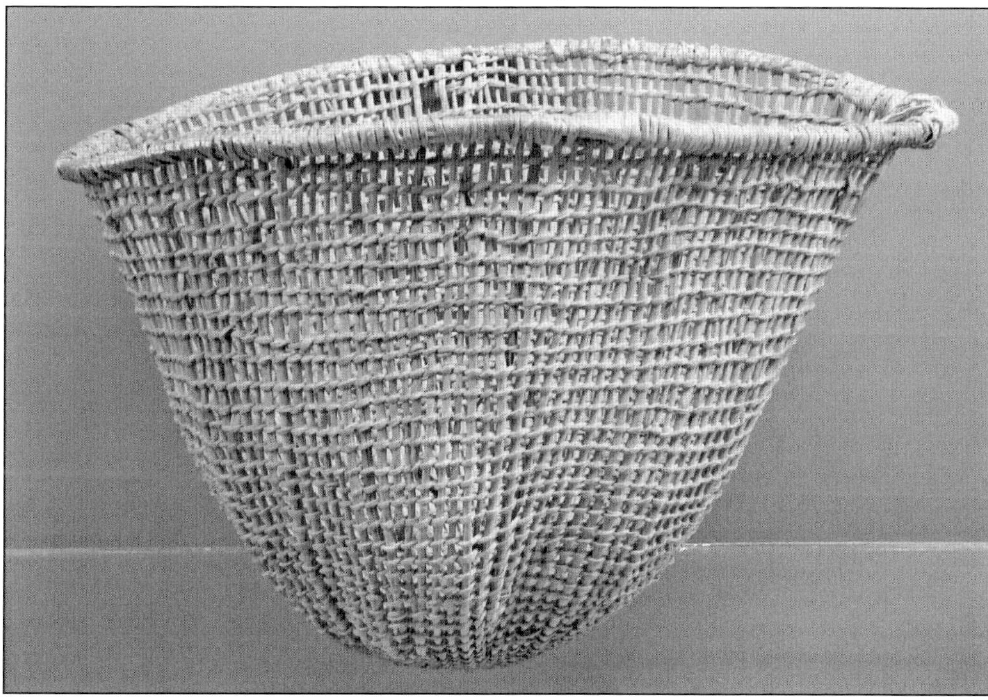

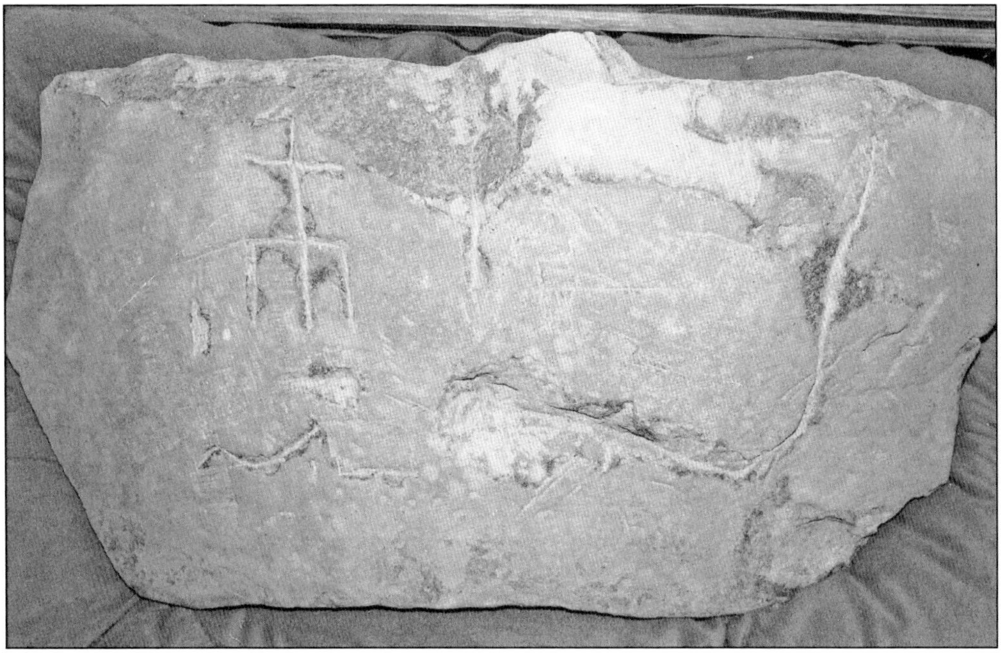

Petroglyphs are images created by removing part of a rock surface by incising, pecking, carving, and abrading. They are found worldwide. This petroglyph was found near Johnson Mill Pond by a Coquille resident. It was given to James Metcalf of Fairview; he was chairman of the Coquille Indian tribe at the time. It is not known if this petroglyph originated in the Coquille Valley or was brought in. (CIT.)

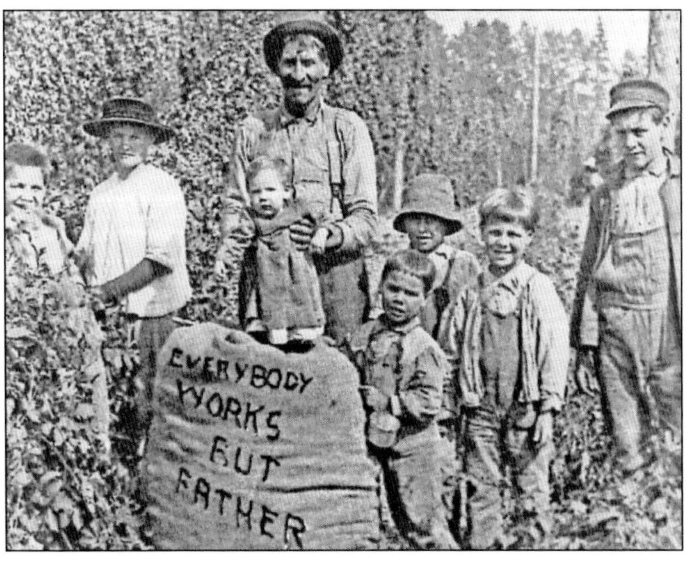

The William Calvin Summers family are the descendants of Upper Coquille people who lived in the Coquille Valley. Chief Washington Tom, Hashe-gali, was headman of a village north of Coquille, and his brother, Tyee ya'ksan was headman of Lhanhashdan to the east. Although many members of this branch of the tribe have always lived in the Coquille Valley, some migrated to the Port Orford and Medford areas. (CIT.)

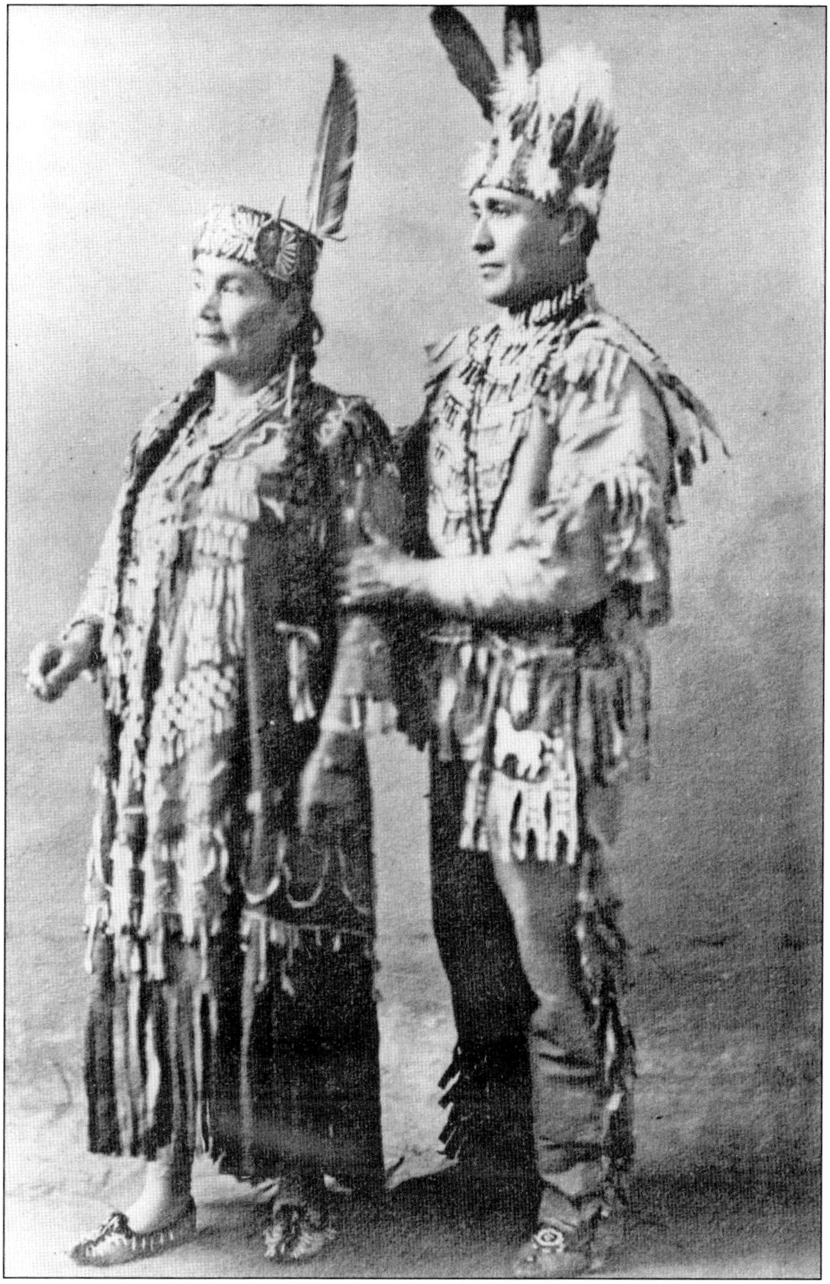

Annie Minor Peterson is pictured around 1910 with an unidentified man wearing native regalia made of leather, dentalium shells, some glass beads, and feathers. Everyday clothing was not so decorative and usually made from plant fibers. During the rainy season, capes and skirts made of cedar bark were worn to keep people dry. Dentalium is a tubular mollusk that was historically harvested from the deep waters on the west coast of Vancouver Island. The shells were strung on iris fiber cordage and used as currency or trade items between tribal groups as well as European trappers. These have been found as far east as the Dakotas. Today, dentalium is the primary decoration on dance regalia. It is still considered a sign of great wealth. Twice a year, on the summer and winter solstice, the Coquille tribe does a ceremony to pray for world renewal. (CIT.)

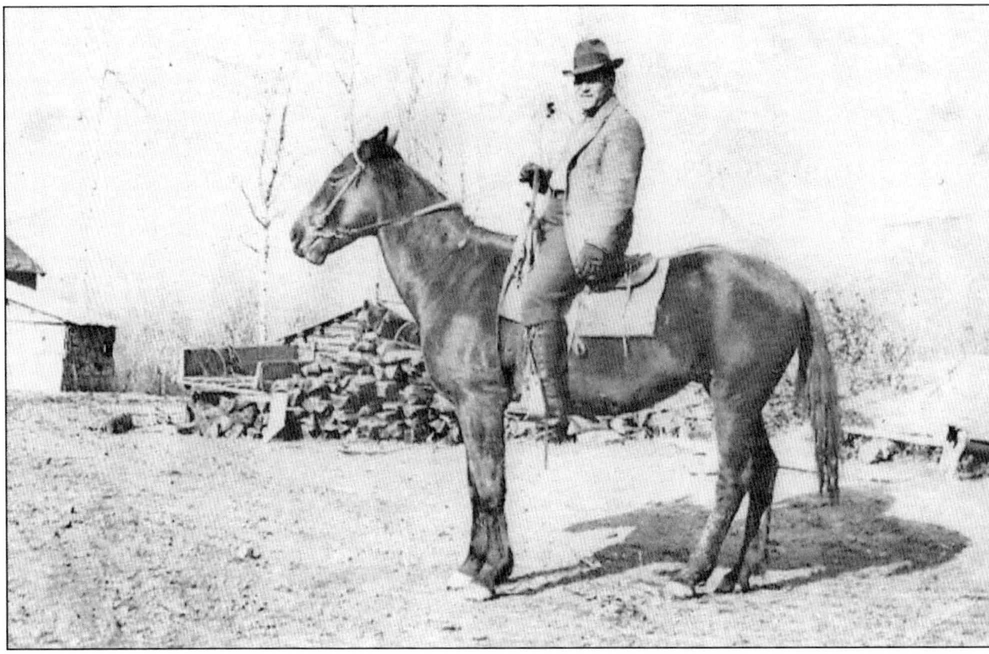

George Bundy Wasson Sr. was a Coos-Coquille Indian. In 1916, he was asked by the Oregon coastal tribes to go to Washington, DC, to research how the tribes could receive payment for their lands, which were taken by the government years earlier. In between trips to DC, George lived in Coquille with his wife and five children. He spent the rest of his life fighting this battle. (CIT.)

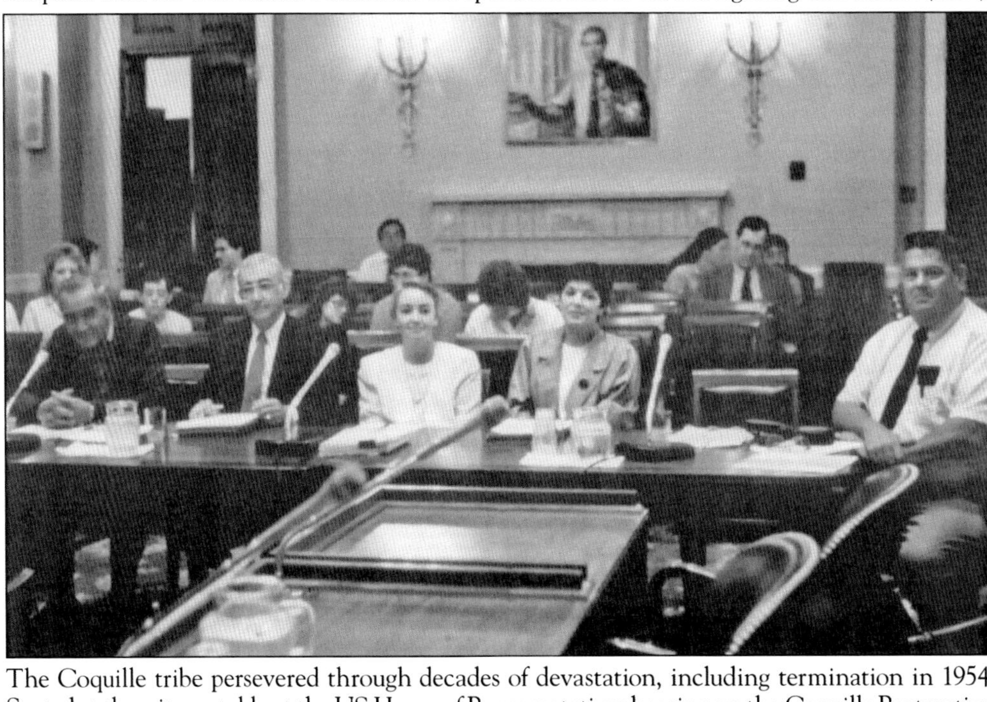

The Coquille tribe persevered through decades of devastation, including termination in 1954. Seated at the witness table at the US House of Representatives hearing on the Coquille Restoration Act in 1988 are, from left to right, Wilfred Wasson, Roy Gilkey, Linda Procter, Michele Burnette, and Joe Thomas. In June 1989, the tribe was restored to federal trust status. (CIT.)

Two

River and Riverboats

The Coquille River provided critical access to Coquille in the city's early years. In a region where existing trails and roads were primitive, the river provided essential transportation. It opened up the Coquille Valley from Bandon to Coquille and Myrtle Point, allowing for exploration and settlement. Thereafter, riverboats provided local passenger and freight service to these towns and points in between. Other boats, including oceangoing schooners and steamers, transported large quantities of lumber and coal for export to other regions, primarily California. The schooners were towed upstream from Bandon. The river provided a means of getting logs to sawmills. Coquille developed a substantial waterfront where the town met the river in response to the traffic. A sawmill occupied the largest wharf, and smaller wharves served the local riverboats.

Riverboats were built in Coquille, Parkersburg, Prosper, and Bandon. Coquille shipyards produced the *Little Annie* in 1877, the first built in Coquille. From 1900 to 1901, Arthur Ellingsen built the *Favorite*, *Pastime*, *Echo*, and *J. Warren*. S.H. Adams built the sternwheeler *Welcome*, and C.H. James built the *Venus*. In 1908, Frank Lowe built the *Coquille*. In 1916, Ellingsen built the *Relief*, the last riverboat built in the area.

Boats that visited but were not built in Coquille included the *Dispatch*, *Telegraph*, *Liberty*, *Dora*, *Wolverine*, *Myrtle*, and *Charm*.

Sternwheelers and propeller-driven riverboats progressed from steam engines fueled with wood and coal to gasoline engines.

The importance of the river for transportation dwindled with the introduction of automobiles and all-weather highways in the area. The completion of a paved highway from Marshfield and a bridge over the river at Coquille further caused the decline.

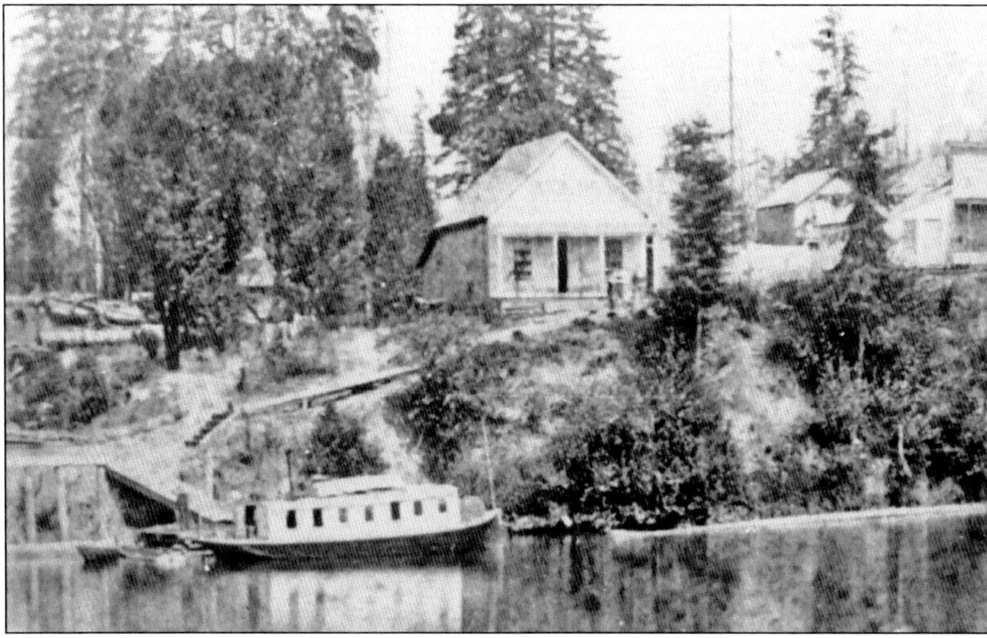

This is the propeller riverboat *Mary* at the waterfront in 1874. Early businesses are shown at upper right. The *Mary* was the first to sail on the Coquille River. It was built in 1874 by William E. Rackleff, who sailed the steamer for a year between the mouth and forks of the Coquille River. After removing machinery, the hull was sold. (CHM 009.16.1895.)

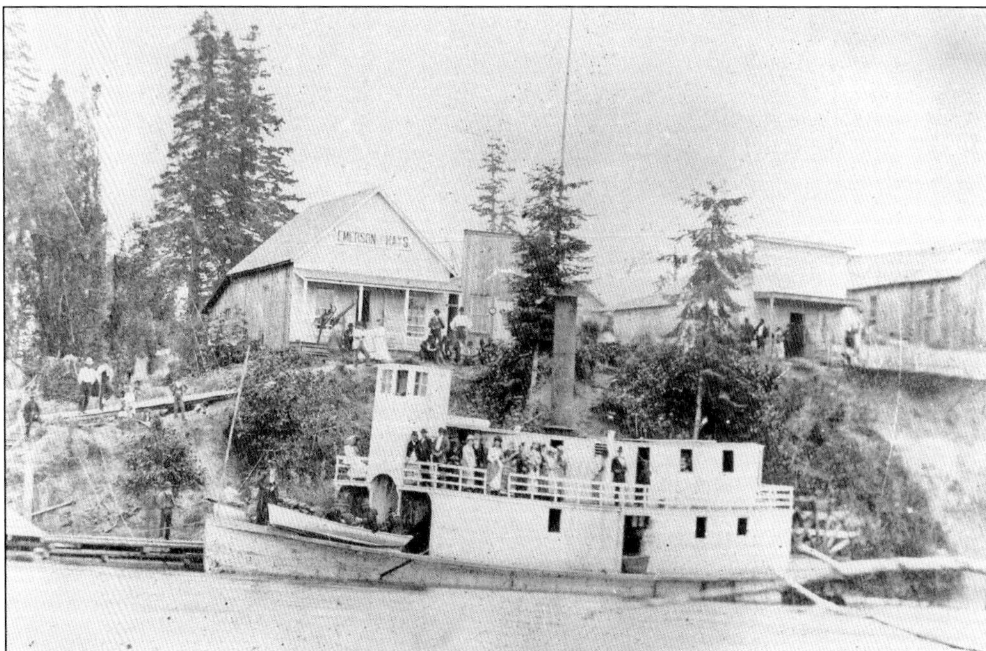

This is the sternwheeler riverboat *Little Annie* at the waterfront around 1876, the year it was built in Myrtle Point. William E. Rackleff, the owner-shipbuilder, operated it on the Coquille River. On June 30, 1890, it sank near Bandon after striking a rock. Emerson & Hays and other stores are visible in the image. (DCM N1344.)

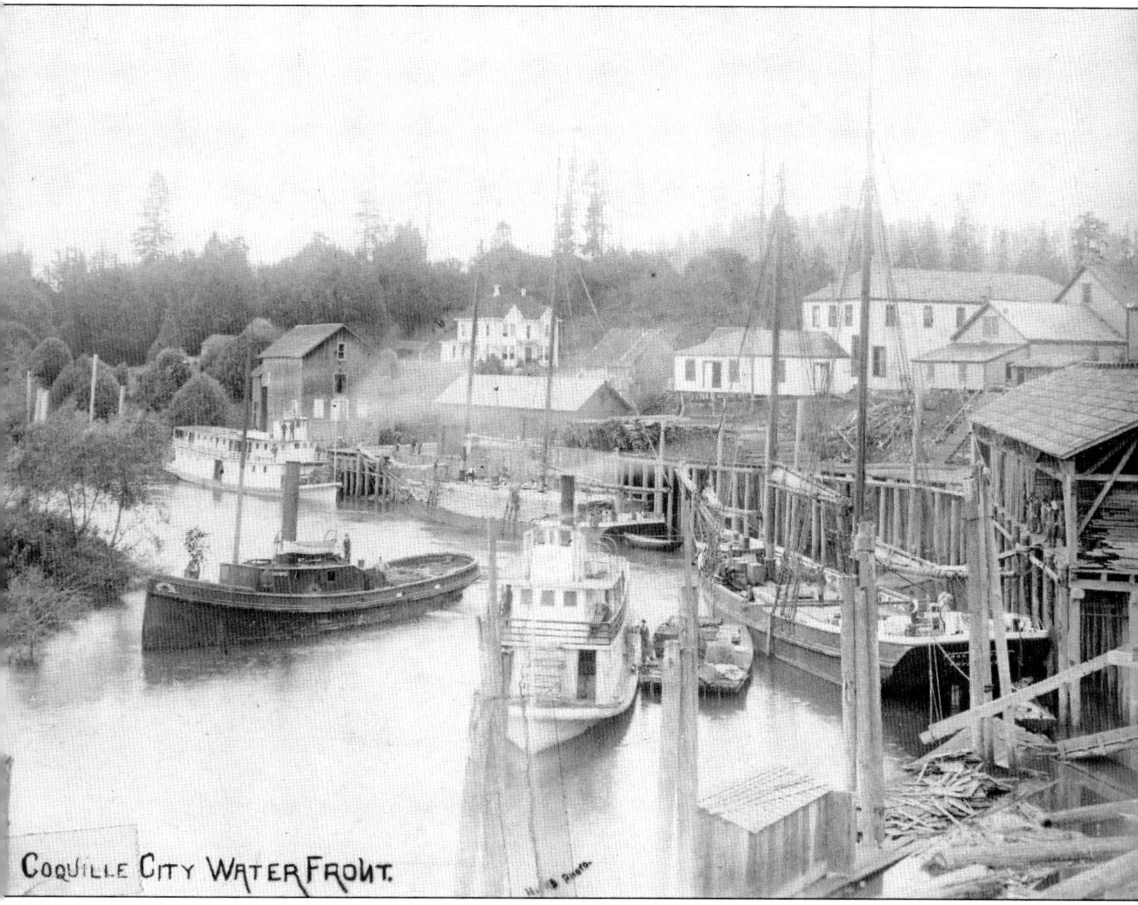

By 1900, the waterfront was busy serving multiple industries and businesses via the river. In 1893, when the railroad arrived, the city became a transportation hub. At the right is an oceangoing schooner loading lumber from the downtown Lyons Sawmill; beyond is a loaded schooner. On the left is the steam tug *Katie Cook*, which towed schooners to and from the ocean. A primary market for the lumber was San Francisco. Schooners brought merchandise for resale back to the city on their return trips. One riverboat is on the river, and another is at the docks in the background. The riverboats provided passenger and freight service on the river for many points between Bandon and Myrtle Point. The Collier house is in the background. (CVM.)

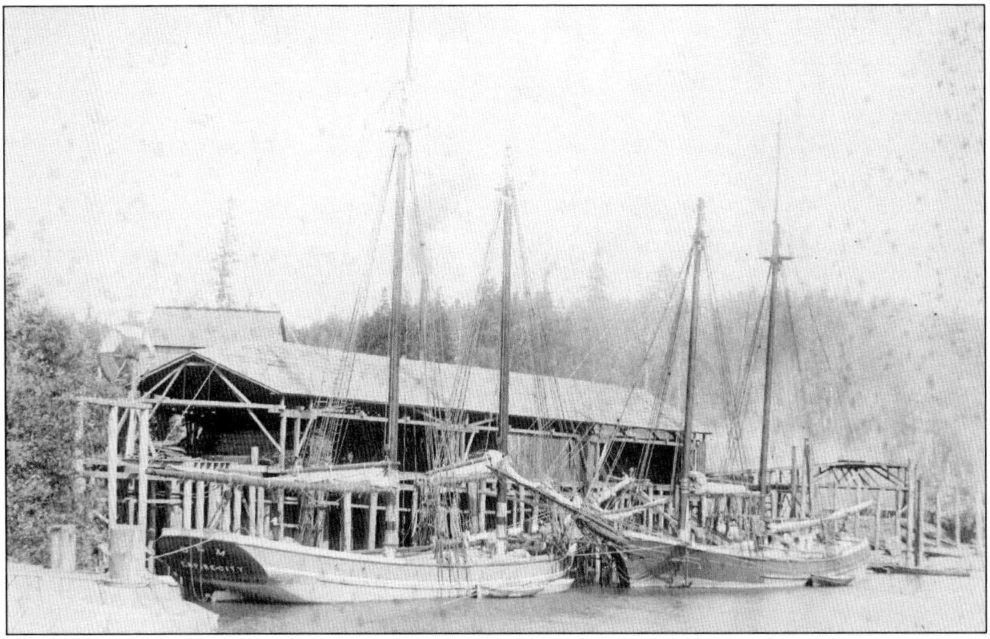

Oceangoing schooners *Empire City* and *Gem* are at the wharf of the downtown Lyons Sawmill around 1900. Sailing ships were towed upriver from Bandon by steam-powered tugboats. Ships loaded with lumber were usually destined for California markets, primarily San Francisco. In 1885, the *Gem* was built at Grub's Mill near Parkersburg by Stein Danielson. (CVM.)

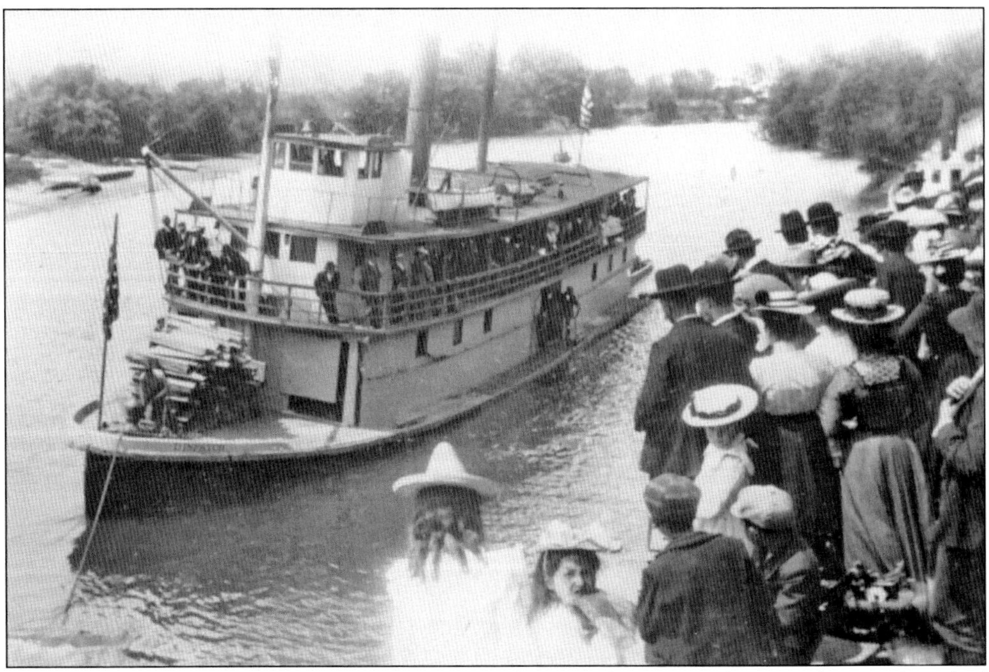

The original sternwheeler *Dispatch* is pictured at the waterfront around 1900. The wood stacked on the bow of the boat was likely fuel for the steam boiler. It was built in 1890 in Bandon and owned by the Coquille River Transportation Company. In 1903, this boat was replaced by a larger *Dispatch*. (CVM.)

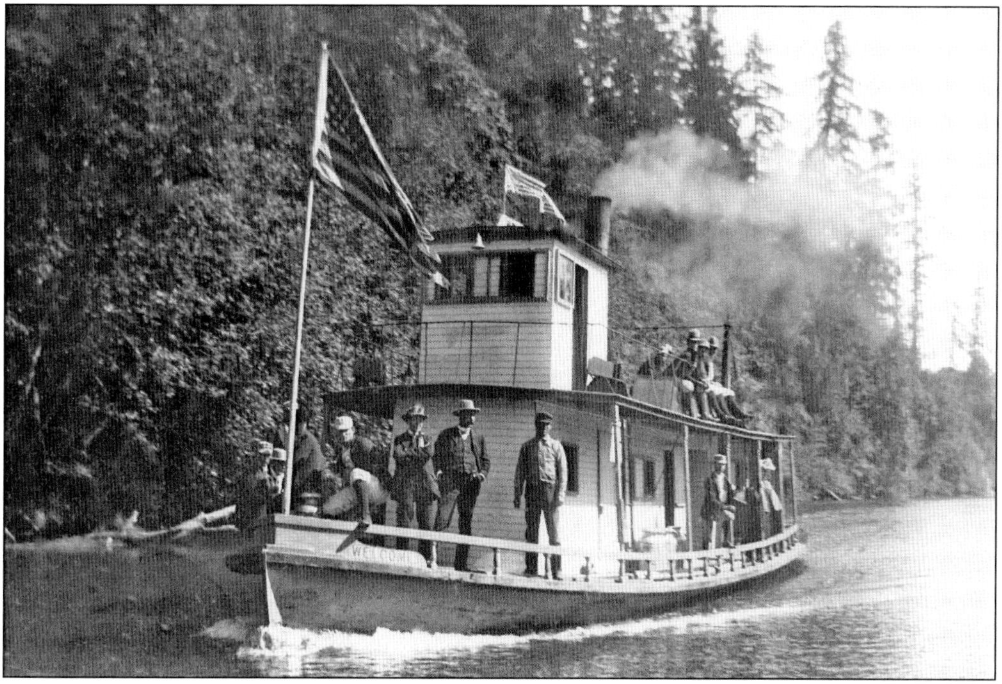

The *Welcome* was a sternwheeler that operated on the Coquille River from 1900 to 1907. In 1900, Samuel H. McAdams built it in Coquille for passenger service. In 1907, it was stranded in a pasture near Myrtle Point after breaking free from its lines and running aground into trees during a high-water event. (BM 28363.)

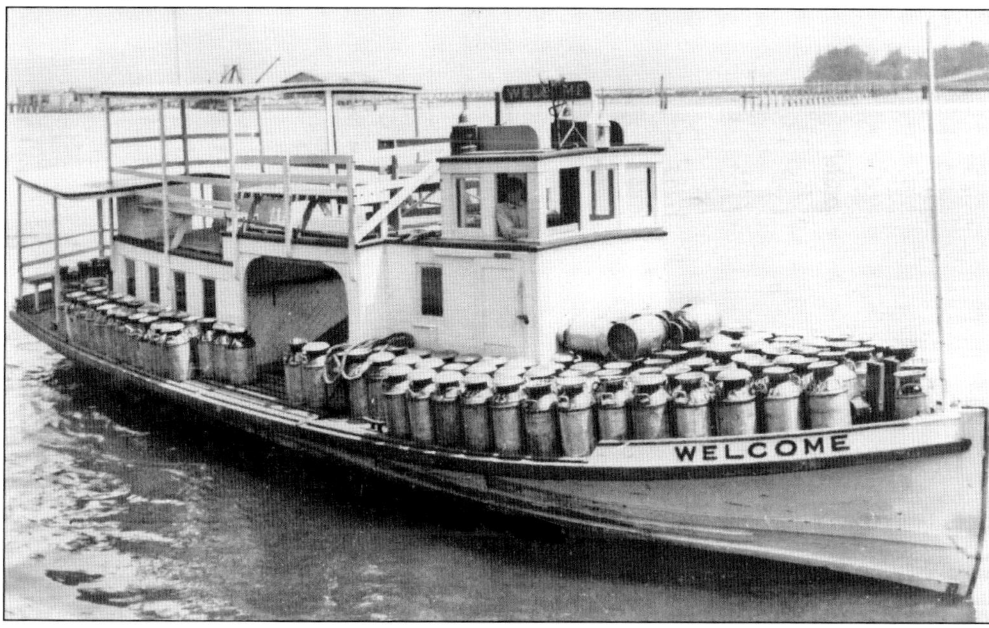

This is the sternwheeler *Welcome* on the lower river loaded with milk cans. Before the advent of highways, riverboats were essential to getting milk from the numerous dairies to creameries operating along the river. Three creameries operated in or near Coquille during the era of riverboats. (BM 29015.)

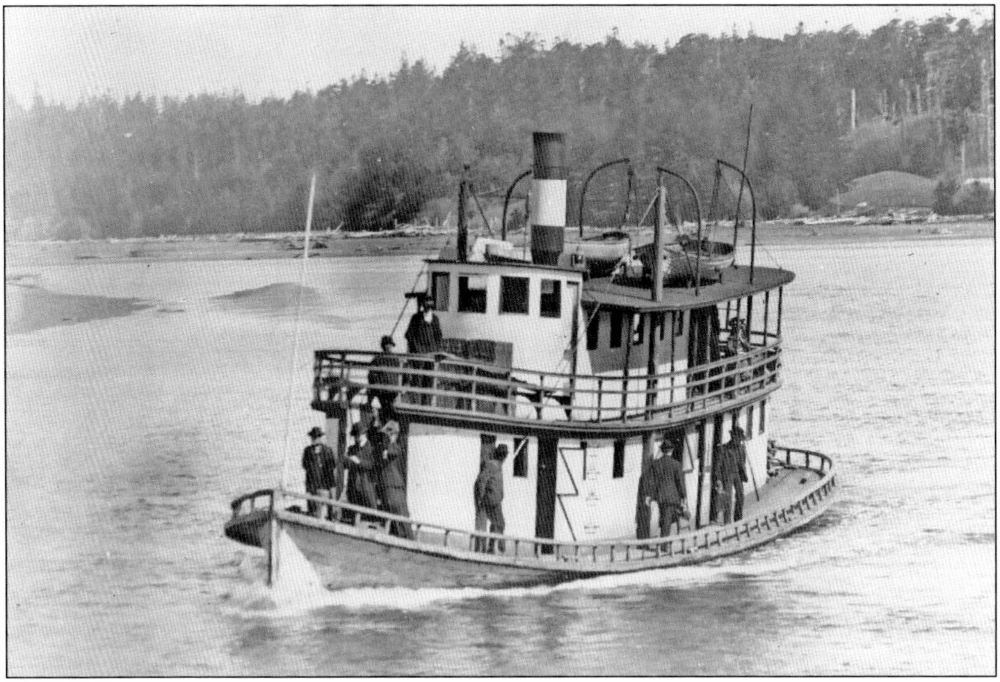

This is the propeller riverboat *Favorite* on the lower river. In 1900, Arthur Ellingsen built it at his shipyard about one mile upriver from Coquille. It was 72 feet in length and displaced 63 tons. It had two cabins and carried 125 passengers. In 1905, its master was J.C. Moomaw, and it made daily trips between Coquille and Bandon. (BM 31022.)

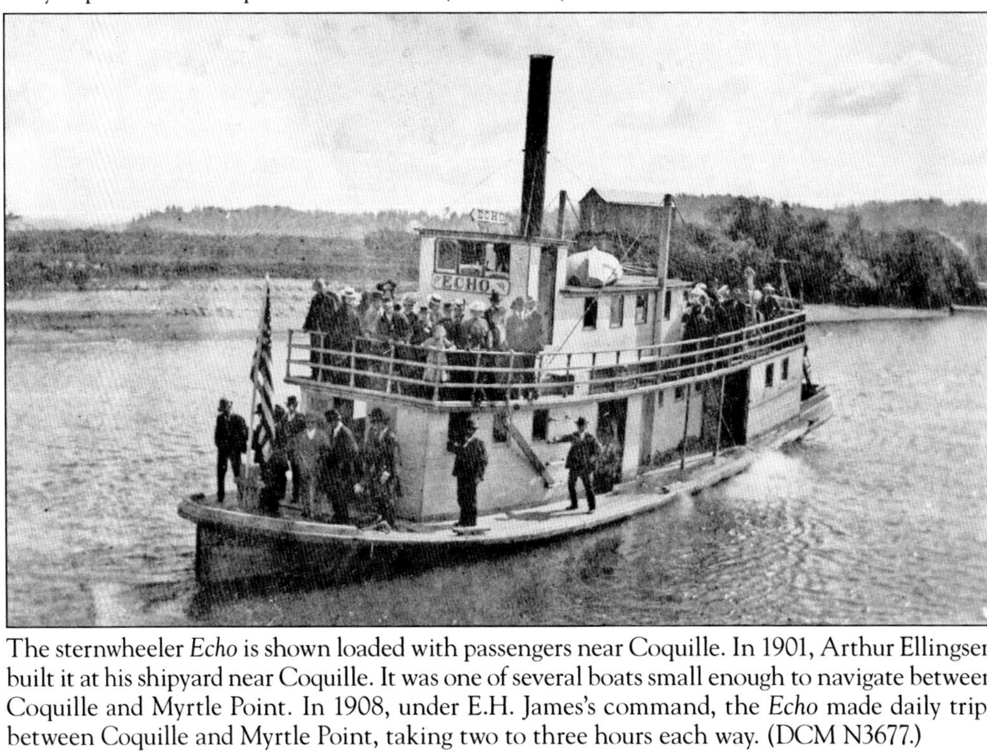

The sternwheeler *Echo* is shown loaded with passengers near Coquille. In 1901, Arthur Ellingsen built it at his shipyard near Coquille. It was one of several boats small enough to navigate between Coquille and Myrtle Point. In 1908, under E.H. James's command, the *Echo* made daily trips between Coquille and Myrtle Point, taking two to three hours each way. (DCM N3677.)

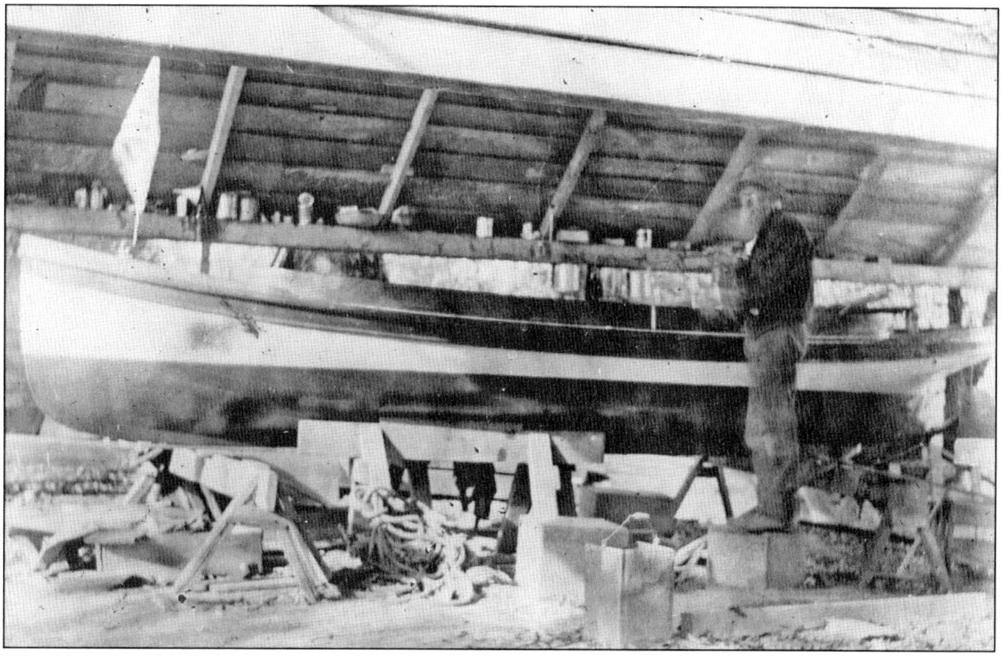

This photograph likely depicts Arthur Ellingsen at his shipyard near Coquille. In addition to several riverboats, Ellingsen built two small oceangoing schooners, *Enterprise* (53 feet and 22 tons) and *Osprey* (58 feet and 43 tons), in 1908. The boats were commissioned for R.D. Hume, who wished to ship merchandise into the Rogue River area. (Ellingsen Collection, BM 49468.)

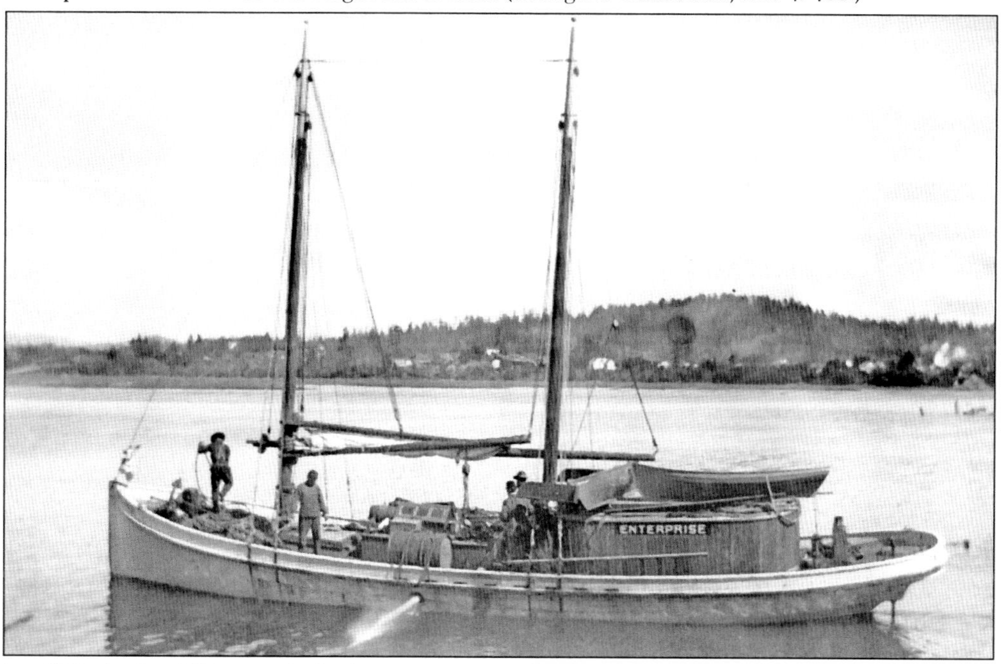

In 1908, Arthur Ellingsen built the oceangoing schooner *Enterprise*. When owned by John R. Miller, the *Enterprise* was intended for service between Bandon and Coos Bay with occasional trips to Port Orford. At this time, O.P. Ellingsen was captain, and Edwin Ellingsen was engineer. In 1914, Capt. Herbert Casaday from Astoria purchased the *Enterprise*. (CHM 009.16.295.)

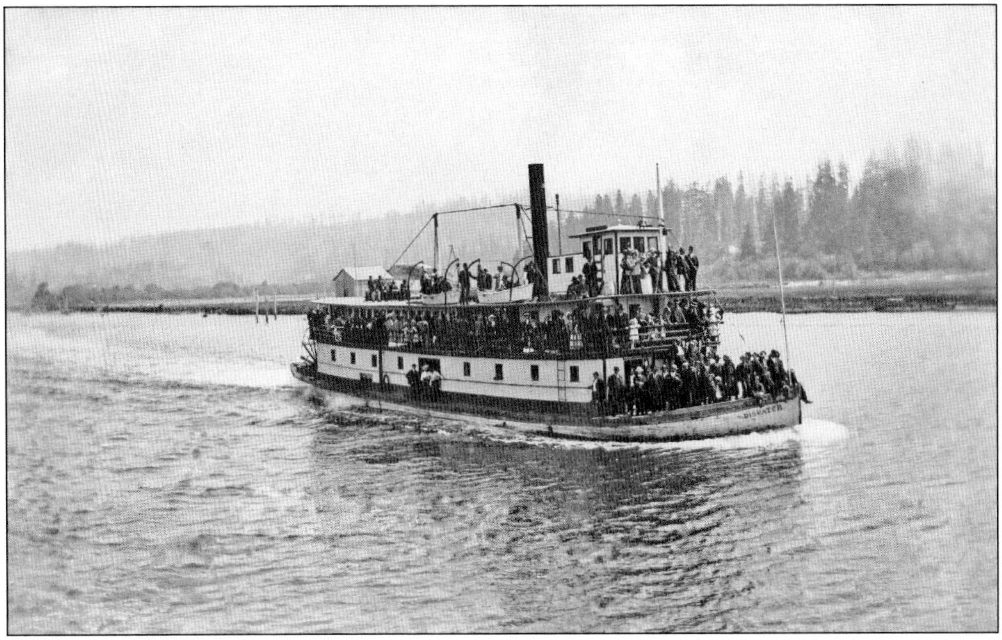

These are pictures of the second and larger sternwheeler *Dispatch*. Above, the boat is on the lower river loaded with passengers. Below, the boat is near Parkersburg and headed for Bandon. In 1903, the second *Dispatch* was built by Charles Trigg at Parkersburg and commissioned by the Coquille River Transportation Company. The boat was 111 feet long and displaced 250 tons. It was the largest boat on the river and required a crew of five. It carried passengers and freight between Coquille and Bandon between 1903 and 1920 with daily service except Sundays. The Coquille-to-Bandon route was generally served by the larger boats and took about three hours each way. In 1920, the *Dispatch* was moved to Coos Bay and renamed the *John Widdi*. (Above, RG; below, VM.)

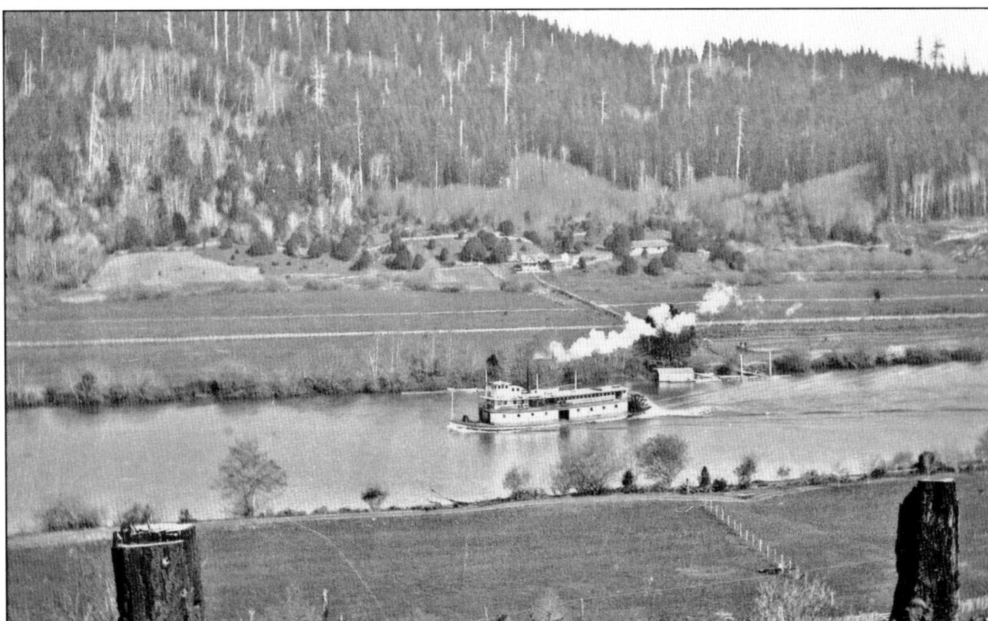

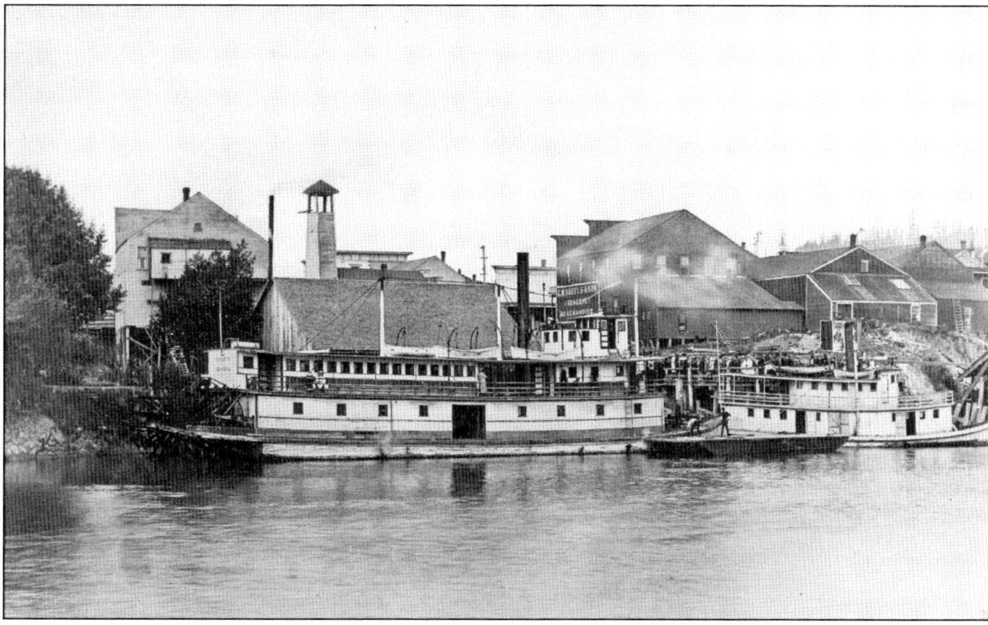

In 1907, the riverboats *Dispatch* and *Favorite* are docked at the waterfront. In the background on Front Street, from left to right, are the Coquille Steam Laundry, a firehose tower, city hall, the large C.M. Skeels store, and the back sides of other Front Street buildings. Immediately behind the *Dispatch* is the covered steamer freight shed. (BM 41029.)

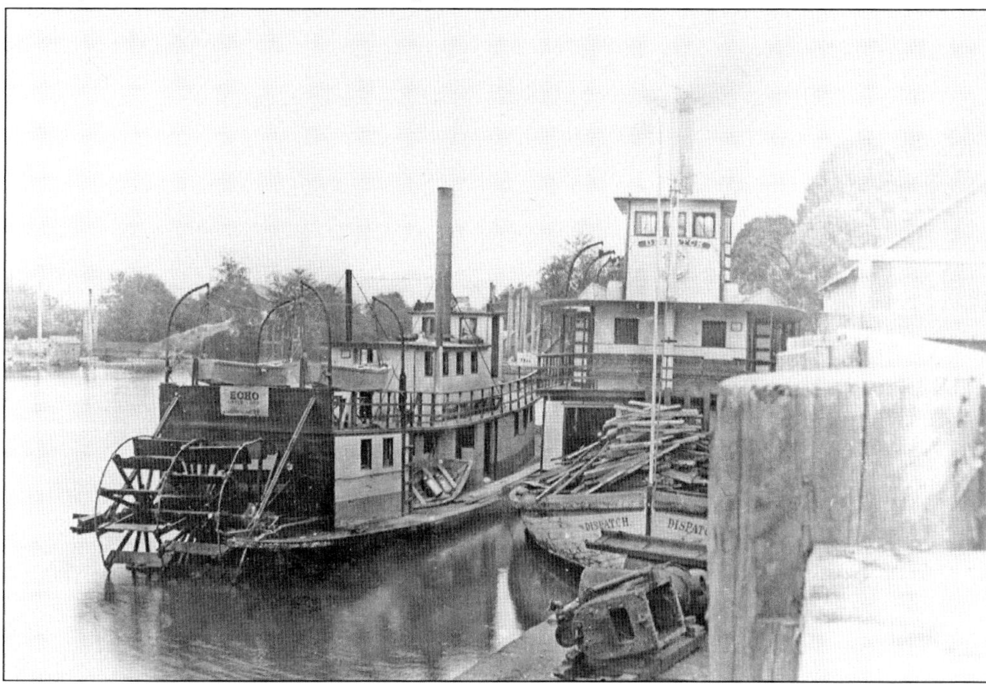

These are the sternwheelers *Echo* and *Dispatch* on the waterfront. The *Echo*, on the left, was a smaller boat that operated between Coquille and Myrtle Point, while the *Dispatch* operated between Coquille and Bandon. Both boats were powered by steam boilers. Wood fuel is stacked on the bow of the *Dispatch*. (DCM N4308.)

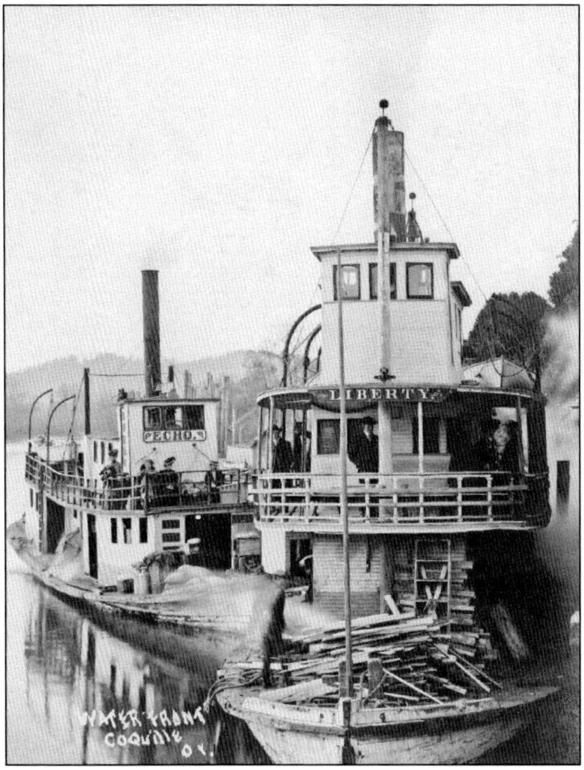

In 1903, the sternwheelers *Echo* and *Liberty* are docked at the waterfront. These boats provided passenger, freight, and towing services. The *Liberty* was built in 1903 by the Herman Brothers at Bandon for businessmen Walter Panter and Oscar Willard. At 174 tons and 91 feet, it was one of the larger boats on the river. It operated between Coquille and Bandon. (BM 20057.)

The *Favorite* is at the waterfront in the foreground. An unidentified boat and the sawmill wharf are in the background on the left. The *Dispatch* is in the distance on the right. Note the well-dressed passengers aboard the *Favorite*. On the boats with two levels, it was common to carry freight on the lower level and passengers on the upper level. (BM 53084.)

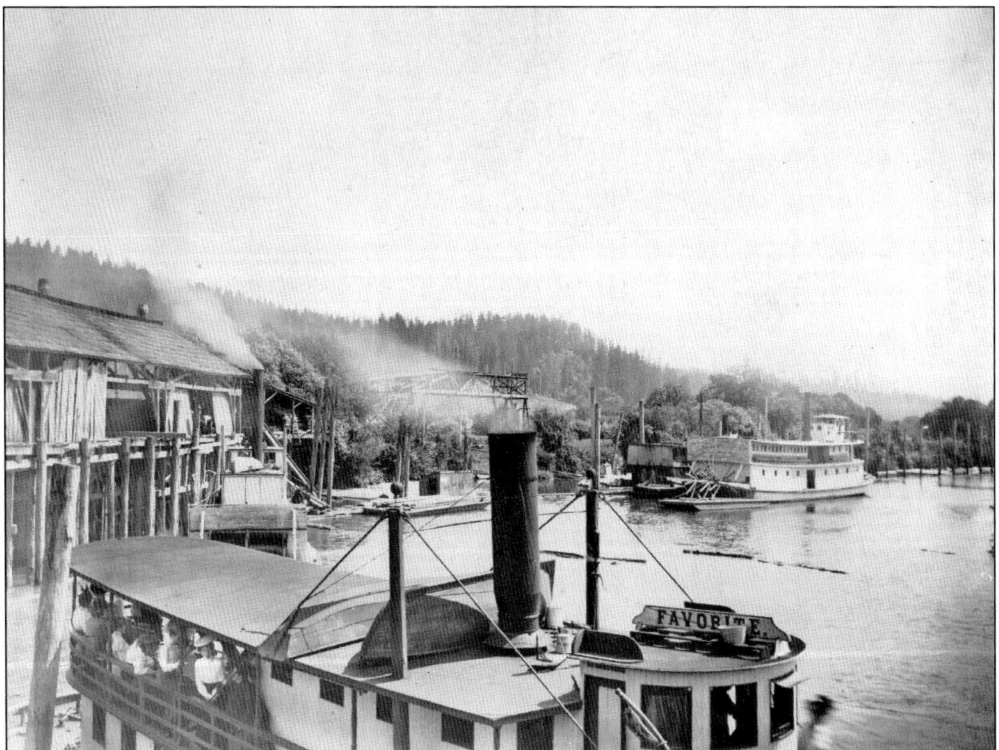

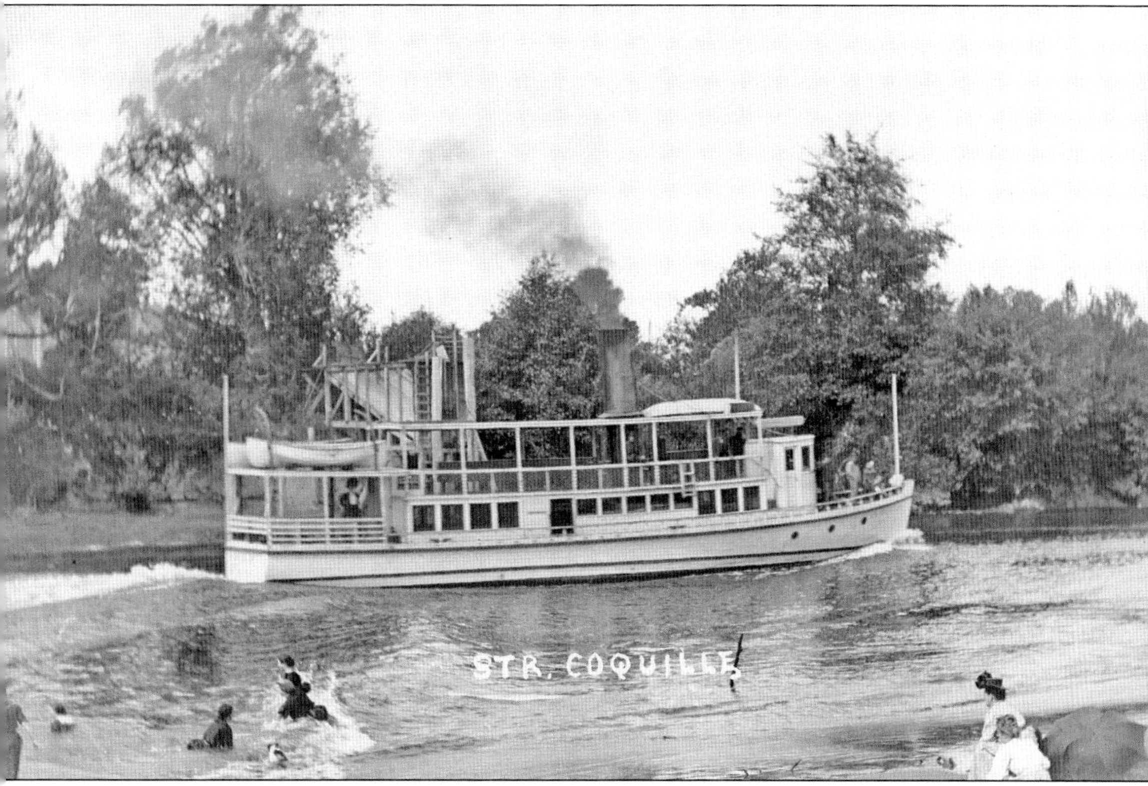

This is the propeller riverboat *Coquille* passing swimmers along the shore of the river near Coquille. The *Coquille* was built in 1908 by Frank Lowe west of downtown near the railroad depot. It was 77 feet in length and displaced 63 tons with a hull built from Port Orford white cedar. Commissioned by the Coquille River Transportation Company, it was intended for passenger service only. It sailed between Coquille and Bandon twice daily, taking two to three hours each way. It was intended as the fastest vessel on the Coquille River but never met that goal. In 1915, it was sold to the Myrtle Point Transportation Company. One year later, it was sold to the Shaver Transportation Company for use on the Willamette River for towing. (BM 49318.)

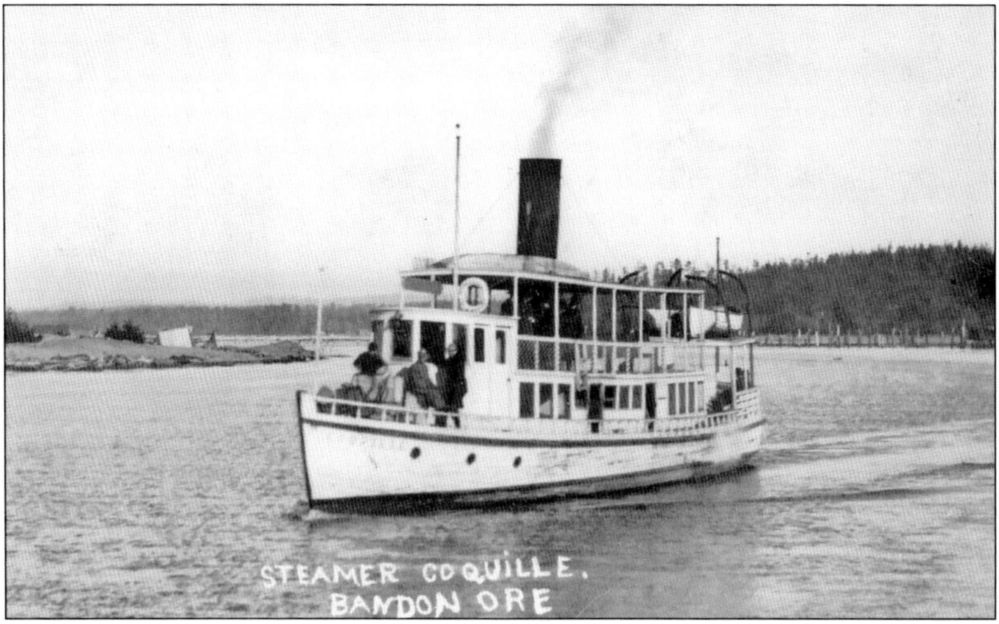

Above, the *Coquille* is shown on the lower river. The *Coquille* was rebuilt several times. Under the direction of Hark Dunham, a larger engine and upper cabin were added around 1912, as shown below where the boat is leaving Coquille. The addition of the upper deck made the vessel top-heavy. When the steamer came around the sharp bend in the river near Prosper, all passengers had to move to the lower cabin to stabilize the boat. The *Coquille* was reconstructed again for passenger service, with the new engine providing enough power for towing. (Both, CVM.)

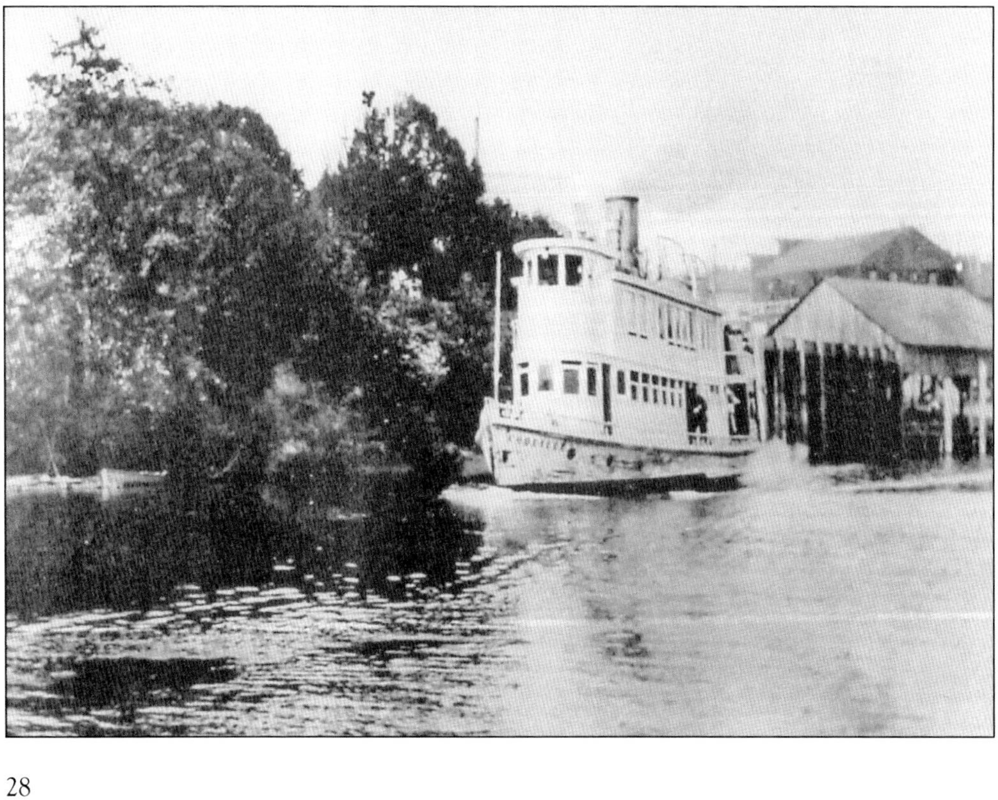

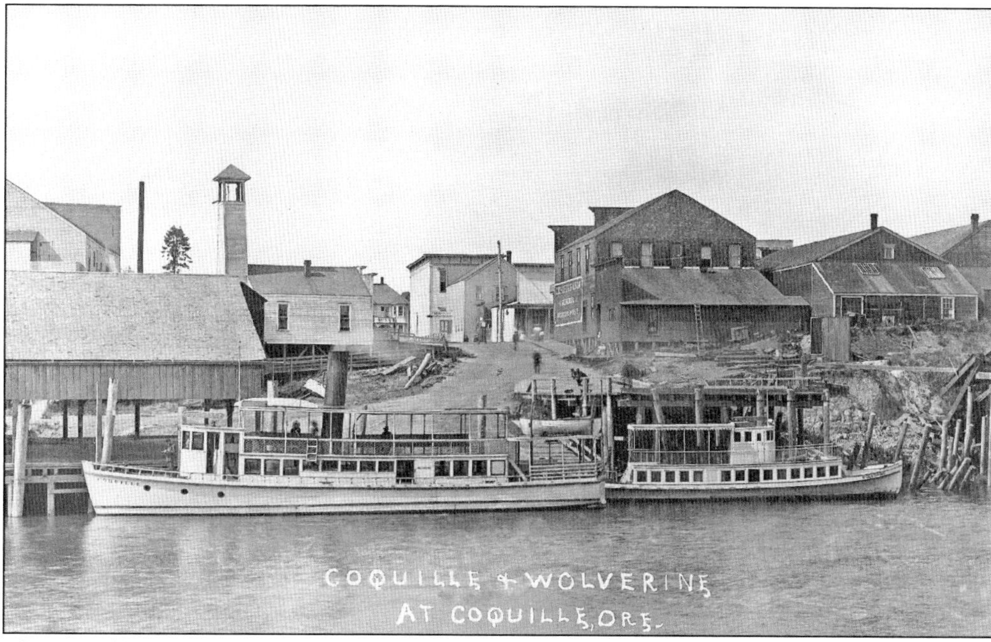

The propeller riverboats *Coquille* and *Wolverine* are pictured at the waterfront. Both boats were built in 1908 and intended for passenger service. The *Coquille* was built in Coquille by Frank Lowe and the *Wolverine* in Marshfield by Max Timmerman. While the *Coquille* was steam-powered, the *Wolverine* was gasoline-powered. (RG.)

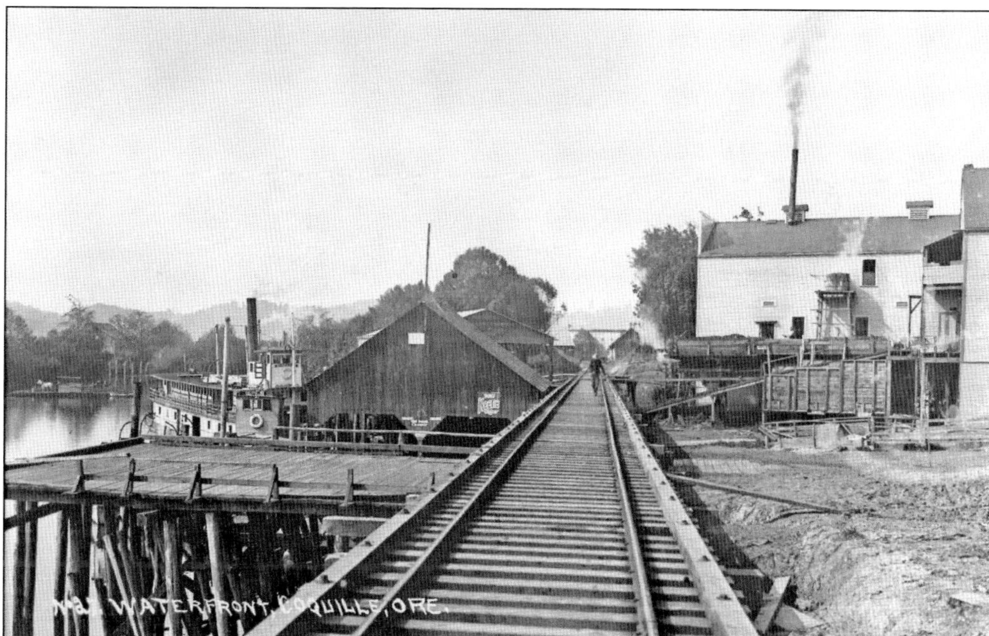

This is the downtown waterfront looking west from the sawmill around 1910. This is after the railroad was moved from Front Street to the waterfront. From left to right are a wharf, the sternwheeler *Dispatch*, the freight shed, the railroad, and the Coquille Steam Laundry. Barely visible down the tracks are the Coquille Valley Creamery and railroad depot. (BM 44322.)

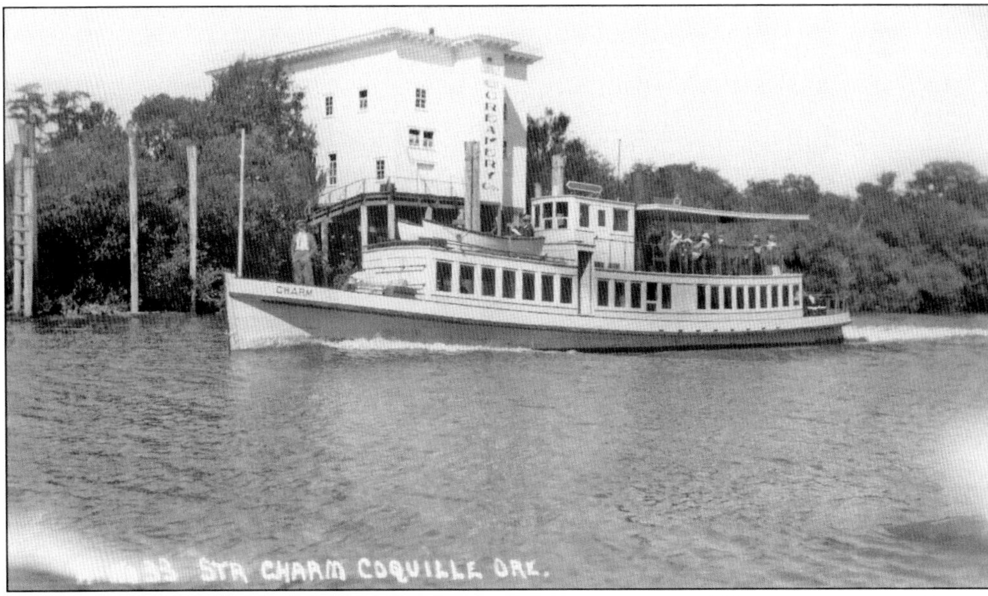

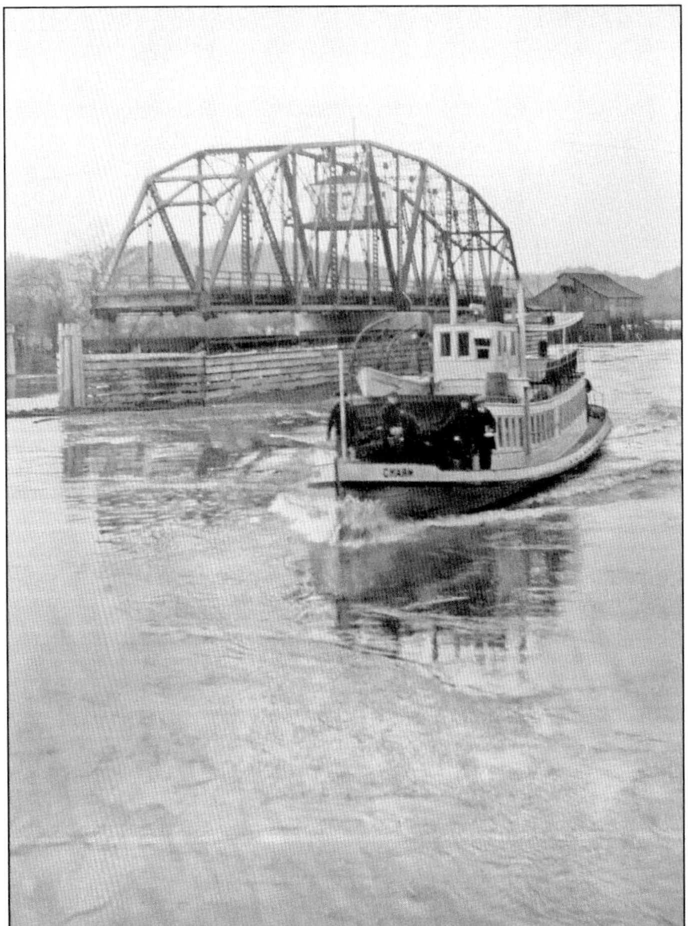

These are pictures of the gasoline-powered propeller boat *Charm*. Above, it is passing the Coquille Valley Creamery about a half-mile west of downtown around 1915. At left, it is passing the steel swing bridge around 1925. The *Charm* was a propeller riverboat built by the Herman Brothers in Prosper in 1913 and was owned by the Coquille River Transportation Company. It was christened by Capt. Oscar R. "Ott" Willard's two small daughters, who were assisted by Dollie Belloni. The *Charm* hauled freight and passengers daily from Coquille to Bandon. In 1924, the *Charm* was sold to the Shaver Transportation Company. (Above, RG; below, BM CHARMONC.)

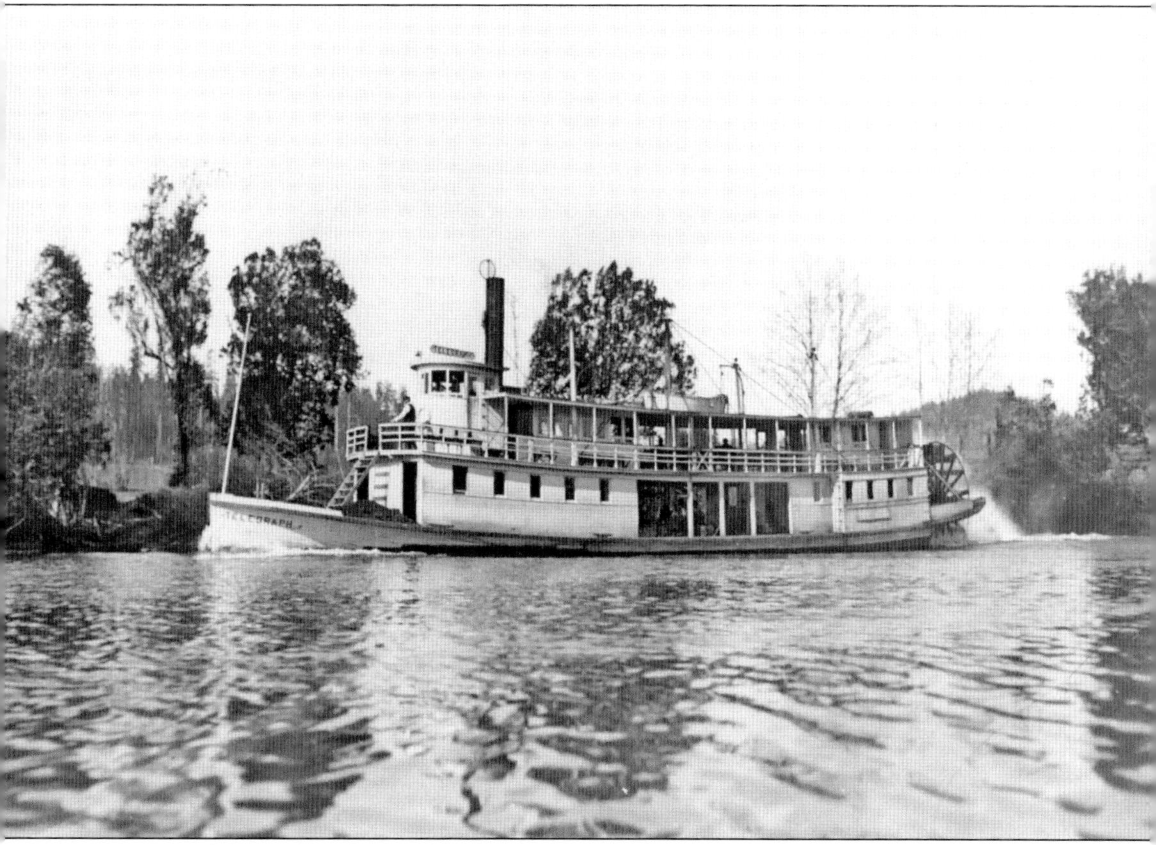

In 1914, toward the end of the riverboat era, the sternwheeler *Telegraph* was built in Prosper by Carl Herman for the Myrtle Point Transportation Company. It joined five other boats in the company's fleet. At 85 feet long and displacing 96 tons, the boat was one of the largest to operate on the river. The steam engine could be fueled by coal or wood. The *Telegraph* sailed between Coquille and Bandon, with the lower deck intended for freight and the upper deck for passengers. The *Telegraph* gained notoriety for collisions, with rival boats resulting in several suspensions. In 1923, the boat was lengthened to 103 feet. While the highway to Bandon was under construction in 1923, the *Telegraph* carried automobiles from Coquille to Bandon. The boat was one of three abandoned on the Paris Ward ranch on the lower river. (CVM.)

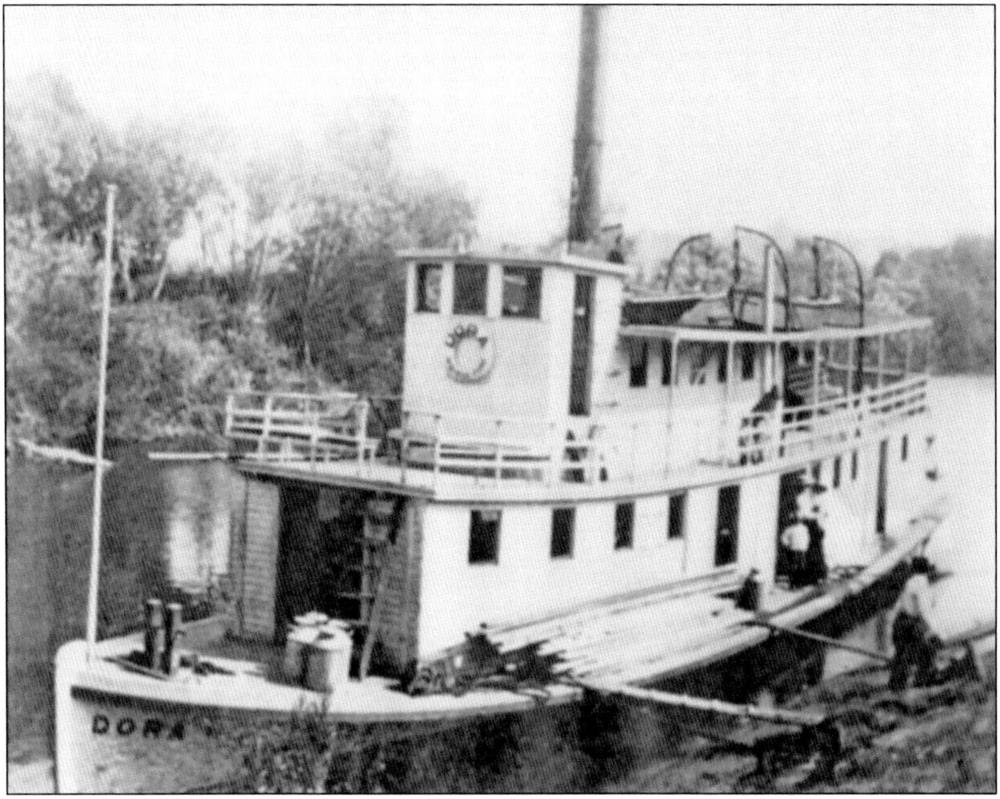

This is the sternwheeler *Dora* with milk cans and lumber at an unimproved landing on the river. The *Dora*, built by the Herman brothers in Randolph, was 64 feet long and displaced 47 tons. It was operated by the Myrtle Point Transportation Company and served points along the river between Myrtle Point and Bandon from 1910 to 1927. (CVM.)

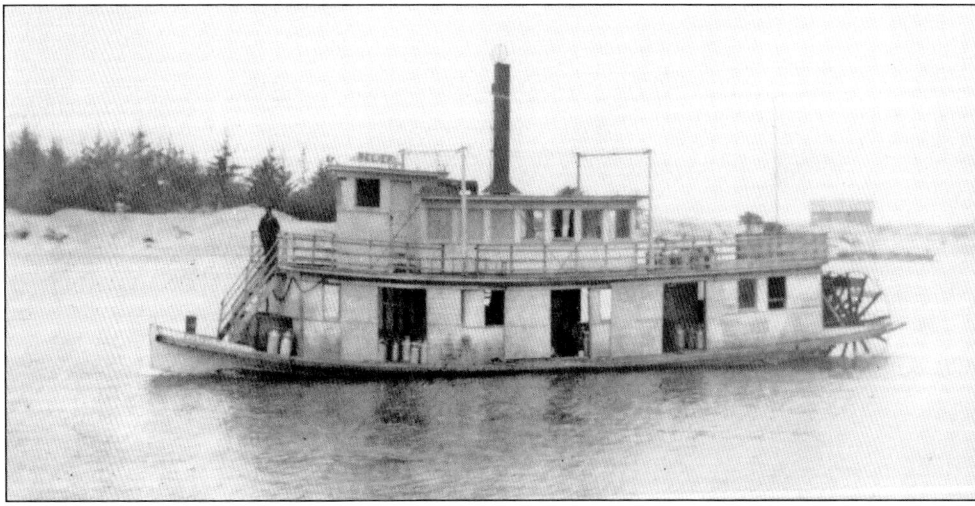

This is the sternwheeler *Relief* on the lower river with milk cans. It was built at the Ellingsen shipyard near Coquille in 1916. This was the last sternwheeler built on the river. The *Relief* was a 44-ton, 64-foot-long boat providing passenger and freight service. It was initially operated by Capt. David Perkins between Coquille and Myrtle Point. (BM 16016.)

Three

Industries

Over the years, a number of industries sustained Coquille, most dependent on the river. The wood products industry dominated business activity since the town was founded. Four major mill sites were developed and operated over time. The first sawmill was built on the downtown waterfront, with later mills built nearby up and down the river.

Coal mining developed early and continued for several decades, with several mines within one mile of Coquille, mostly on the north side of town. For a short time, natural gas wells operated in the Fat Elk area to supply the city.

The dairy industry was vital; three creameries were established in the Coquille area, with the Swift and Company Creamery near the railroad depot. It became one of the largest creameries on the Pacific Coast.

Other agriculture important to the area was truck farming of crops, including potatoes, corn, green beans, and fruit. For a while, cranberry processing was conducted in Coquille.

One of the most interesting and unique enterprises was a three-year experiment in the late 1800s to produce silk by the Southern Oregon Silk Station founded in 1893 at Coquille City.

Today, industrial activity is greatly reduced, with the Roseburg Forest Products plywood mill remaining as the only large industry in the city. Wood products harvesting and processing were greatly reduced after changes in federal timber management.

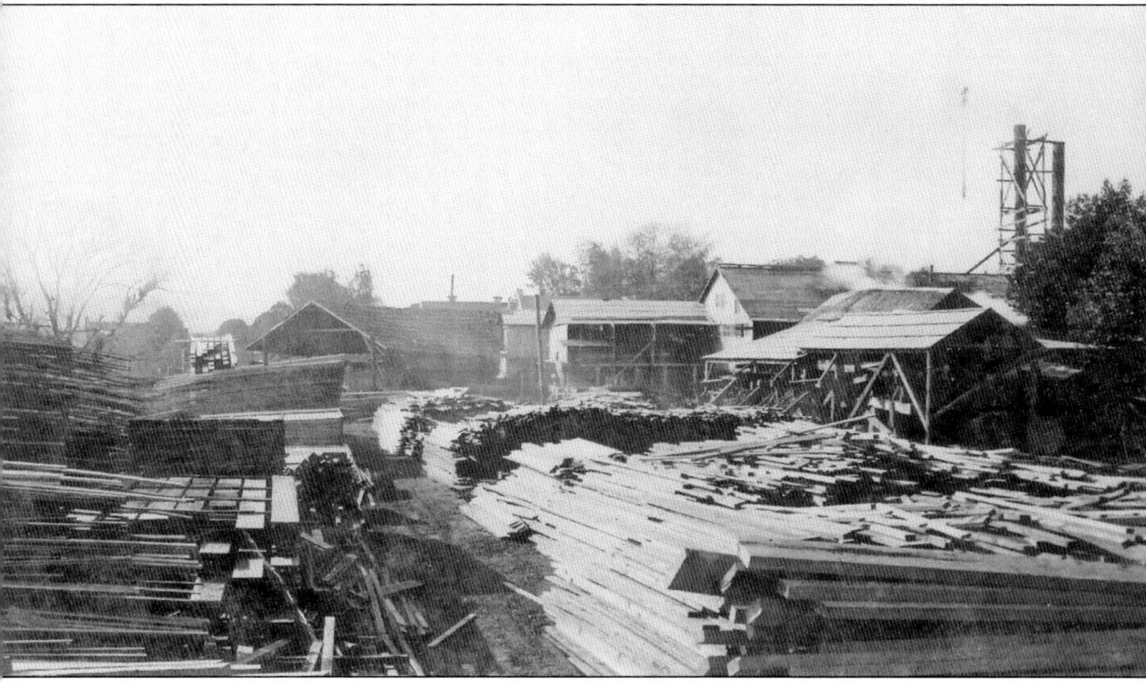

This is the Coquille Mill and Mercantile Company sawmill on the downtown waterfront around 1909. The mill was built in 1880 by Bunch, Bennett & Company, but Binger Hermann soon assumed ownership. J.A. Lyons bought the mill from Binger Hermann, at which time the capacity was 8,000 feet per day. Lyons took over the plant and increased the capacity to 20,000 feet. He then established a nearby general merchandise store. The mill had 400 feet of water frontage and sufficient dockage to load four schooners at once. Lyons employed 50 to 60 men at the mill and logging camps year-round. Later, the mill was owned by Coquille Mill and Mercantile and finally by E.E. "Eck" Johnson. After 1913, the mill supplied steam for the Oregon Power Company to generate electricity for the community. This mill escaped the big downtown fires of 1892 and March 1918 only to be destroyed by fire in June 1918. The mill was an important local industry for decades. (CVM.)

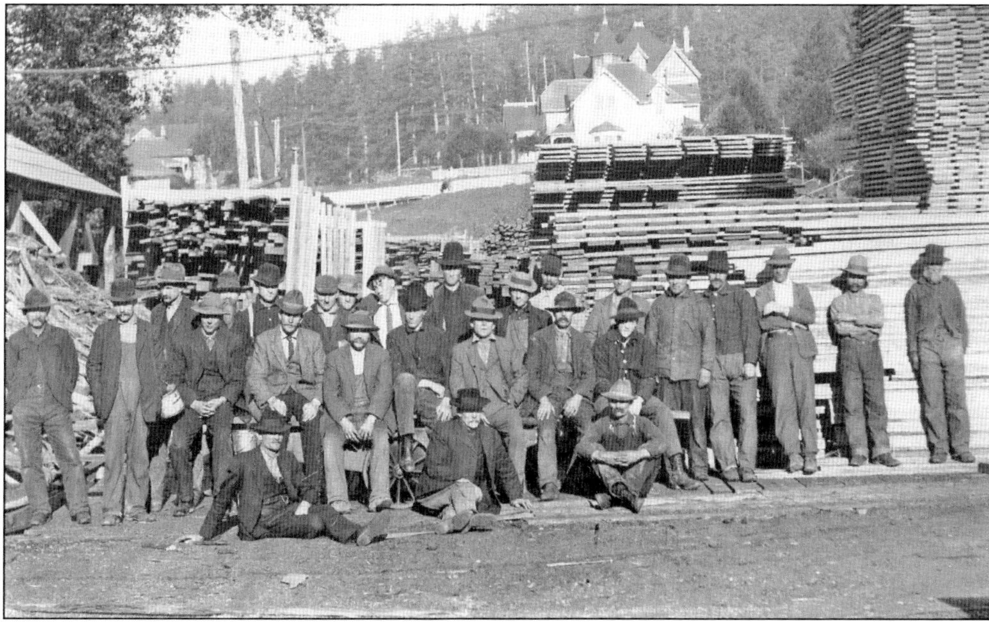

Workers of the downtown waterfront sawmill are pictured standing in front of lumber stacked for drying. The lumber produced in the mill was sold locally and exported to Californian markets. In the background looking east are three homes appearing to be one. The Mehl home is in front, and behind it are the Sherwood and Harlocker homes. (CVM.)

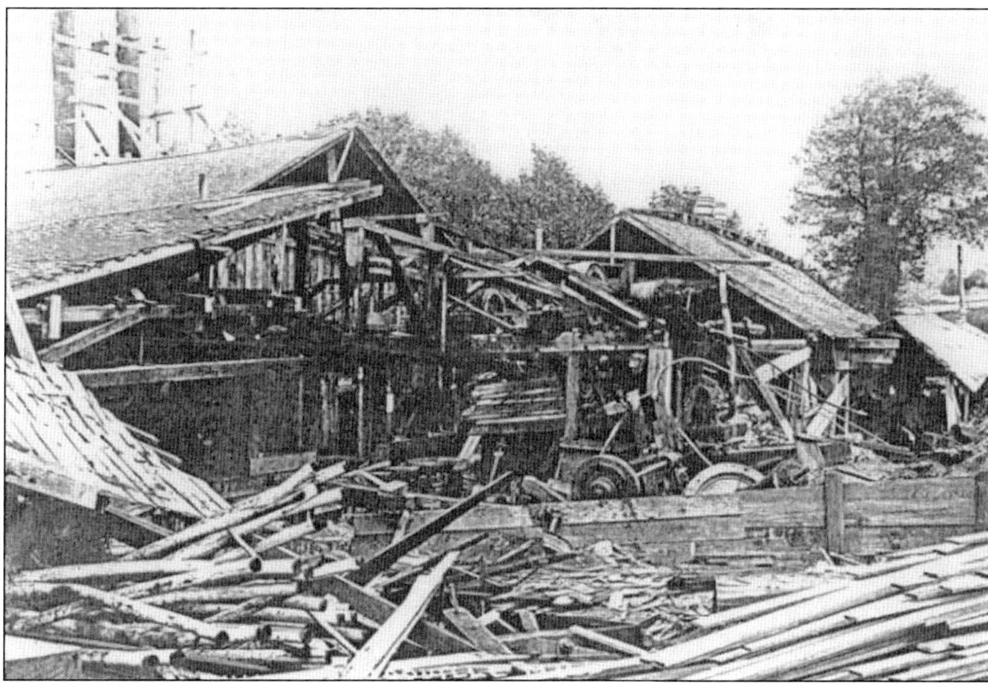

The Coquille Mill and Mercantile Company sawmill on the waterfront was destroyed by a boiler explosion on July 26, 1910. The explosion was so forceful that windows were broken throughout town. Residents feared an earthquake. Eight workers at the mill were injured and buried in debris. Engineer F.F. McCalley was killed in the explosion. (CVM.)

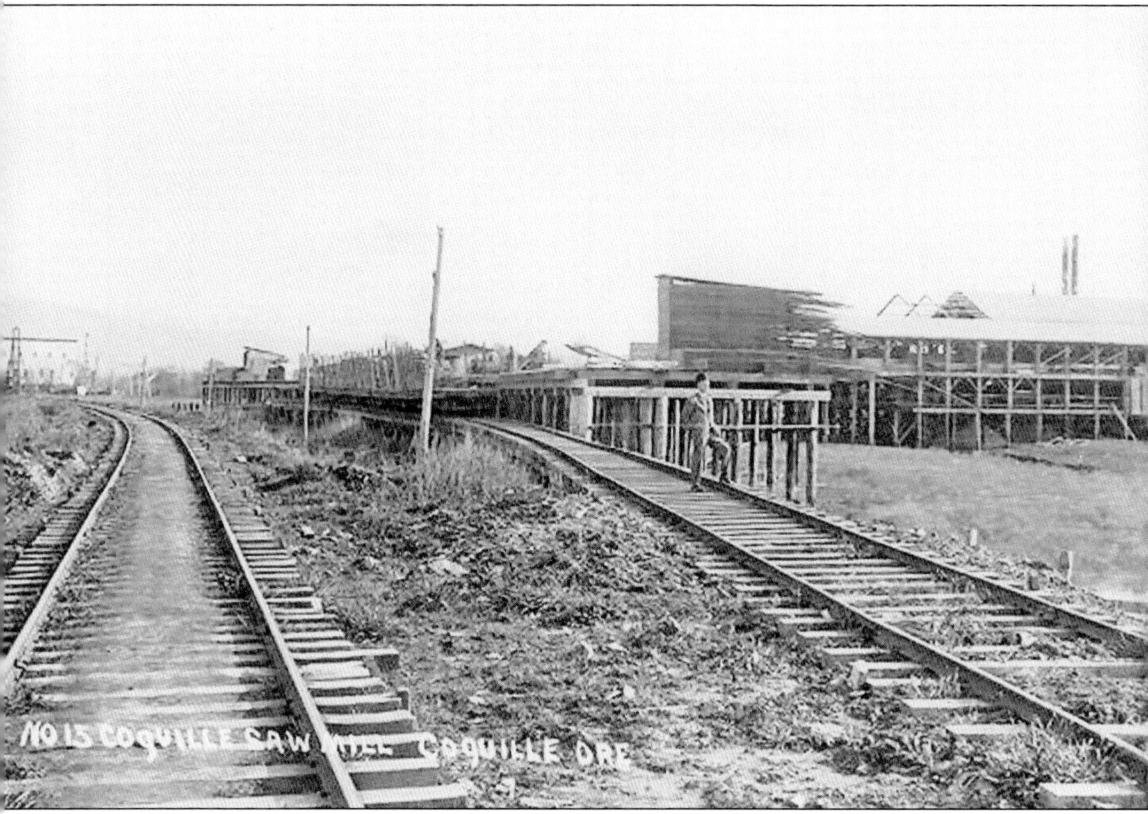

In 1911, Coquille Lumber Company built a sawmill where Sturdivant Park is now. The company was formed by Joseph A. Collier and other local investors, including Louis J. Simpson of North Bend. After financial setbacks, the mill shut down. Later, it was purchased by the Robert Dollar Lumber Company of California. During World War I, it was modified by the Sitka Spruce Company to provide Sitka spruce aircraft materials for the US Army. Soldiers were even assigned to work at the mill. Barracks and a cafeteria were built for the workers next to the plant. Extensive preparations were made to harvest Sitka spruce timber in the Beaver Hill area. The plant operated after the war as the Coquille Lumber Mills and later as Dimmick Lumber Company. It was ultimately dismantled in the late 1930s. Roy Wernich was the mill manager for many years. (CVM.)

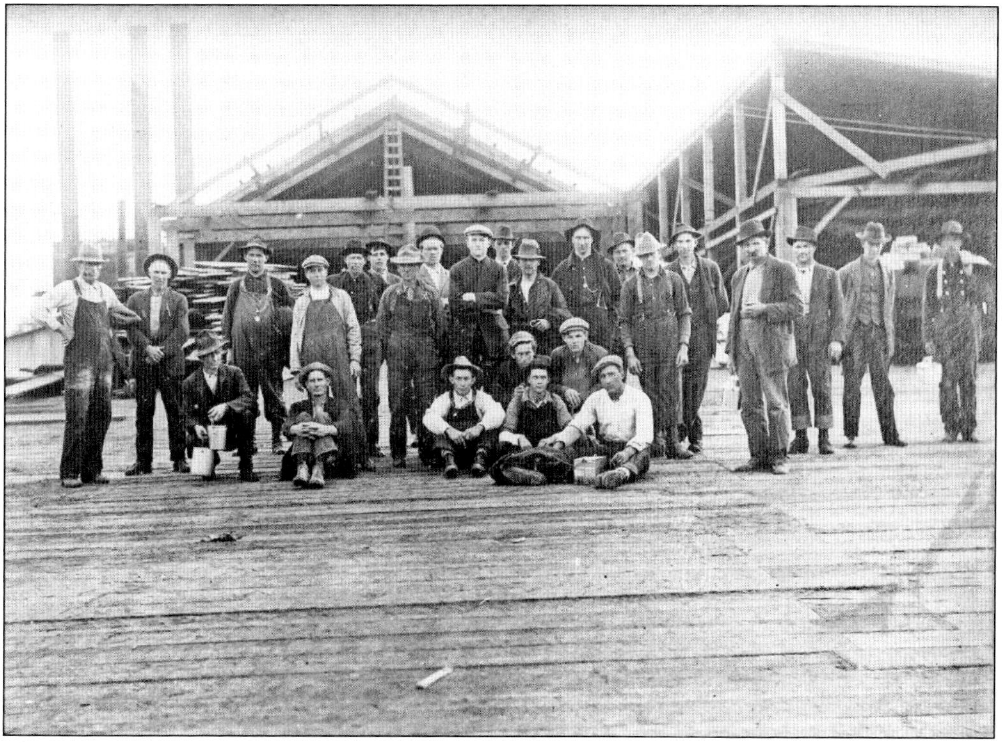

These are civilian workers of the Coquille Lumber Company sawmill around 1913. The mill was west of the downtown and became the Sitka Spruce Sawmill during World War I, with soldiers operating the mill. These men are on a raised wooden platform with boiler smokestacks and mill buildings in the background. (DCM N2399.)

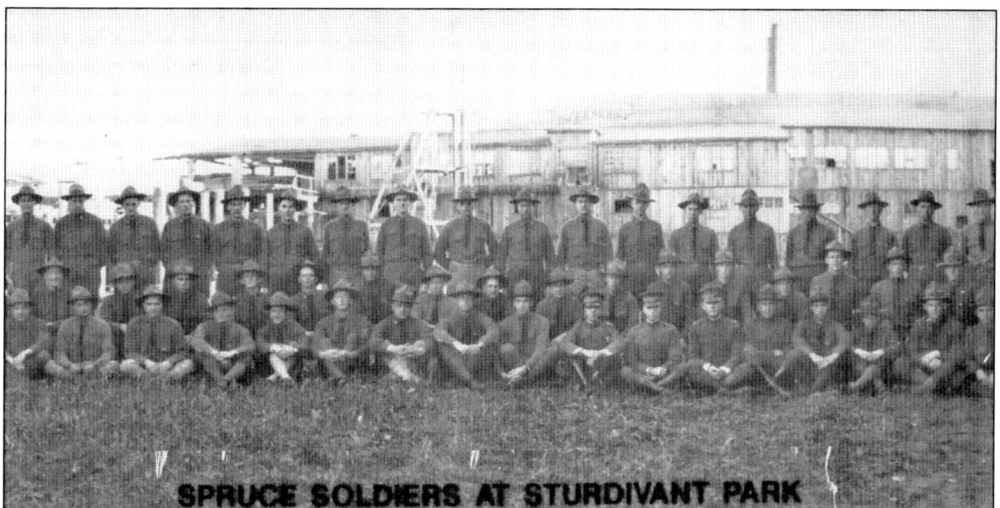

These are soldier workers of the Sitka Spruce Sawmill during World War I. They were members of the 103rd Spruce Squadron, US Army. For a time, they operated the mill to support the war effort. The main focus of the mill during the war was processing Sitka spruce lumber for aircraft. In 1917, a two-story barracks was erected for the 52 soldiers and 2 officers. (CVM.)

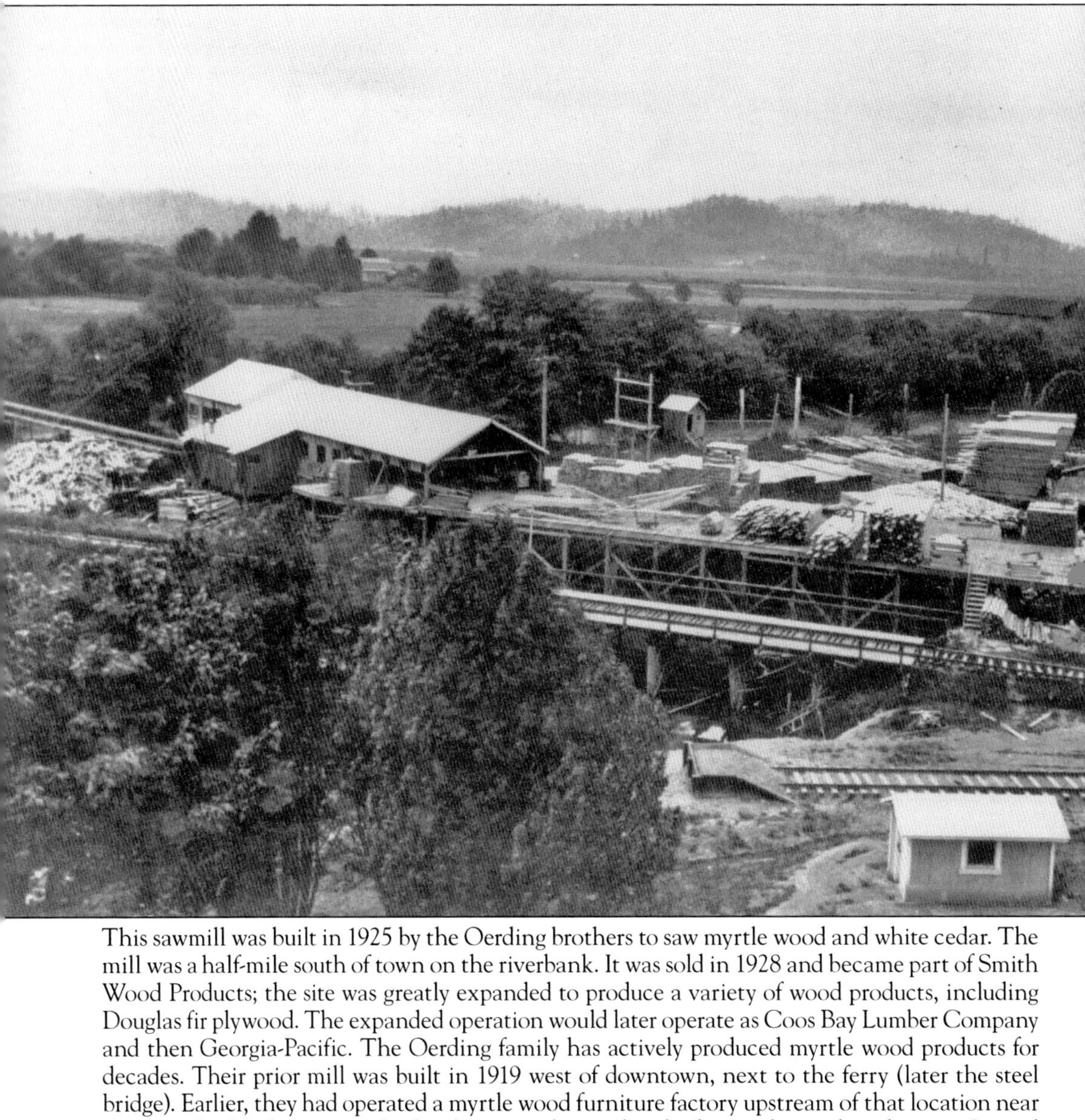

This sawmill was built in 1925 by the Oerding brothers to saw myrtle wood and white cedar. The mill was a half-mile south of town on the riverbank. It was sold in 1928 and became part of Smith Wood Products; the site was greatly expanded to produce a variety of wood products, including Douglas fir plywood. The expanded operation would later operate as Coos Bay Lumber Company and then Georgia-Pacific. The Oerding family has actively produced myrtle wood products for decades. Their prior mill was built in 1919 west of downtown, next to the ferry (later the steel bridge). Earlier, they had operated a myrtle wood furniture factory upstream of that location near the city wharf. In later years, the family operated a retail outlet for myrtle wood products on Central Boulevard near today's high school. One of their early customers was author Jack London, who commissioned the construction of furniture in 1907 for his ranch in California. (CVM.)

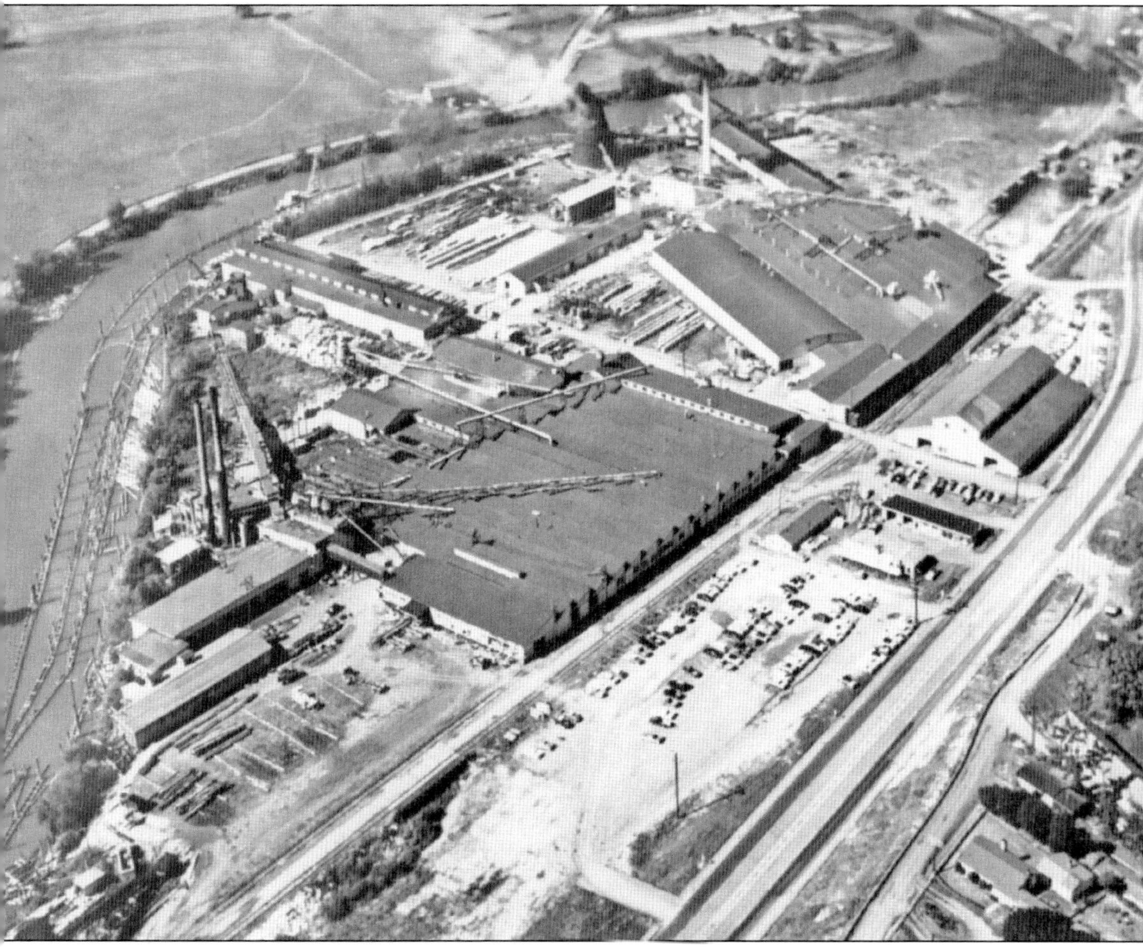

This is an aerial view of the Coos Bay Lumber Company or Georgia-Pacific mill. The dominant mill for the community was south of the downtown between the highway and the river. The first mill at this site was a sawmill built by the Oerding brothers. Thereafter, Smith Wood Products purchased the mill. By 1929, with the assistance of George Ulett, the mill was expanded with a new focus on battery separators and venetian blinds, both made from white cedar. Ulett saw the potential of expanding the operation to produce Douglas fir plywood and added a new plant by 1936. The mill was purchased by Coos Bay Lumber Company in 1946 and finally Georgia-Pacific in 1956. At one time, the plant employed 700 workers. (CVM.)

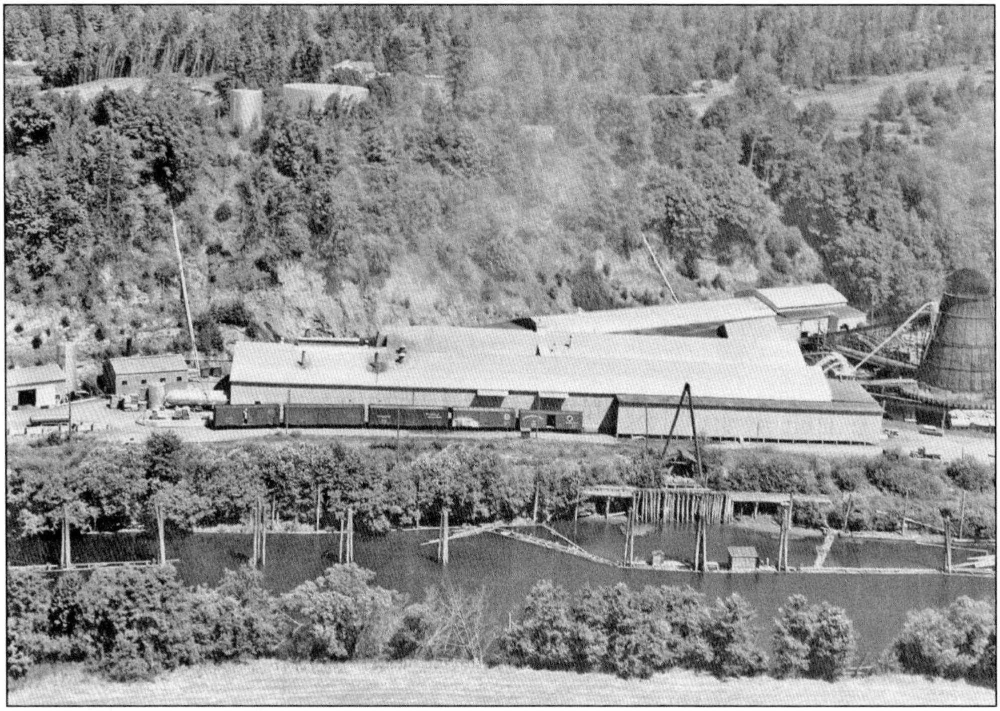

This is the original Coquille Plywood Mill north of town at Cedar Point, next to the river. In 1952, George Ulett supported the completion of this plant. It was sold to Textron in 1955 but kept the name. Later, it was sold to Roseburg Lumber Company, which became Roseburg Forest Products. The plant has expanded over time and is still in operation. (CVM.)

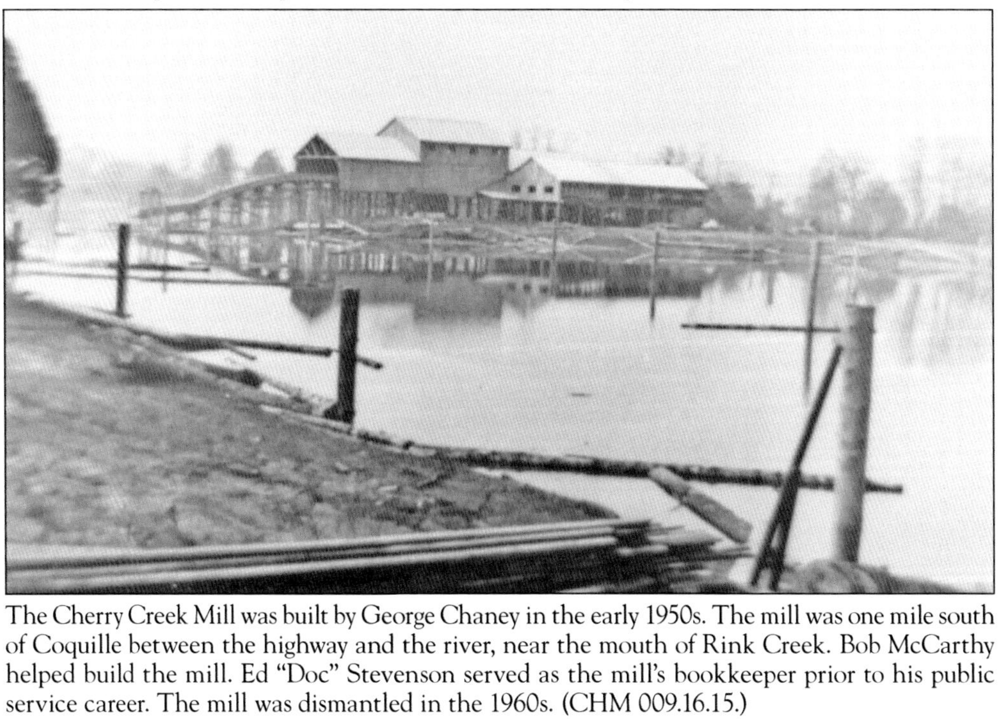

The Cherry Creek Mill was built by George Chaney in the early 1950s. The mill was one mile south of Coquille between the highway and the river, near the mouth of Rink Creek. Bob McCarthy helped build the mill. Ed "Doc" Stevenson served as the mill's bookkeeper prior to his public service career. The mill was dismantled in the 1960s. (CHM 009.16.15.)

Fallers are at work on a big fir on Cunningham Creek north of town. Smith-Powers had a logging camp on Cunningham Creek and later constructed a logging railroad up Cunningham Creek and on to Fairview. Smith-Powers also built a logging railroad from Myrtle Point to the Powers area. Their extensive logging operations supported their large Marshfield sawmill. (DCM N2399.)

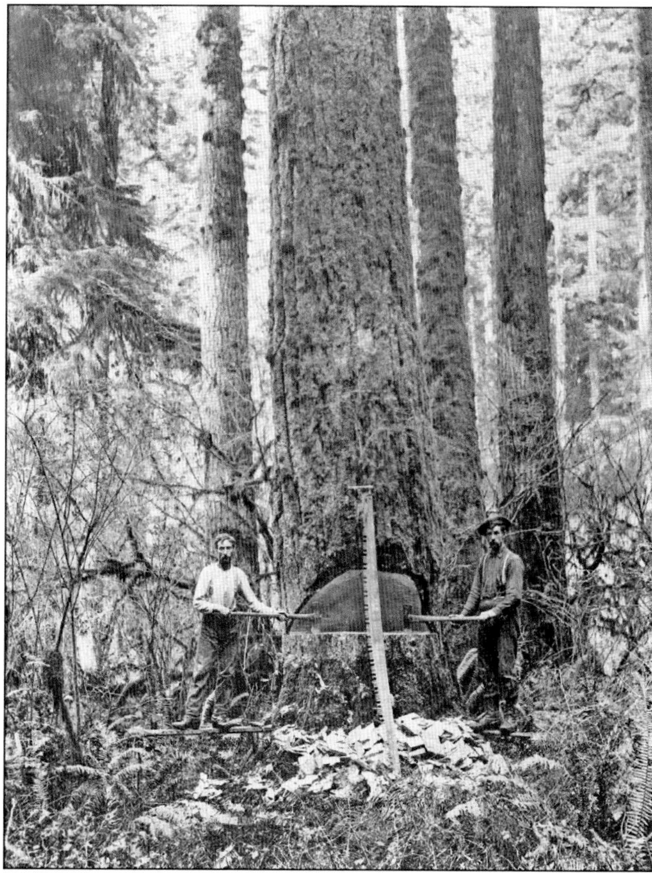

Ox teams were used in early logging to move logs out of the forest. The oxen were strong and economical to maintain, the same qualities sought by pioneer settlers earlier. The ends of the logs were beveled to ease the pulling. Later, steam-powered "donkeys" and small railroads would reduce the use of the ox teams. (CVM.)

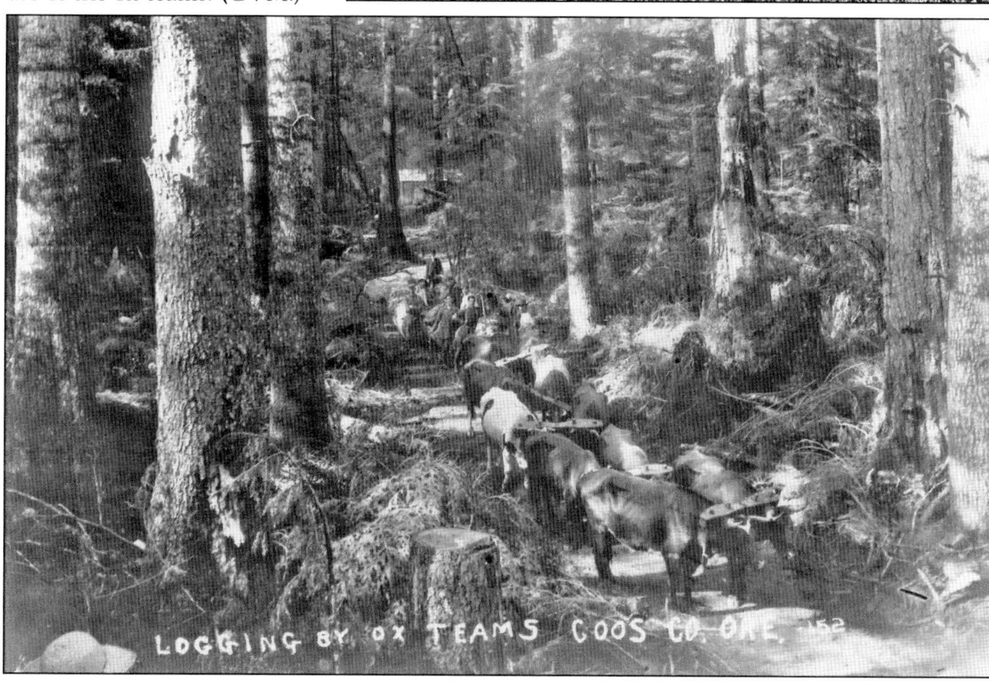

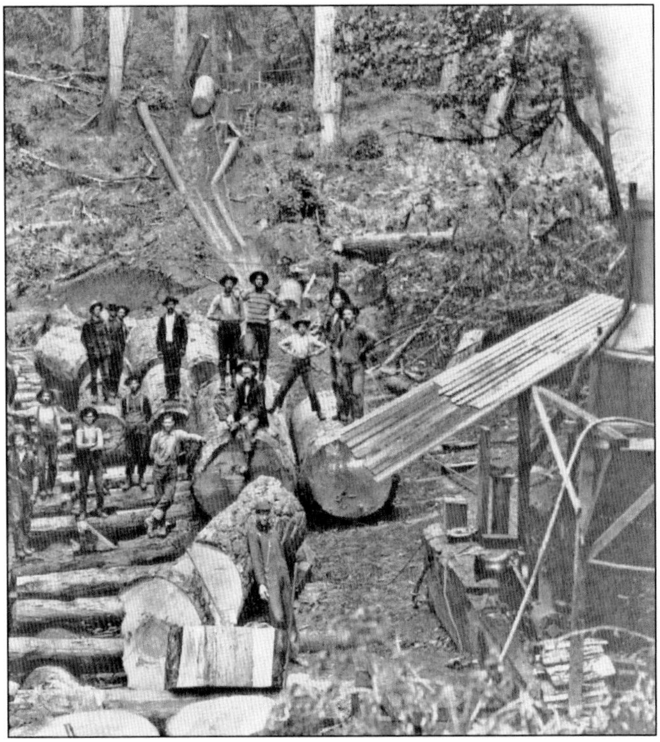

In 1906, the Aasen brothers actively logged on Rink Creek about one mile south of town. They leased the downtown sawmill prior to its purchase by E.E. "Eck" Johnson. At left is the Aasen brothers' logging crew in 1910 beside the steam donkey they used to pull logs to a landing. From the 1890s until the 1920s, most steam donkeys were wood-fired. By the late 1930s, with internal-combustion engines, the need to pipe water to the donkeys was eliminated. Below are the Aasen brothers' small steam locomotive and railroad used to haul logs out of the little valley to the river nearby. The cut wood piled along the tracks was used to fuel the locomotive. (Left, BM 40113; below, BM 45407.)

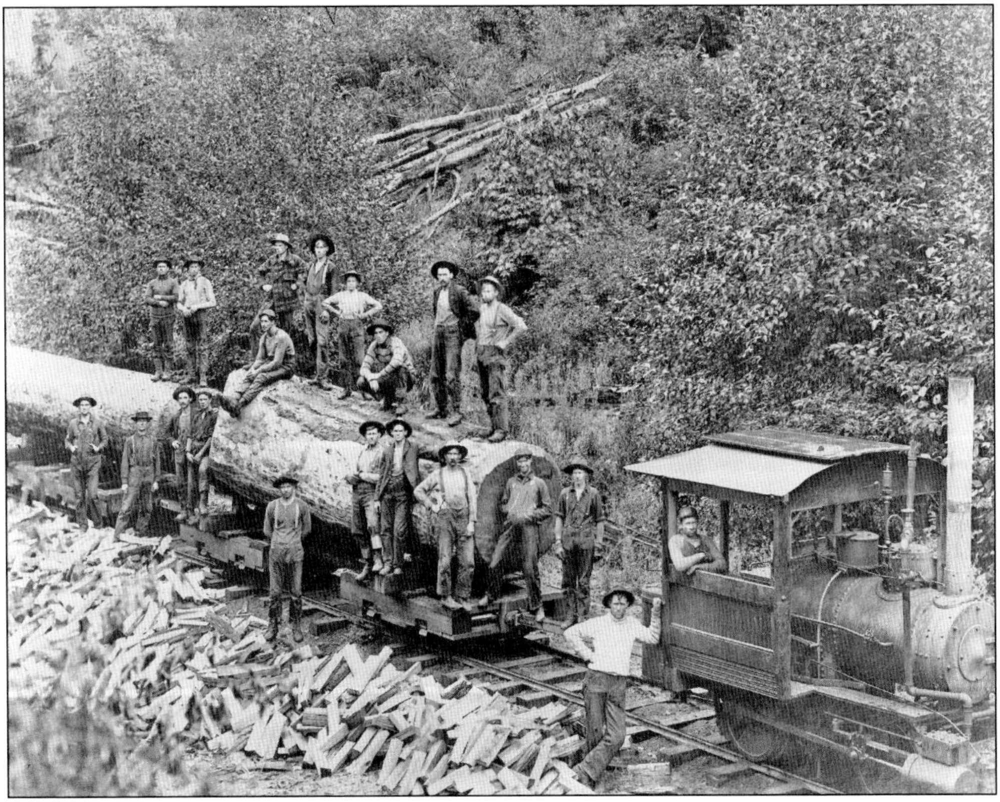

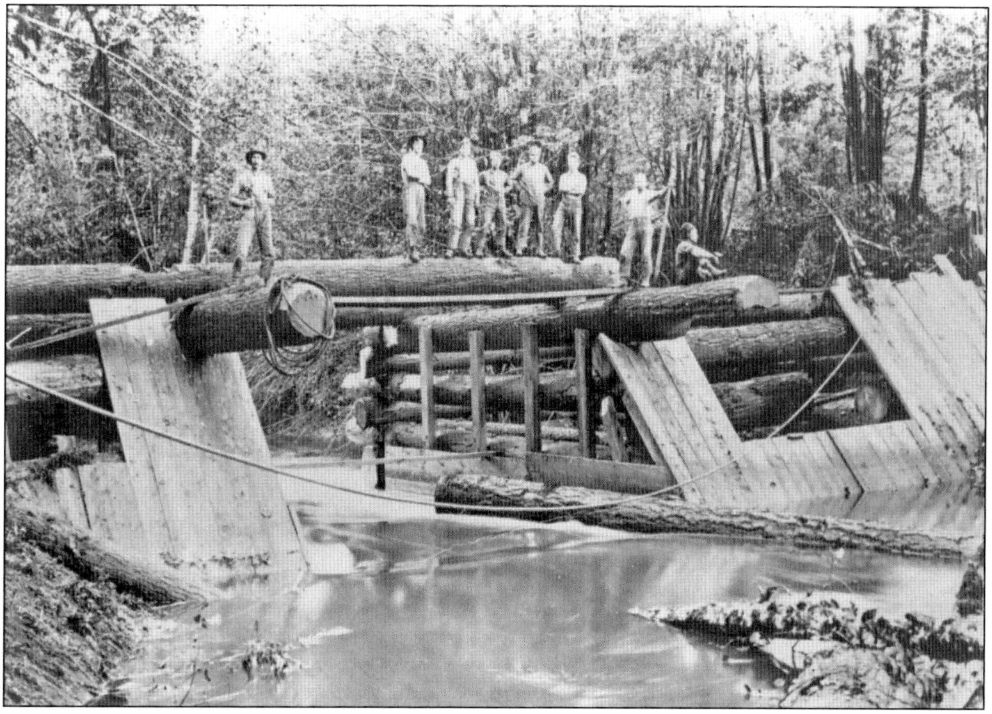

This is an Aasen brothers splash dam on Middle Creek. The dam would create an upstream reservoir in which water and logs were stored until the spillway was opened to release a large flood. This was done on the upper reaches of the river. Once the flood brought the logs to the lower portions of the river, they were more manageable. (CVM.)

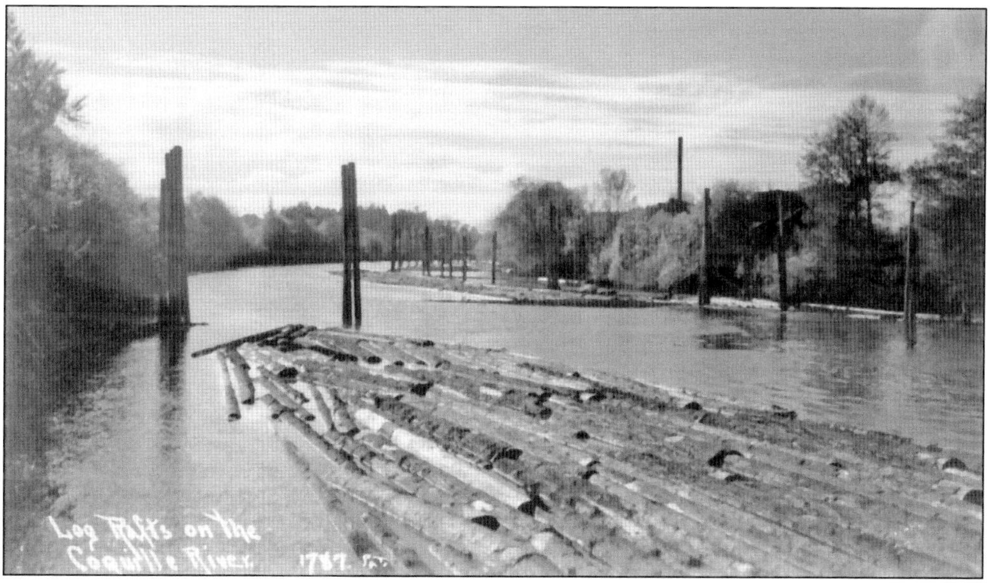

The lower portions of the river from Myrtle Point to Bandon were useful for transportation, sorting, and storing of logs. Pilings, common still in the lower river, provided a means to anchor the logs. Moorage rights to tie logs to pilings were bought and sold and were most valuable near the mills. (CVM.)

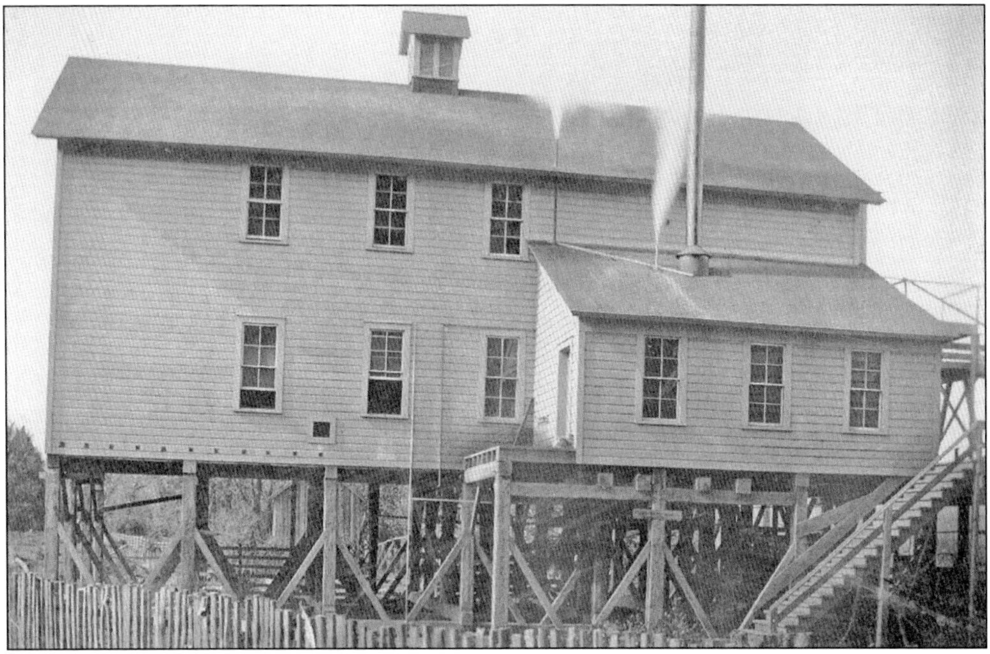

The Coquille Creamery was situated on the bank of the river one mile south of town. In 1897, the Coquille Dairymen's Union rented the creamery as a cooperative business. In 1901, it was the oldest creamery in operation in the county. Owned by Hillmer & Bredhoff of San Francisco, it was operated under a lease by C. Romander. In April 1908, the O.K. Creamery purchased the Coquille Creamery. (CVM.)

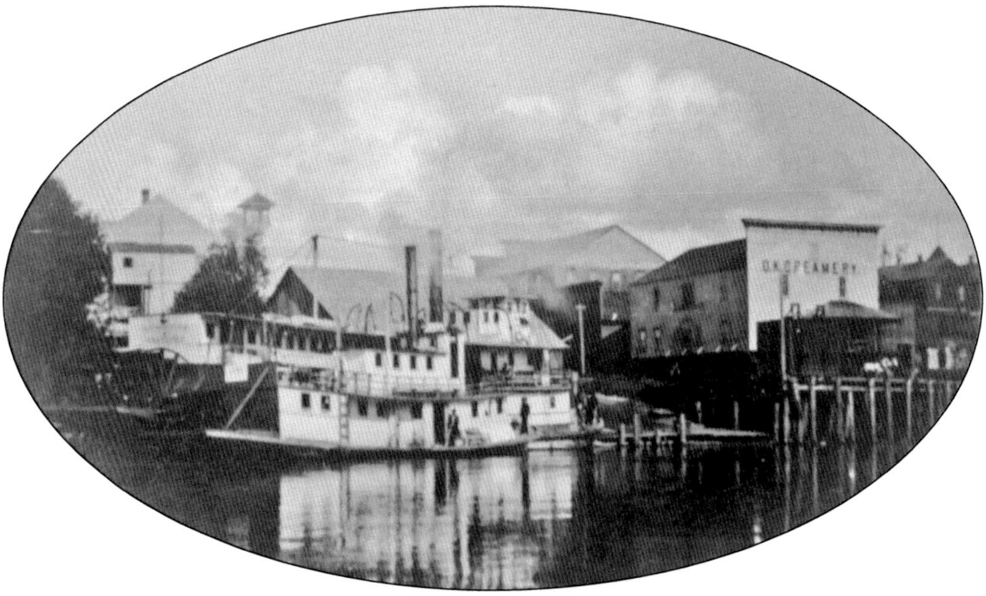

The O.K. Creamery was located on the downtown waterfront. Articles of incorporation were filed in 1907 by owner Fred B. Haight and Company. George E. Peoples was the manager. During 1910, the creamery produced 154,937 pounds of butter and 72,342 pounds of cheese, with sales amounting to $59,317. In 1911, local dairymen incorporated and operated the O.K. Creamery as a cooperative. (CHM 992.8.1767.)

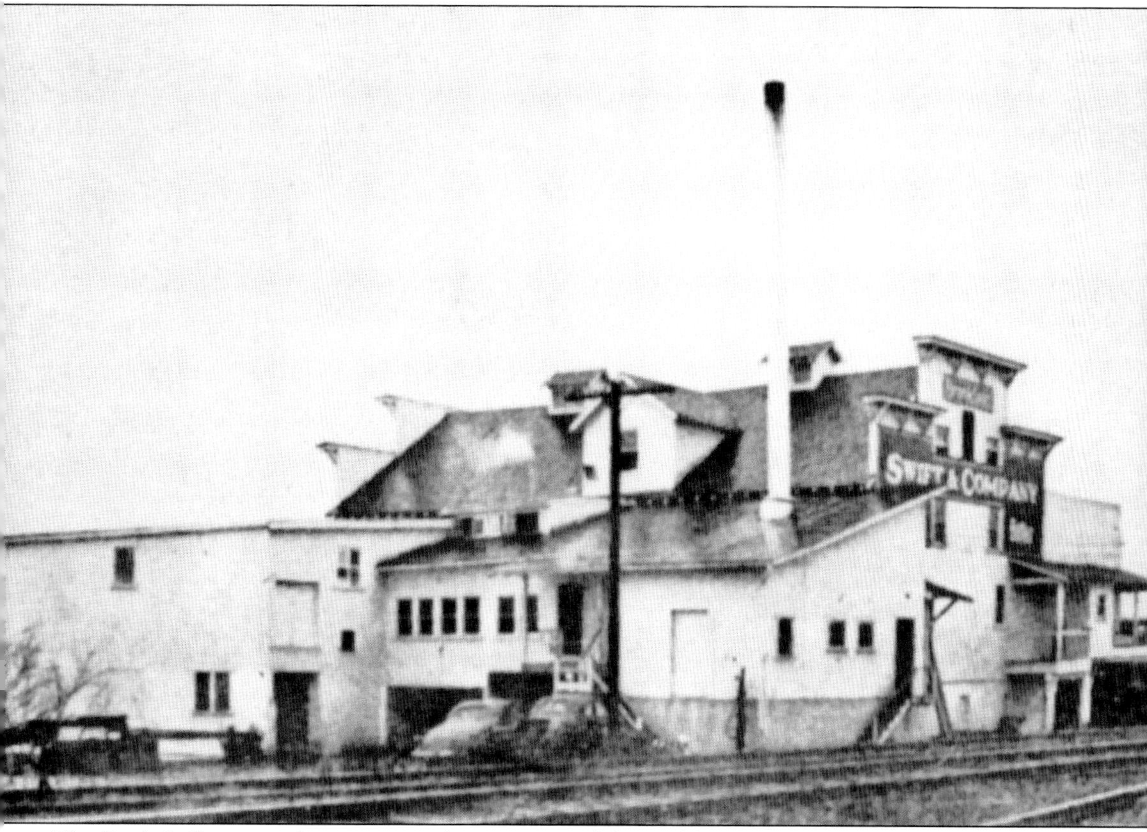

The Swift & Company Creamery, on the river west of the steel bridge and railroad depot, is shown here around 1940. Swift had purchased the plant from the Coquille Valley Creamery in 1928. The original Coquille Valley Creamery was destroyed by fire and rebuilt in 1916. At the time of the fire, the officers in the creamery were C.E. McCurdy, Fred Belloni, Charles Skeels, W.G. Mehl, and Frank Willard. After buying out several local small creameries, Swift & Company became the largest cheese and butter maker on the Pacific Coast. The main plant was in Coquille, with sister plants in Norway, Myrtle Point, Sixes, Reedsport, and Cushman. Henry Belloni worked at the creamery and received many awards for his butter. In 1948, the Swift & Company Creamery building was condemned, and owners in Chicago decided not to rebuild. (CHM 009.16.5612.)

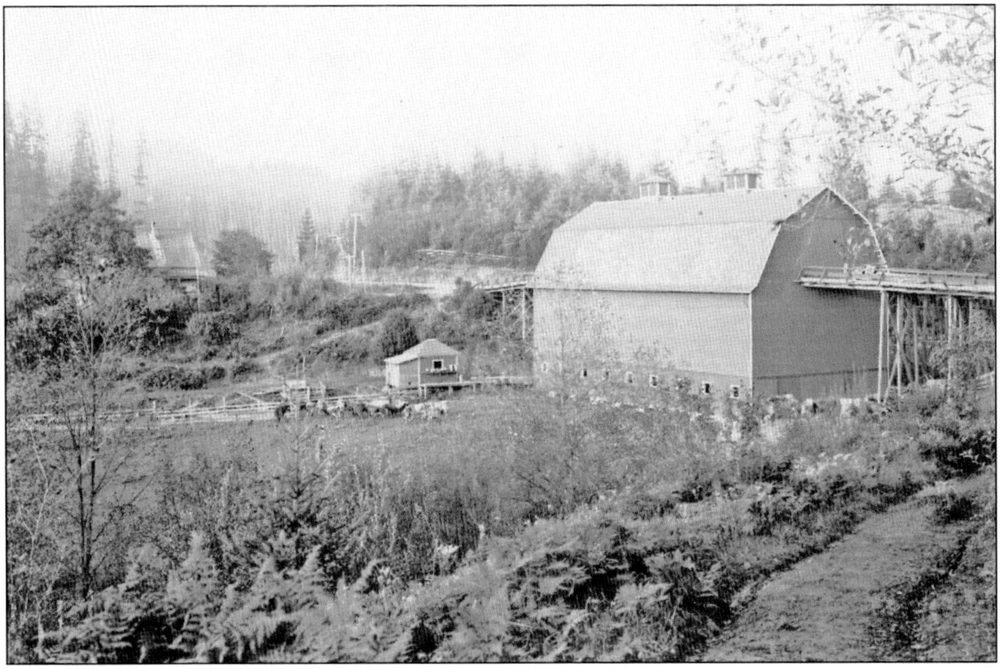

The Watson dairy barn on Cunningham Creek was one of many in the area. It was noted for its use as a detour for cars while work was being done on Fairview Road. Traffic was temporarily rerouted through the upper level of the barn. (CVM.)

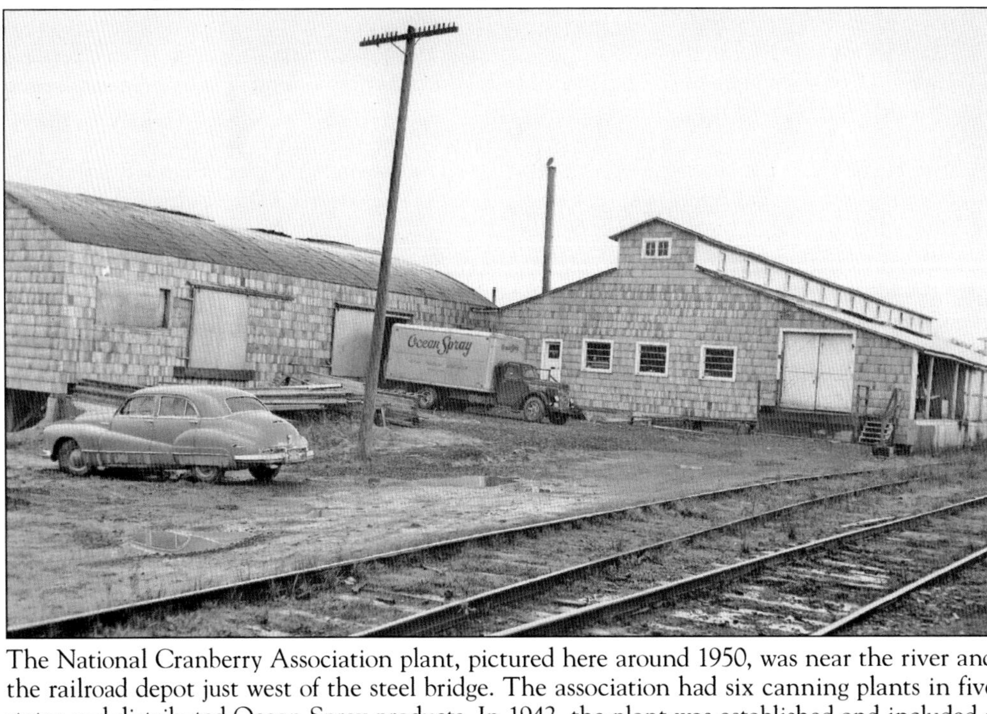

The National Cranberry Association plant, pictured here around 1950, was near the river and the railroad depot just west of the steel bridge. The association had six canning plants in five states and distributed Ocean Spray products. In 1942, the plant was established and included a cold storage facility. In prior years, the large building on the right was the Collier Warehouse. (CHM 973-90-C.)

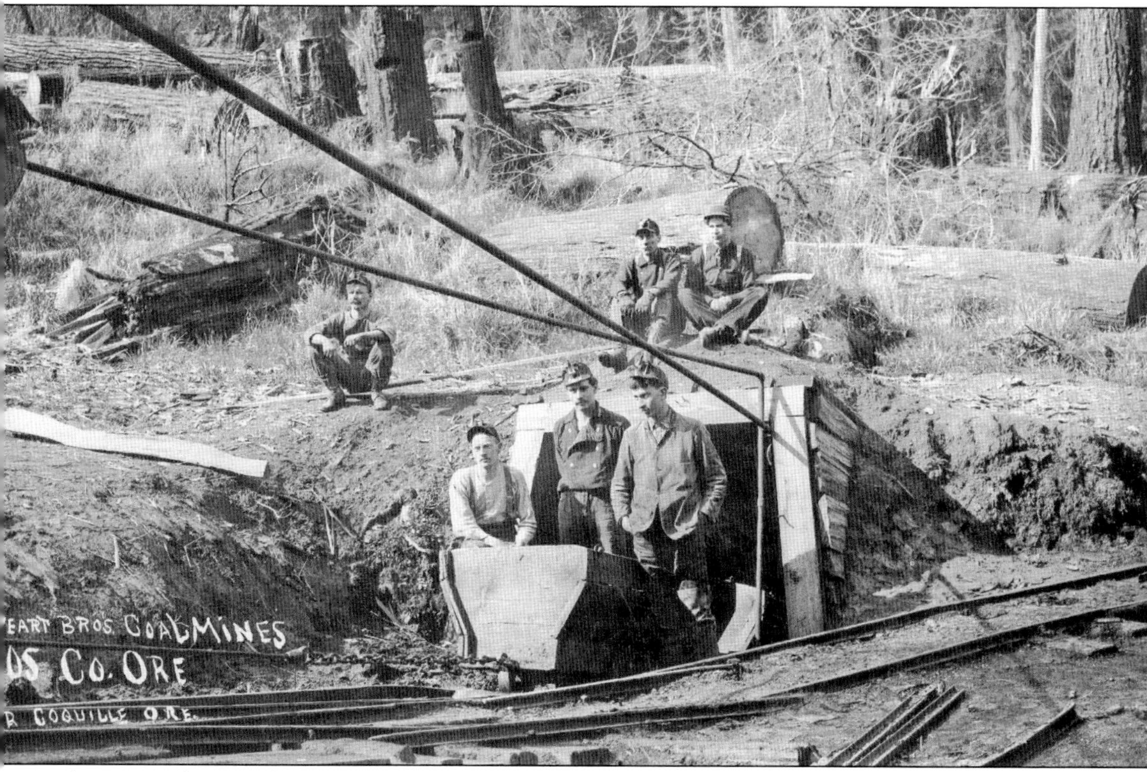

This is one of two coal mines the Peart brothers owned about one mile northwest of downtown. The Peart mines were among several local mines that mostly served local residential and commercial heating markets. In 1902, a tramway and trestle were built totaling 3,500 feet to move the coal from their first mine to the main railroad and the river. The trestle was washed out by high water in 1903. In 1904, the mine was sold to the Coquille Coal and Lumber Company. In 1905, John Peart opened a new mine nearby on Budd Creek. By 1907, a bunker was built on the downtown waterfront, and the new mine was supplying coal for the river trade and the sternwheeler *Dispatch*. In 1910, Frank Morse purchased an interest in the mine and installed a power plant nearby to produce electricity for Coquille and Myrtle Point after the Johnson Mill fire destroyed the power plant there. His enterprise was the Coquille River Power Company. (CHM 981.75.)

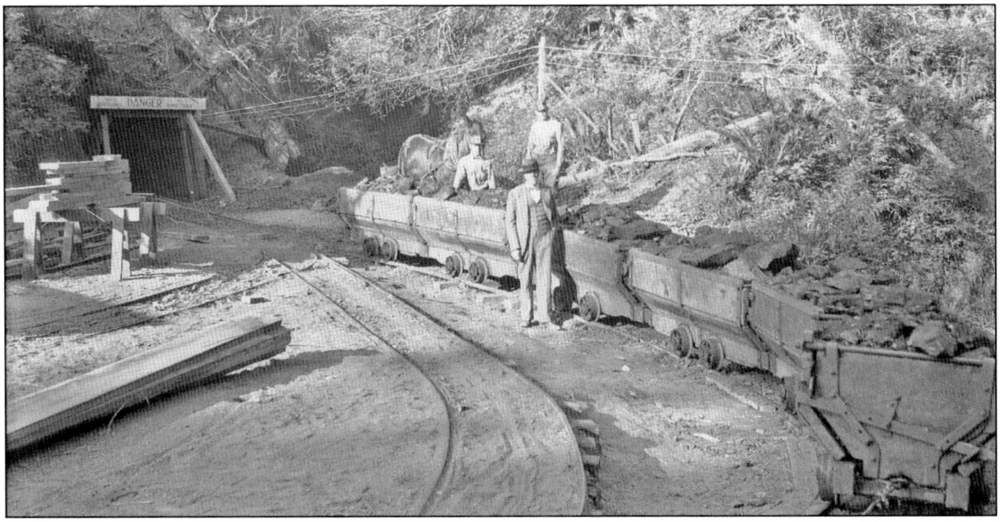

The McClain coal mine, northwest of downtown near the two Peart mines, operated from 1929 to 1930. The Bituminous Coal Company mine was nearby. These four mines were located northwest of Coquille between Cunningham Creek and Cedar Point. The Barrow mine operated in the Shelley Road area. All of the local mines were considered part of the Riverton coal basin and worked the same coal vein. (CHM 009.16.5639.)

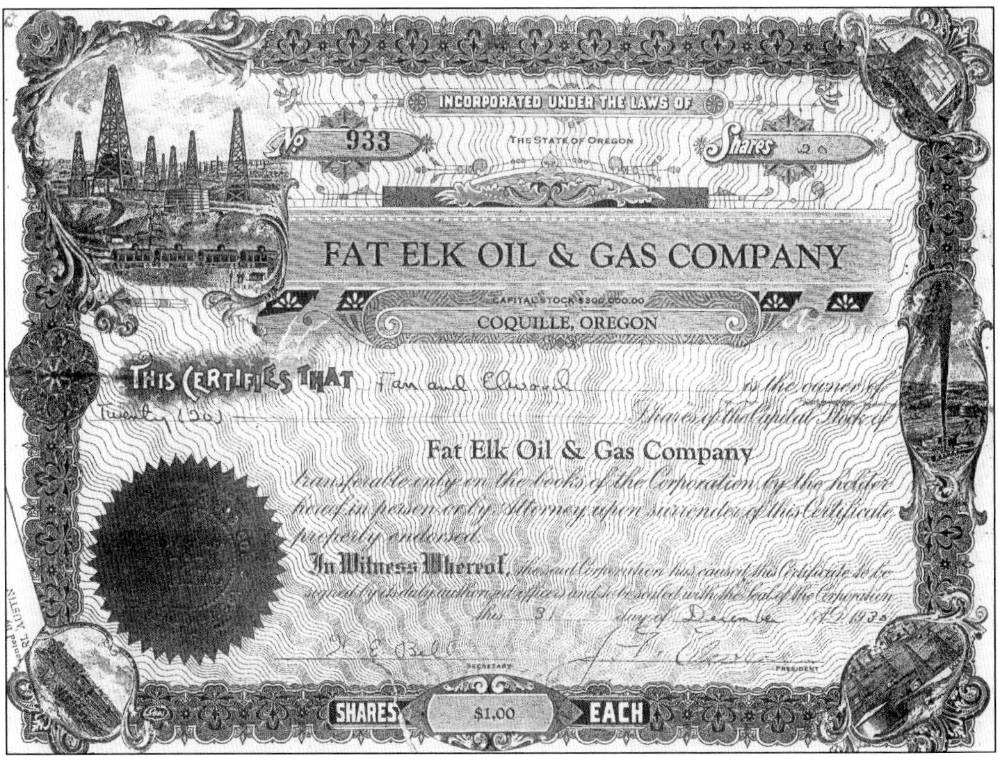
INCORPORATED UNDER THE LAWS OF THE STATE OF OREGON

No 933 — Shares 20

FAT ELK OIL & GAS COMPANY

CAPITAL STOCK $300,000.00

COQUILLE, OREGON

This Certifies that ______ is the owner of Twenty (20) Shares of the Capital Stock of

Fat Elk Oil & Gas Company

transferable only on the books of the Corporation by the holder hereof in person or by Attorney upon surrender of this Certificate properly endorsed.

In Witness Whereof, the said Corporation has caused this Certificate to be signed by its duly authorized officers and to be sealed with the Seal of the Corporation this 31 day of Decembe 193_

SECRETARY — PRESIDENT

SHARES $1.00 EACH

During the 1920s and 1930s, companies drilled for oil and gas in the Fat Elk area. The earliest venture was by the Fat Elk Oil & Gas Company, which included local investors and had limited success. In 1938, W.E. Marrion of the Coast Oil Company drilled new wells and put a pipeline across the valley and under the river to deliver gas to the city. (JF.)

Four

Buildings and Businesses

In 1871, the Coquille business district began when Tilman Vowell opened a general store. Vowell later sold his merchandise to Alkaney Nosler. James Moulton soon purchased the goods, enlarged the stock, and erected the first frame building in the town.

Soon, other businesses were established along the waterfront on what would be named Front Street. In 1873, M.W. Miller erected a small hotel called the Elk Horn. Its defining feature was a pair of massive elk horns that graced the front of the inn. In 1875, the Robinson House, a plain and substantial hotel known for its excellent accommodations, was built nearby.

In the summer of 1880, Bunch, Bennett & Company erected a sawmill and gristmill between Front Street and the river. By 1883, the Olive Hotel was built, replacing the Elk Horn. In 1890, the Coquille River Bank was established. Both businesses were on Front Street.

The district suffered a major blow when, at about 1:00 a.m. on May 31, 1892, a fire broke out on Front Street. This devastating fire effectively destroyed most of the city's commercial business district.

The city quickly rebuilt, still centered on Front Street, largely on the expected arrival of a railroad from Marshfield. The largest addition was the Hotel Coquille, an impressive wood-frame structure on Front Street. The business district grew, with the river and the railroad providing essential transportation. In 1909–1910, three major masonry buildings were constructed, including the First National Bank Building and the Laird Building on First Street and the Richmond-Barker Building on Front Street. In addition, creameries were established and more sawmills were built.

In 1918, another large fire downtown caused a setback. However, the completion of a paved highway from Marshfield in 1921 provided a major economic boost. In 1922, the wood-frame Baxter Hotel (former the Hotel Coquille) was destroyed by a fire. The hotel was rebuilt in concrete and substantially enlarged. Businesses flourished, and new buildings continued to be erected until Highway 101 was rerouted to bypass Coquille in 1960.

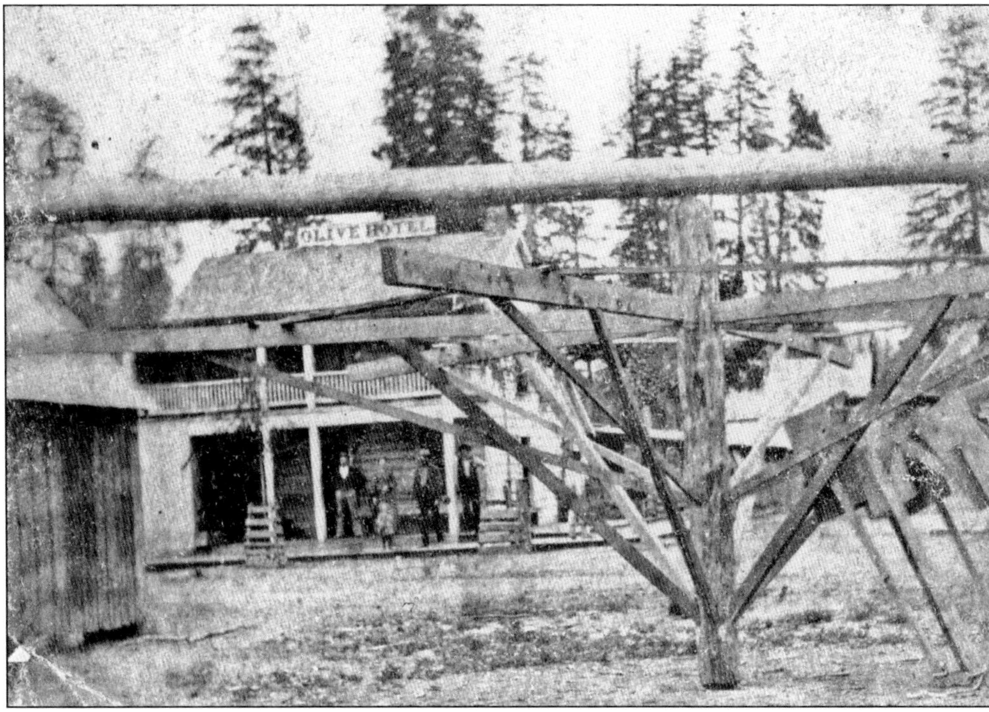

The Olive Hotel was on the northwest corner of Front Street and Central Boulevard in 1873. A member of the Nosler family built the Elk Horn Hotel for M.W. Miller. Later, Charles Olive purchased the hotel and renamed it the Olive Hotel. In 1890, the Olive was considered the best hotel in Coquille. The Olive was destroyed in the fire of 1892. (CHM 992-8-2048.)

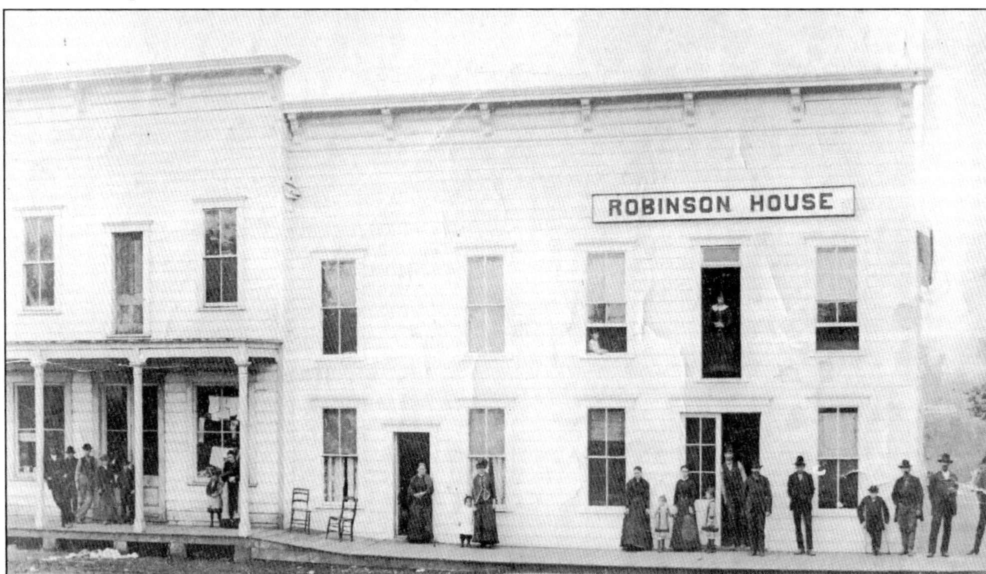

The Robinson House was on the south side of Front Street. It was built in 1875 and noted for its comfortable sitting room with a fireplace. The hotel was destroyed in the 1892 fire. At the time, it was operated by R.H. Lewis. The monetary loss due to the fire was $3,500, but it was only insured for $2,500. (CHM 988.P2.)

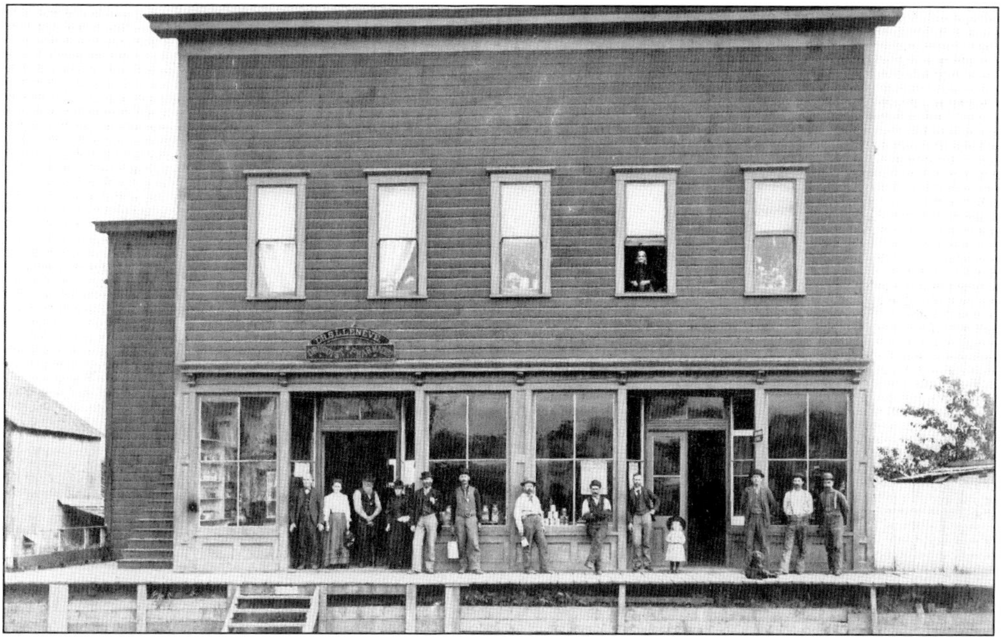

In 1877, Dr. Samuel L. Leneve built his drugstore on the south side of Front Street. He was the pioneer druggist for the entire Coquille Valley and was also postmaster. The pharmacy carried Chamberlain's cough remedy, pain balm, and colic, cholera, and diarrhea remedy and Oregon Kidney Tea. The building was destroyed in the fire of 1892. (CHM 975-100n.)

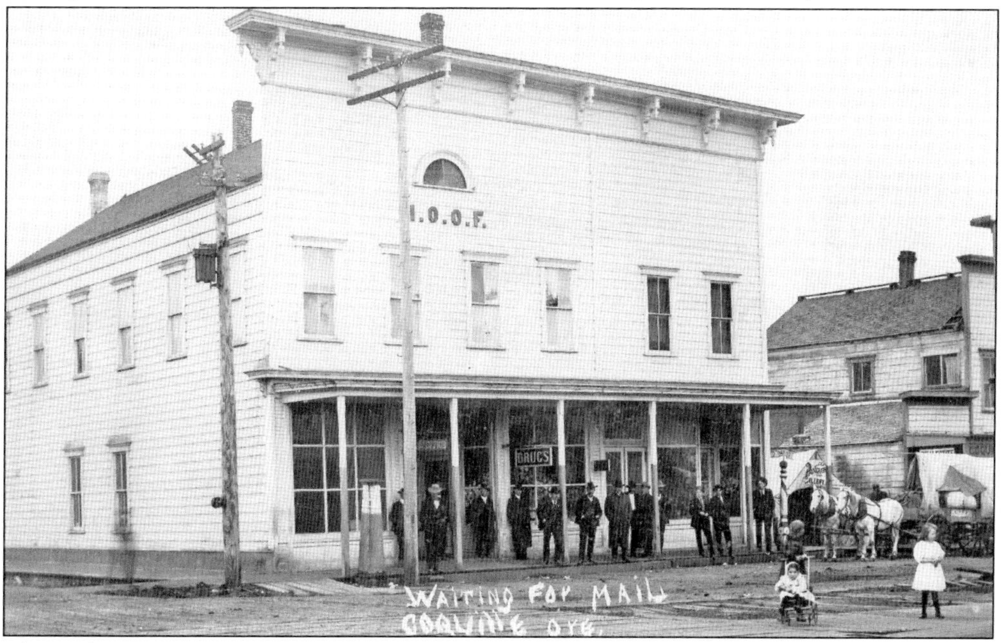

This is the original wood-frame Odd Fellows building on the southeast corner of First Street and Central Boulevard, the same location as the current building. On the ground floor, Fuhrman's Drug Store and the post office occupied the left side, while the McDonald Barbershop occupied the right side. The upstairs was used for Independent Order of Odd Fellows (IOOF) Lodge 53, which was formed in 1875. (CVM.)

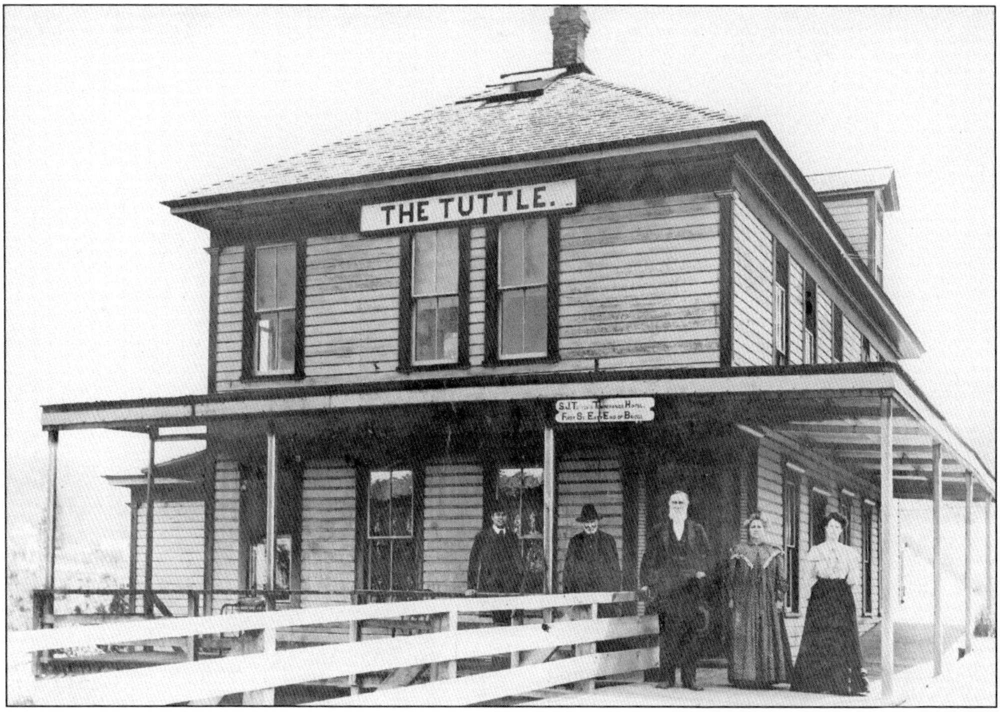

The Tuttle Hotel, at the east end of Front Street, was built in 1890 by Thomas Krewson and owned by Samuel Jackson Tuttle. Note the raised, wood-plank street or bridge. In an 1897 advertisement, the business noted "Only White Labor Employed," reflecting the attitude of some toward the Chinese. At the time, hotel rates were $1 per day, $4 per week for regular boarders, and $5 per week for transients. (CVM.)

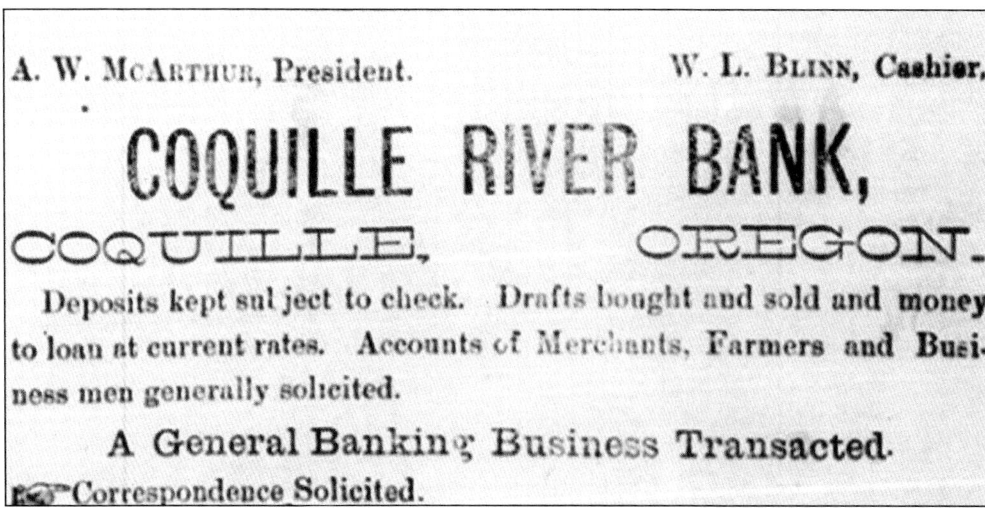

The first bank in the town was the Coquille River Bank, which was established in 1889. Located east of Leneve's Drug Store on Front Street, the building had a 25-foot front with two stories. A.W. McArthur was president, and W.L. Blinn was the cashier. The building was destroyed in the fire of 1892. (CH.)

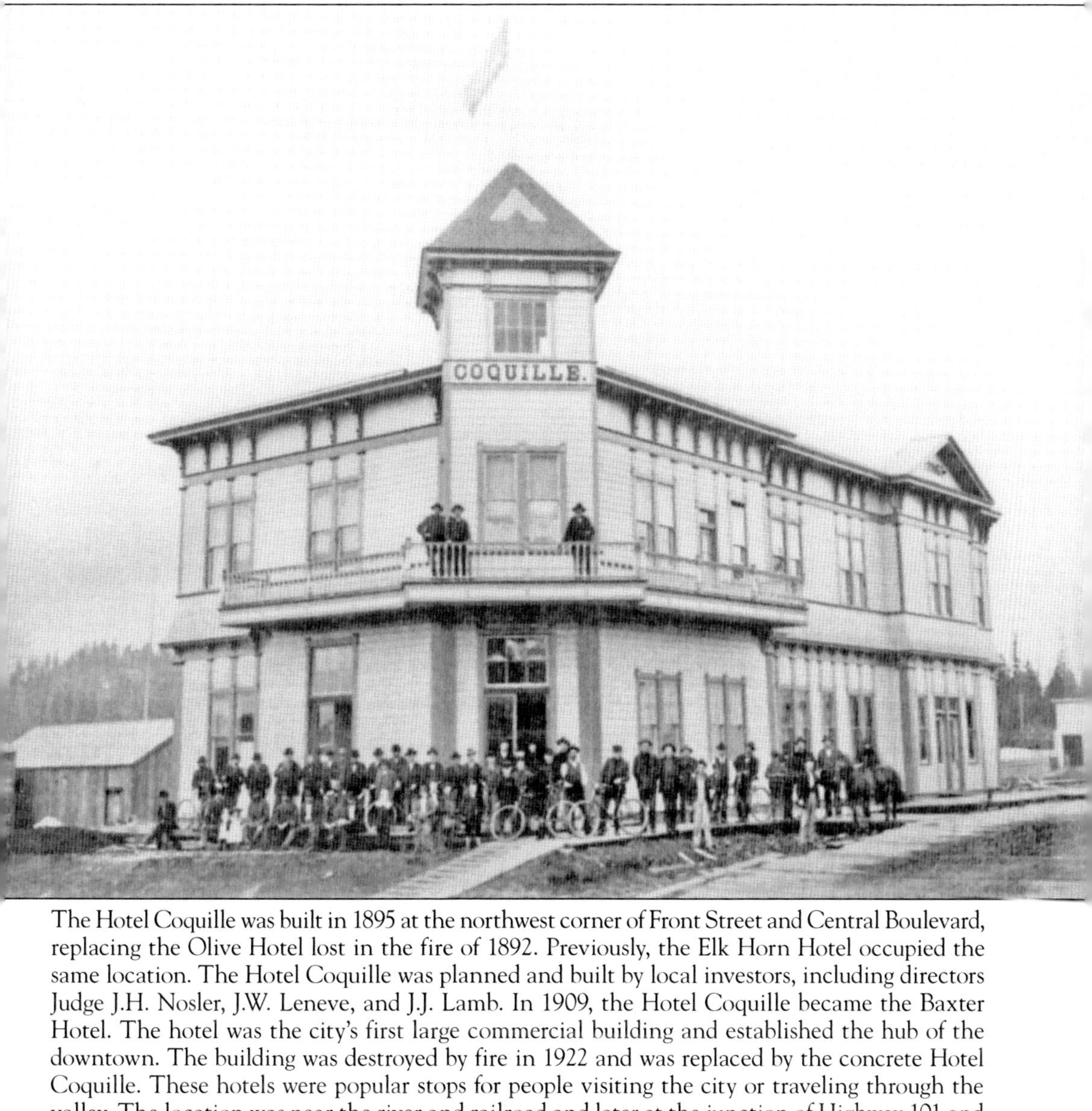

The Hotel Coquille was built in 1895 at the northwest corner of Front Street and Central Boulevard, replacing the Olive Hotel lost in the fire of 1892. Previously, the Elk Horn Hotel occupied the same location. The Hotel Coquille was planned and built by local investors, including directors Judge J.H. Nosler, J.W. Leneve, and J.J. Lamb. In 1909, the Hotel Coquille became the Baxter Hotel. The hotel was the city's first large commercial building and established the hub of the downtown. The building was destroyed by fire in 1922 and was replaced by the concrete Hotel Coquille. These hotels were popular stops for people visiting the city or traveling through the valley. The location was near the river and railroad and later at the junction of Highway 101 and Highway 42. (CVM.)

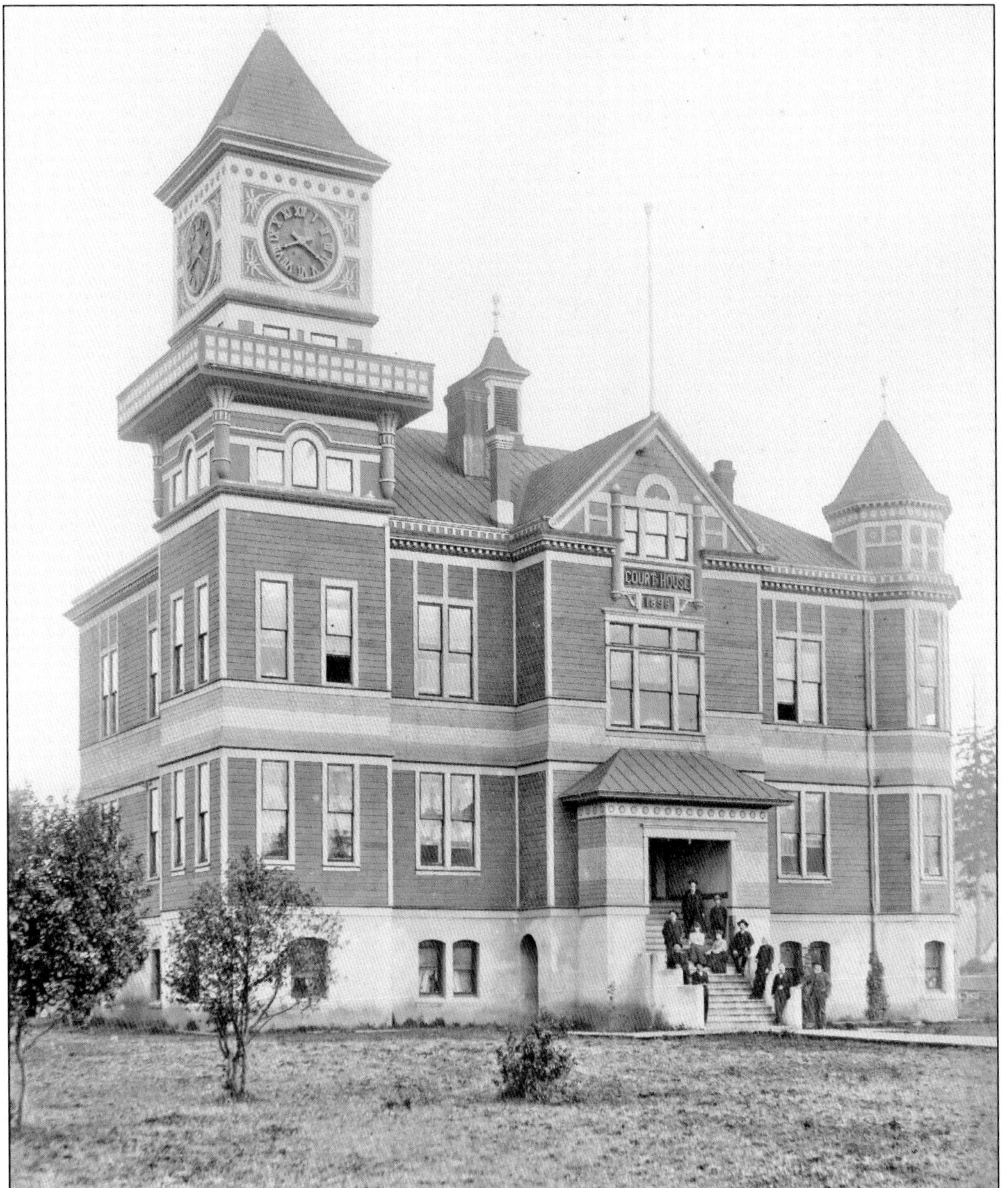

The Coos County Courthouse was built in 1898 by contractor Harmon Snook of Salem after the county seat was moved from Empire to Coquille in 1897. The two-story building with a basement faced south and was built of wood and brick and trimmed with stone. The lumber was furnished by the Lyons Sawmill, and the interior was trimmed with hardwood, myrtle wood, and white cedar. The basement held the jail, the sheriff's residence, and the furnace. The first floor held the offices of the judge, county clerk, sheriff, treasurer, assessor and surveyor, and recorder. The second floor housed the office of the superintendent of schools and the courtroom. Before the courthouse was built, court was held in the bottom floor of the original Masonic hall. In 1916, the hall of records was built to expand the courthouse, and the new three-story building housed the jail on the top floor. The courthouse served the county until 1953, when it was demolished to make way for a new concrete courthouse. (CVM.)

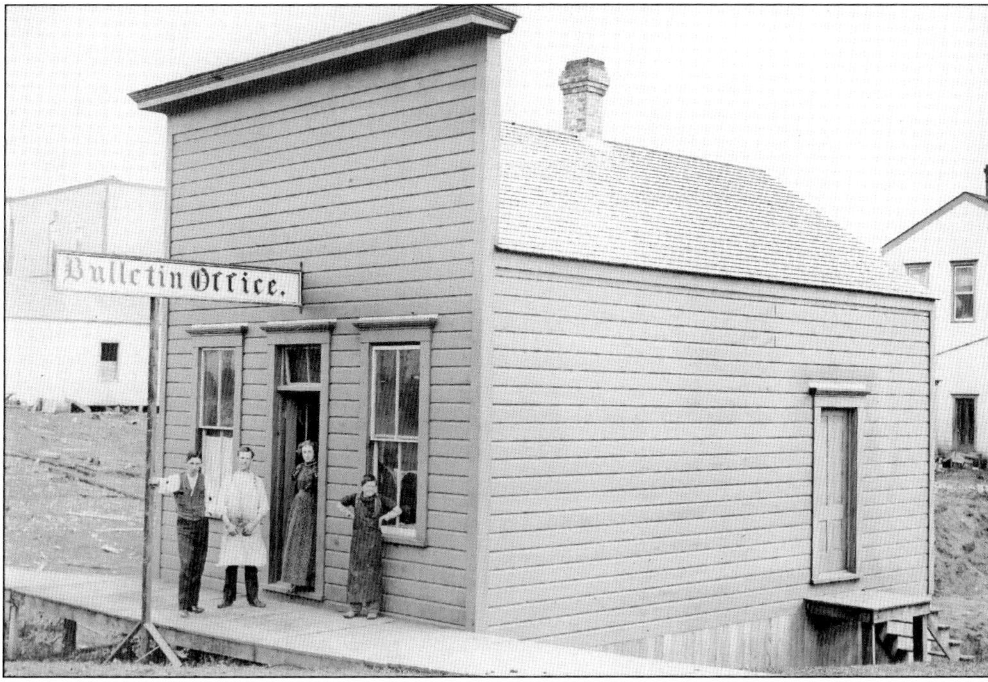

The second newspaper published in Coquille was the *Coquille Bulletin*. The first printing of the *Bulletin* was on December 7, 1894, by John M. Lasswell. It was a weekly independent newspaper printed every Friday until 1899. In 1904, J.J. Stanley sold his interest in the *Bulletin* to Dr. Franklin Dean, who combined it with the *Coquille Herald* and issued a semiweekly newspaper. (CHM 988-P487.)

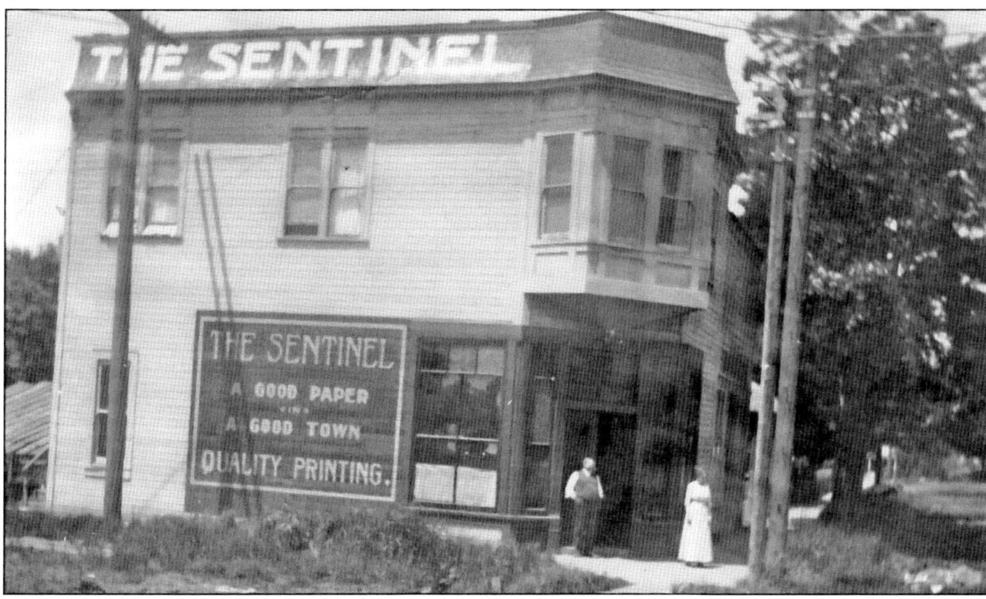

Pictured here are the *Coquille Valley Sentinel* newspaper, printing office, and staff at the northwest corner of Second Street and Central Boulevard around 1915. The first newspapers published in the city were the *Coquille Herald* and the *Coquille Bulletin*. The *Herald* was sold to H.W. Young in 1914 and merged with the *Coquille Valley Sentinel* in 1917. (CHM 995.D64.)

I. J. LAMB, Pres. L. HARLOCKER, Vice-Pres. G. W. WHITE Cashier.

COQUILLE VALLEY BANK.

CAPITAL - - - - - $50,000

COQUILLE, OREGON.

Does a general banking business. Has money to loan on approved personal and real estate security, buys county, town and school district warrants, draws notes, mortgages, deeds and all kinds of legal instruments—Notarial work.

Issues fire insurance at lowest rates in following companies: Ætna, Springfield, Connecticut, Orient and Magdeburg.

BOARD OF DIRECTORS.

A. J. SHERWOOD, ISAIAH HACKER, J. J LAMB, L. HARLOCKER, and G. W. WHITE.

In May 1900, G.W. White established the Coquille Valley Bank in association with John Jones Lamb and Lintner Harlocker. Lamb was president, Harlocker vice president, and White cashier. The bank building was completed in 1900, and the bank was in operation until its dissolution in 1903. The First National Bank opened soon after purchasing the business and building at the northwest corner of First Street and Central Boulevard. (CCH.)

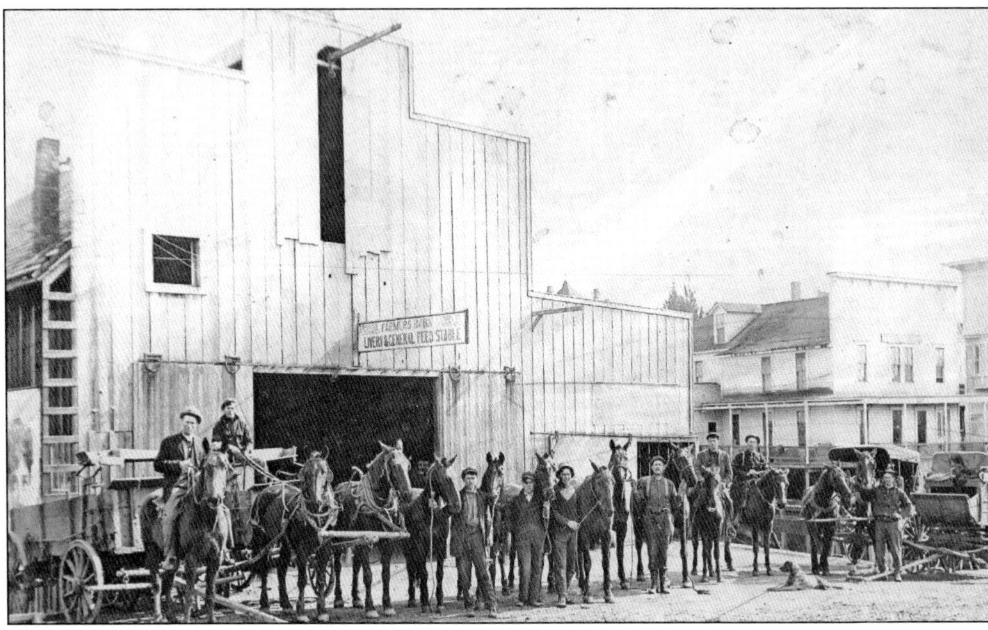

This is the J.B. Pointer Livery in the early 1900s at the southeast corner of First Street and Adams Street. R.E. Buck established the first livery in Coquille. Other liveries included the Pioneer Livery and Feed Stable, at the northwest corner of First Street and Central Boulevard, and the Dunham & Whites Livery, on the north side of First Street between Central Boulevard and Adams Street. (CVM.)

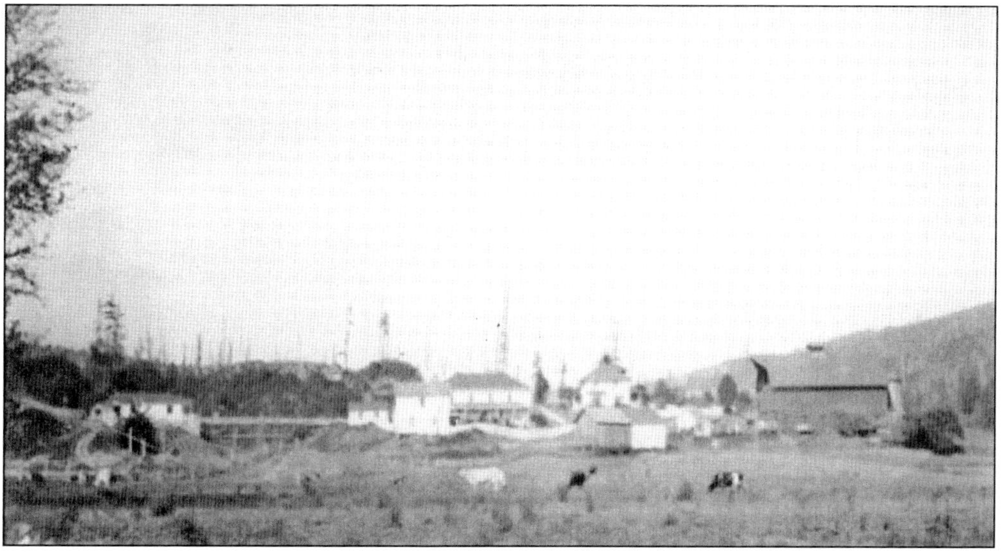

The county poor farm was relocated from Empire to Fairview Road north of town in 1897. It served the indigent and unfortunate who had nowhere else to go. Those living on the farm resented the name and requested it be renamed the Cunningham Farm. It consisted of a dairy, a birthing shed, a cookhouse, and a cemetery. There was a "lepers field" for those with leprosy. (CVM.)

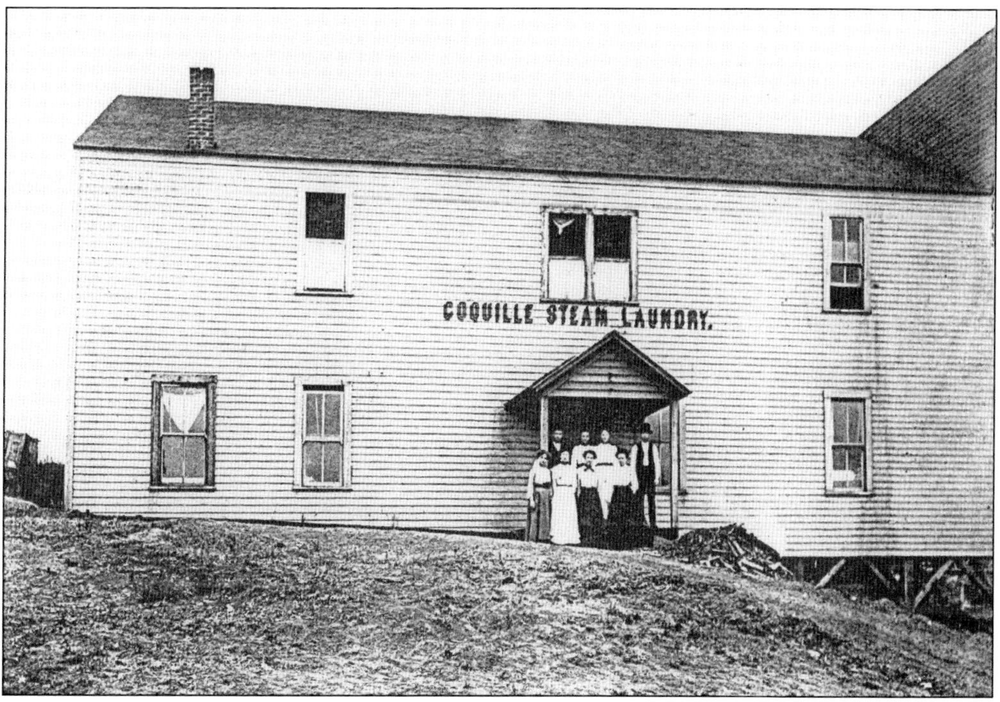

In 1903, Sam Nosler and Will Lyons established the Coquille Steam Laundry on the west end of Front Street. In 1907, their services included sorting, ironing, washing, and mangling. They purchased a wagon, picked up laundry on Mondays, and delivered on Fridays. By 1908, Nosler had a new partner by the name of Morrison, and a three-ton ice-making plant was installed. (CVM.)

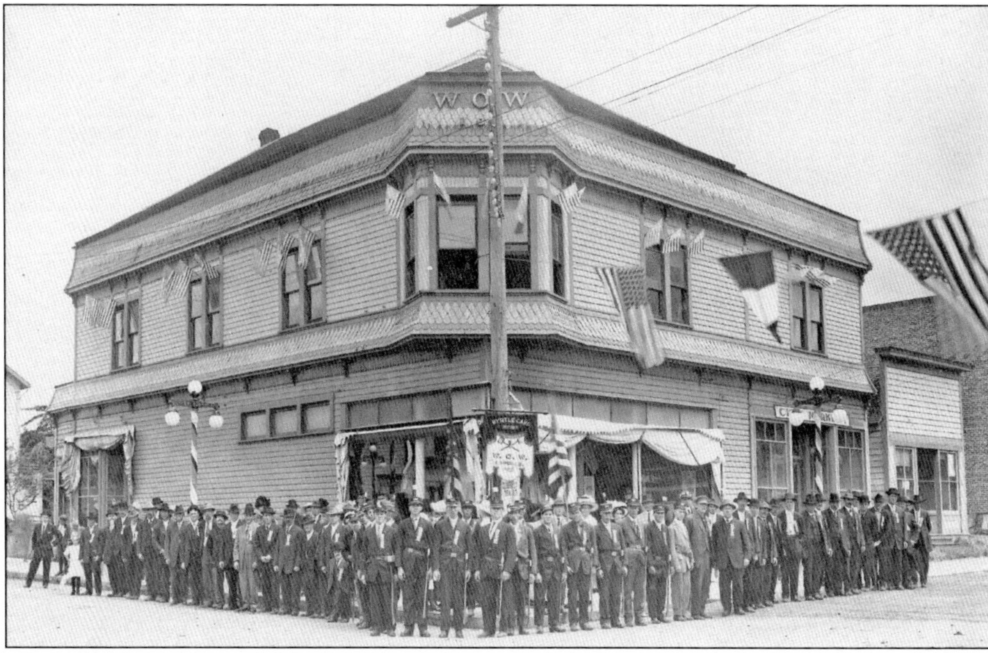

This is the Woodmen of the World building in the early 1900s on the northeast corner of First Street and Central Boulevard. The local Myrtle Camp No. 197 was organized in 1895 by Prof. J.P. Fiester, and A.J. Sherwood was the first consul. The women's organization was the Order of Women of Woodcraft. The upper floor was later removed with the lower portion still in use. (CVM.)

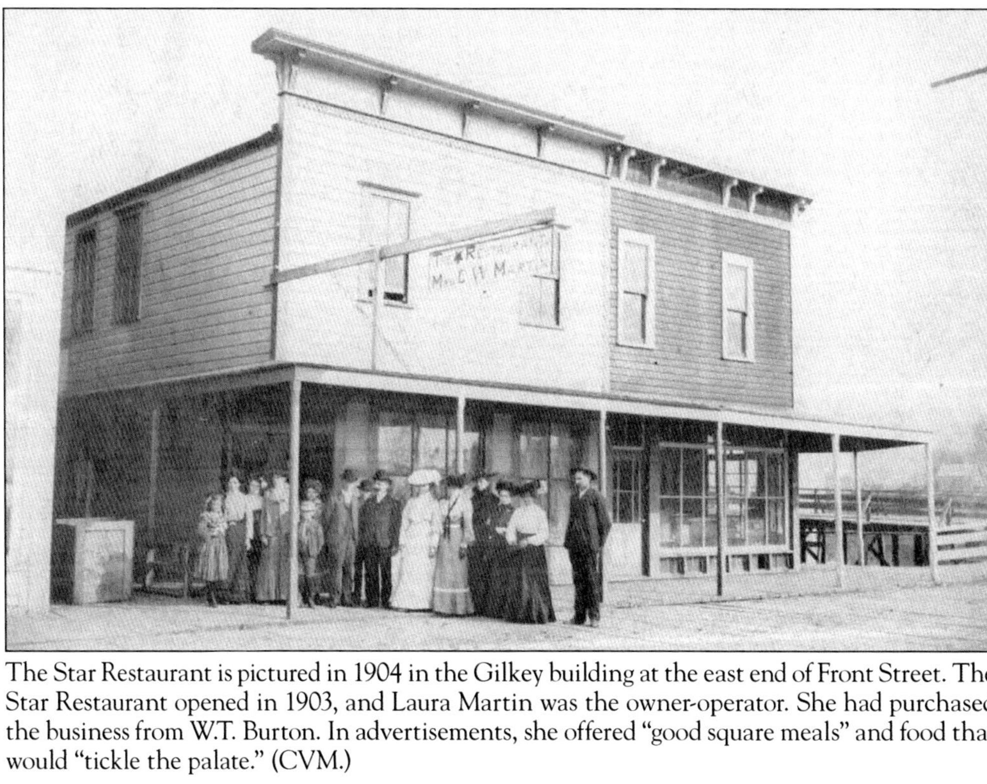

The Star Restaurant is pictured in 1904 in the Gilkey building at the east end of Front Street. The Star Restaurant opened in 1903, and Laura Martin was the owner-operator. She had purchased the business from W.T. Burton. In advertisements, she offered "good square meals" and food that would "tickle the palate." (CVM.)

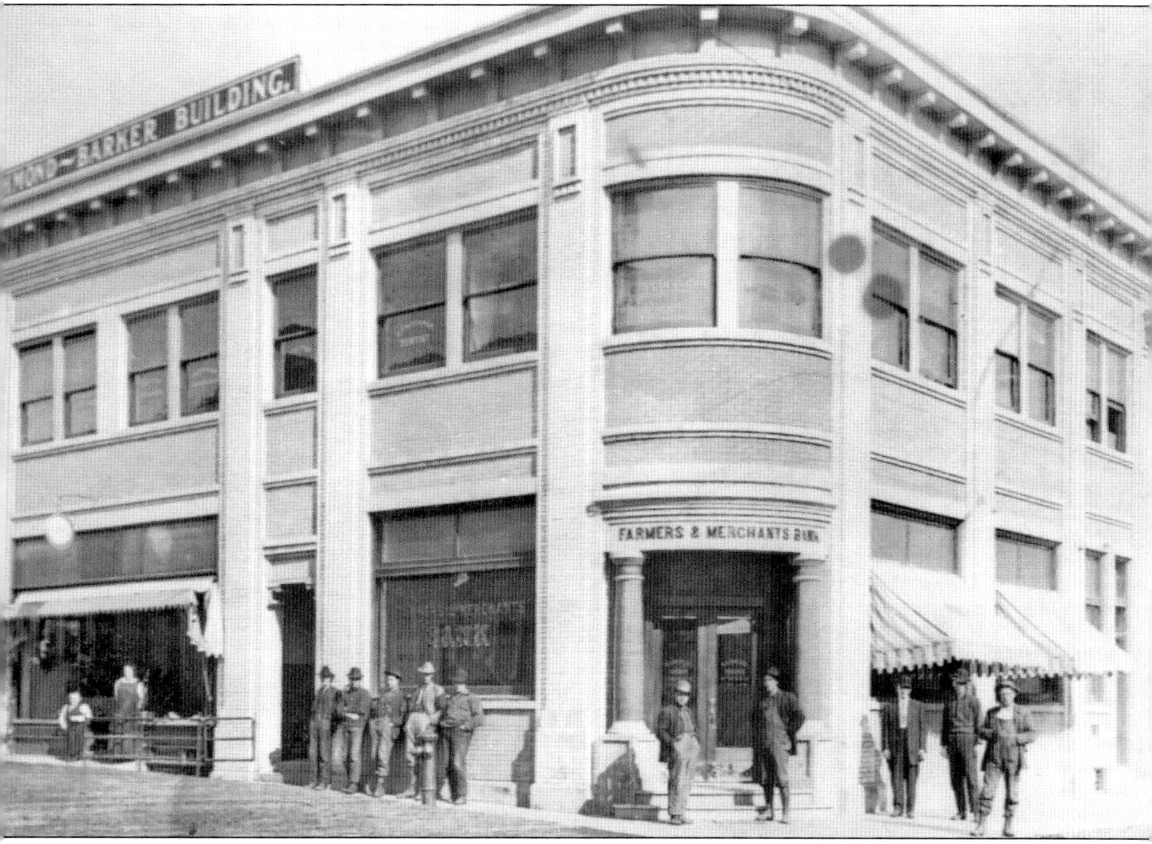

The Richmond-Barker Building, at Front Street and Central Boulevard, was constructed in 1909. The primary tenant was the Farmers & Merchants Bank at street level. To the left were two spaces for commercial businesses, with a basement for additional businesses accessed by a sidewalk staircase. William Schroeder is standing at the far left in front of his jewelry store, with a candy store to the right. In the basement were the Coquille Power & Gas Company and an ice-cream factory. The upstairs was intended for professional offices. Later, the Ellingson Building was constructed surrounding this building with entrances on both streets. Organizers of the Farmers & Merchants Bank included Rudolphus S. Knowlton and Reuben H. Mast. The bank opened its doors in 1909, with Knowlton elected the president. The bank failed during the Great Depression. Later, the building served as the Belle Knife and Falk Hospitals. The building is now occupied by the Coquille Broiler restaurant. (CVM.)

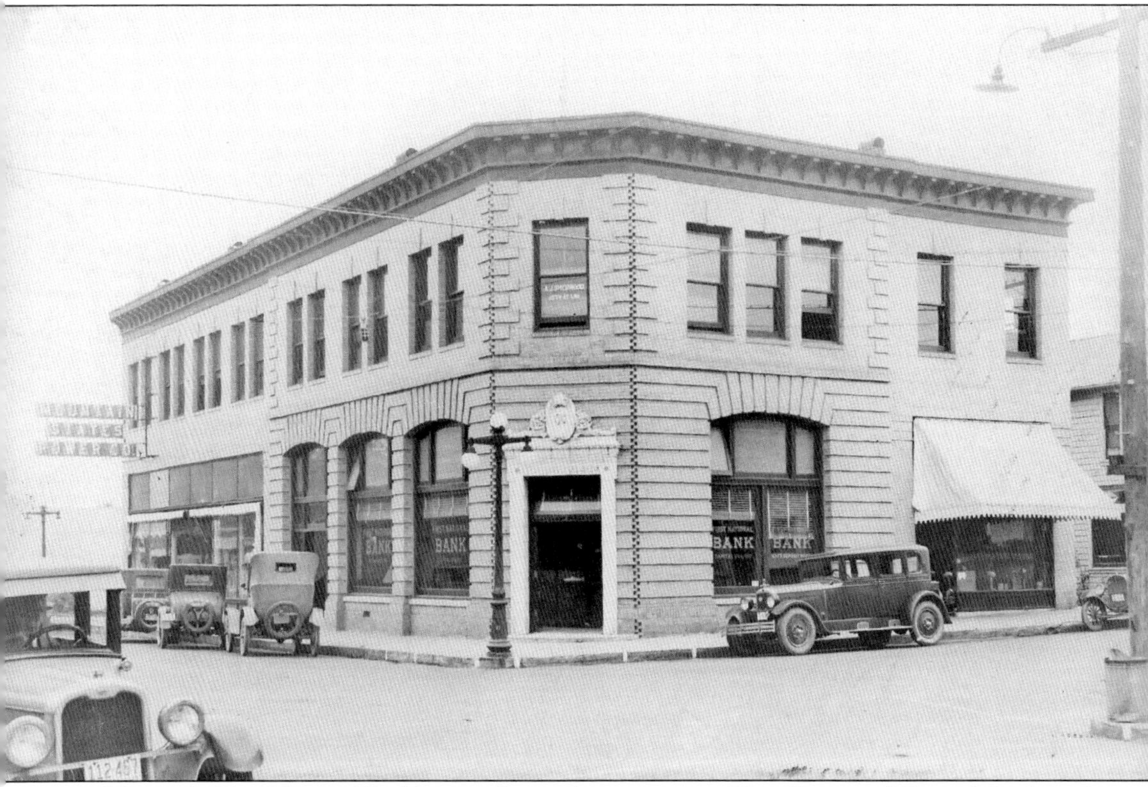

This is the First National Building, at the northwest corner of First Street and Central Boulevard, around 1920. The brick building was built in 1910 and replaced a wood-frame building, which was relocated next door (visible at the far right). The building housed the First National Bank and three street-level businesses, including Mountain States Power Company. The second floor contained professional offices. A substantial basement was accessed by a stairwell in the adjoining alley. The First National Bank of Coquille was founded in 1903 by Andrew Jackson Sherwood, who was a prominent lawyer. He served as bank president for 26 years until his death in 1929. The application for the formation of the bank was submitted by R.E. Shine and others. The First National Bank printed $204,360 worth of national currency before it stopped printing money in 1935. The bank issued eight different types and denominations. (CVM.)

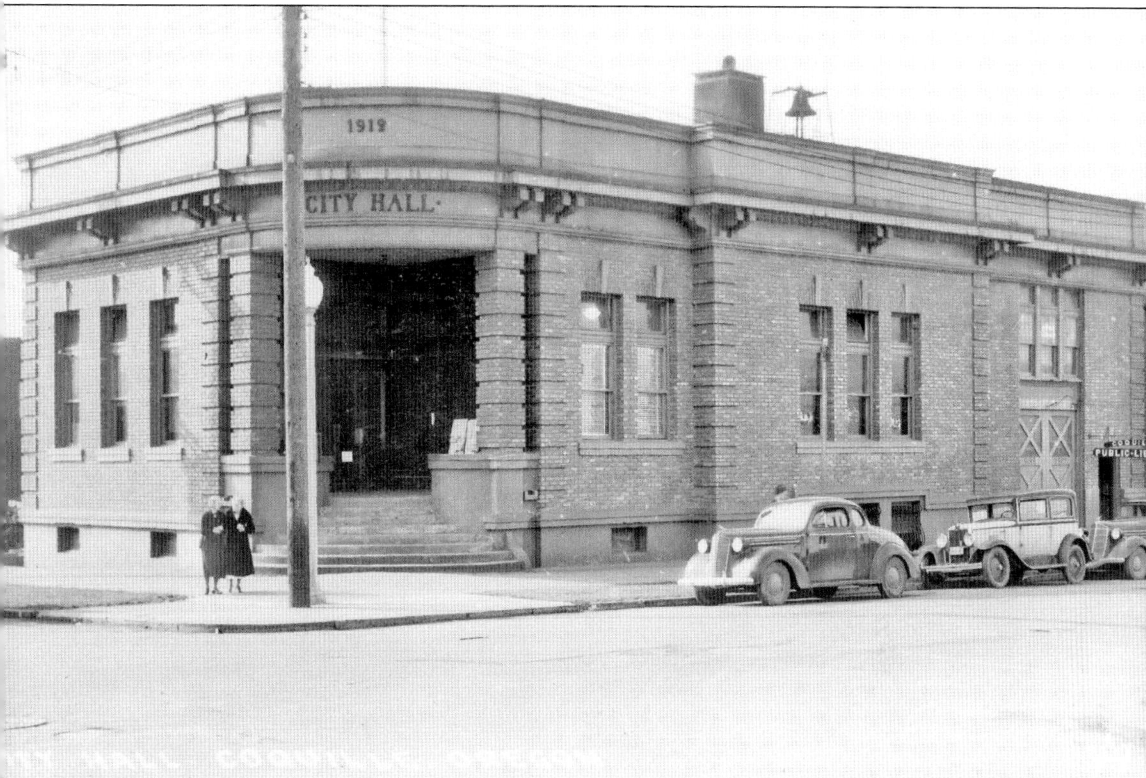

City hall was constructed in 1912 on the southwest corner of Second Street and Adams Street by Longston and Bayliss at a cost of $11,292. It replaced a nondescript wood-frame building erected on the waterfront in 1904 mainly for the protection of fire equipment. Construction of the building marked the first time all city functions were gathered together under one roof. The eastern two-thirds of city hall is one story with a basement. The western third is a two-story structure. The building included offices, a library, fire and police departments, and a jail in the basement. Upon entering the building, the city manager's office was to the left, with other offices immediately to the right. A hallway extended to the west to access public works. The police department was on the south side, with a stairway to the council chambers, which was originally the library. It was built with bricks from the Arago brickyard. It is the best example of the American Renaissance style in the city. (CVM.)

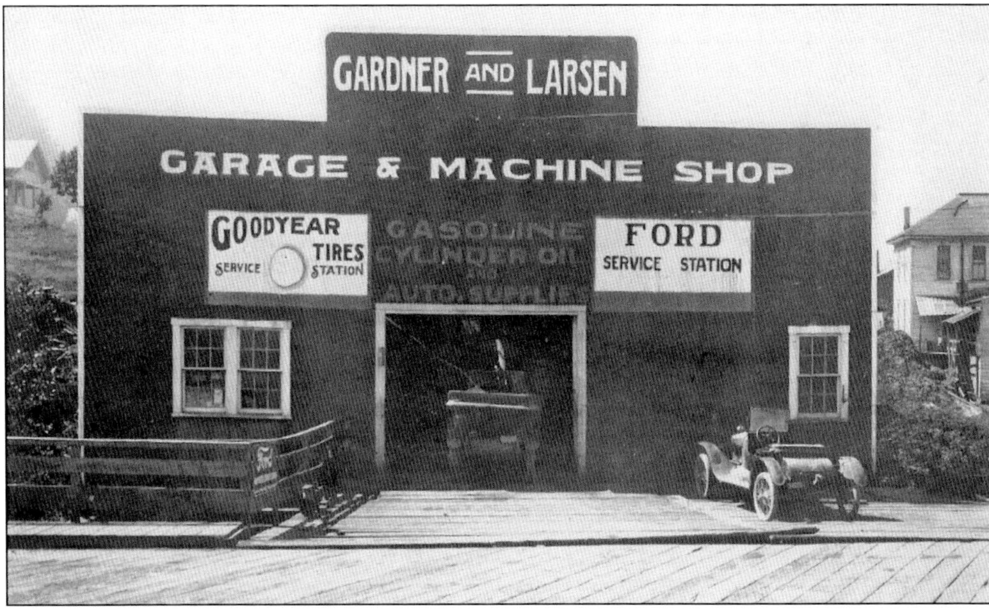

In 1915, the Gardner and Larsen Machine Shop was on the southwest corner of First Street and Baxter Street. It was owned by Charles W. Gardner and Atlin A. Larsen. They specialized in Ford parts and repairs and oxygen-acetylene welding. The ground in this area was very low, requiring a raised, wood-plank street and sidewalks with railings. (CVM.)

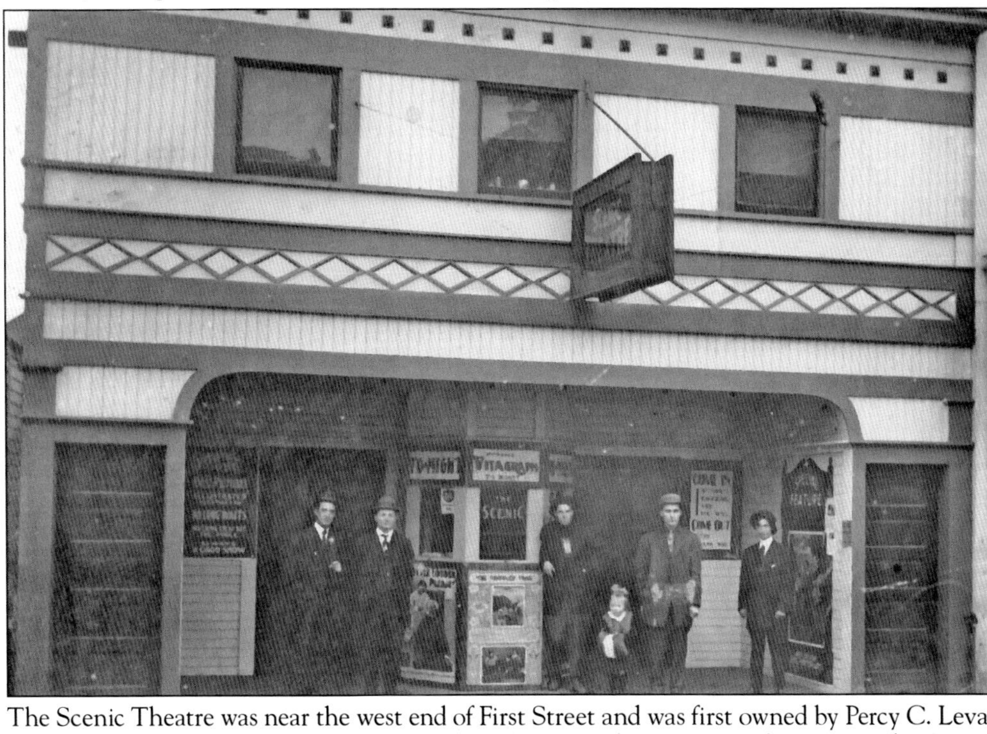

The Scenic Theatre was near the west end of First Street and was first owned by Percy C. Levar and later by C.S. Pendleton. Movies were played on Mondays. On March 17, 1918, the Scenic Theatre and several nearby buildings were destroyed by a fire that started in a second-hand store located at the rear of the theater. (CHM 982-133.)

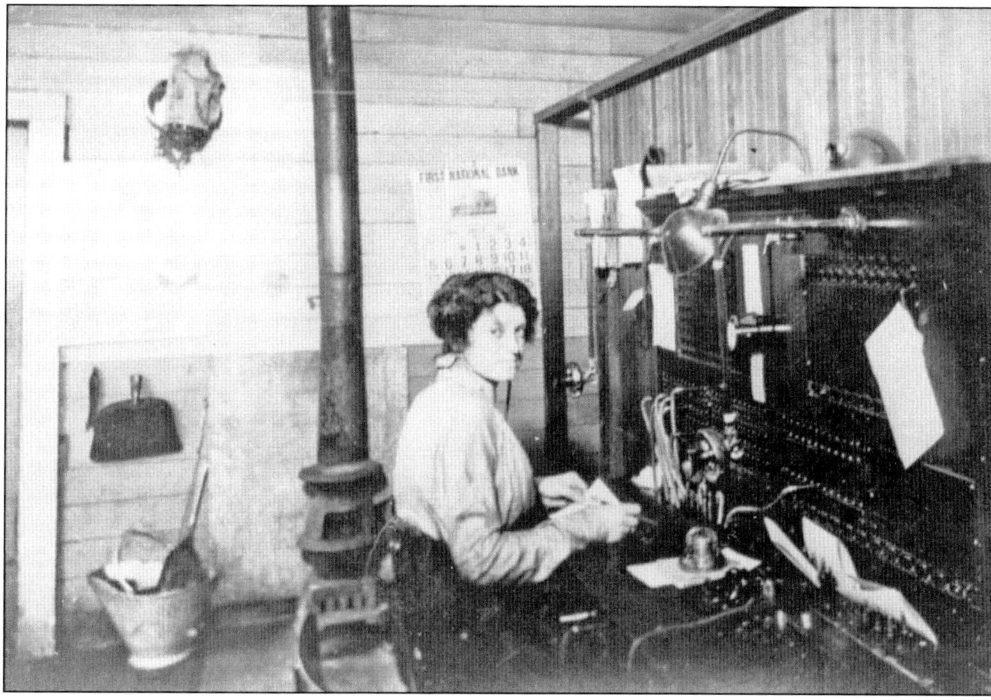

Above is telephone switchboard operator Alta Stanley in 1914. Below is the Coquille Telephone and Telegraph Office in 1945. This building is still standing next to Farr's True Value Hardware on Central Boulevard. The telephone office and switchboard were first located in the Martin building on First Street. In 1889, the telegraph line was completed between Coquille and Empire. In 1903, the telephone company erected telephone poles in the business part of town. Once the telephone was established, the two entities combined, working out of the same office. In 1910, Coquille and Myrtle Point were connected. (Both, CVM.)

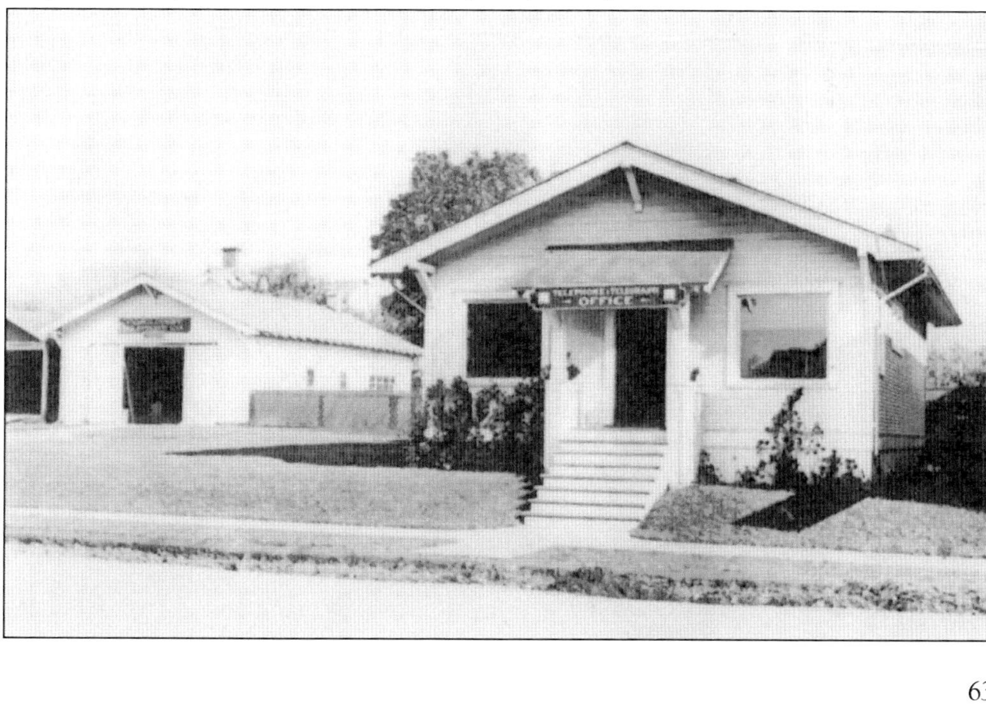

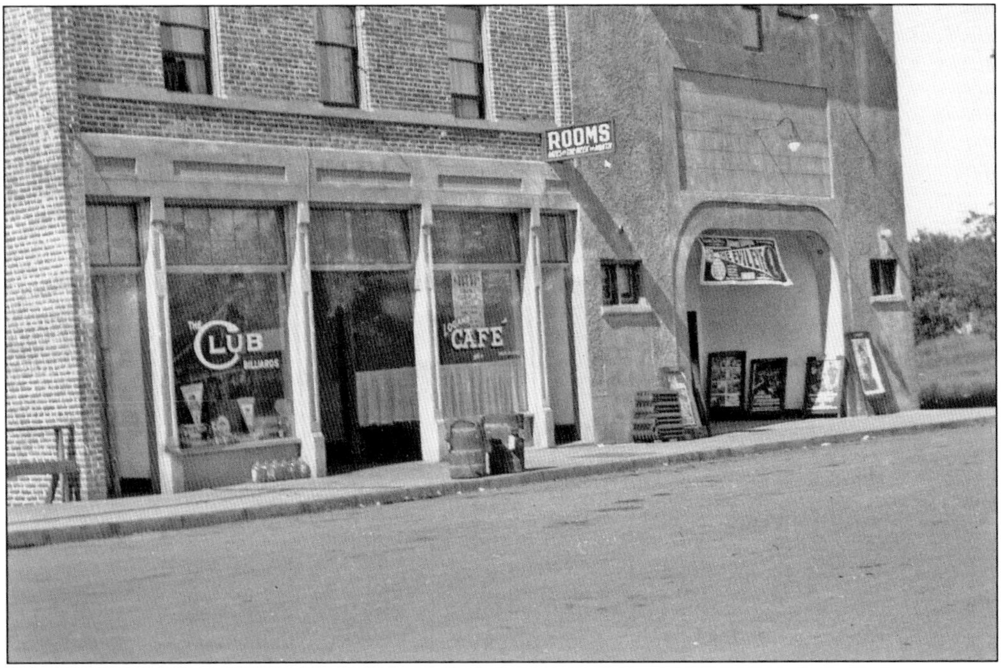

Pictured around 1920, the Machon Building is on the left at the west end of First Street; it was built after the fire of 1918. On the ground floor, it houses the Club Billiards and Logan's Café. Second-floor rooms are for rent by the week or month. Later, these businesses would be Bill's Place, Cagley's Barber Shop, and the Tourist Hotel. (CVM.)

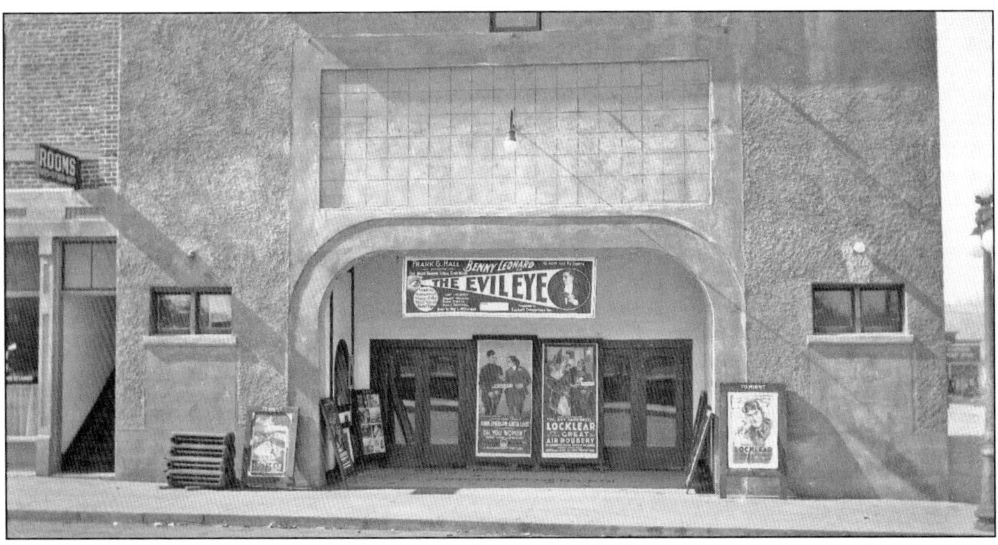

This is the Liberty Theatre around 1920 at the west end of First Street. This building and the building to the left were built by Charles Machon after the fire of 1918. In 1934, Lloyd and Ruth Claver and Orville and Marion Wood purchased the theater. The theater would later be renamed the Roxy Theatre after the original Roxy Theatre at Second Street and Adams Street burned. (CVM.)

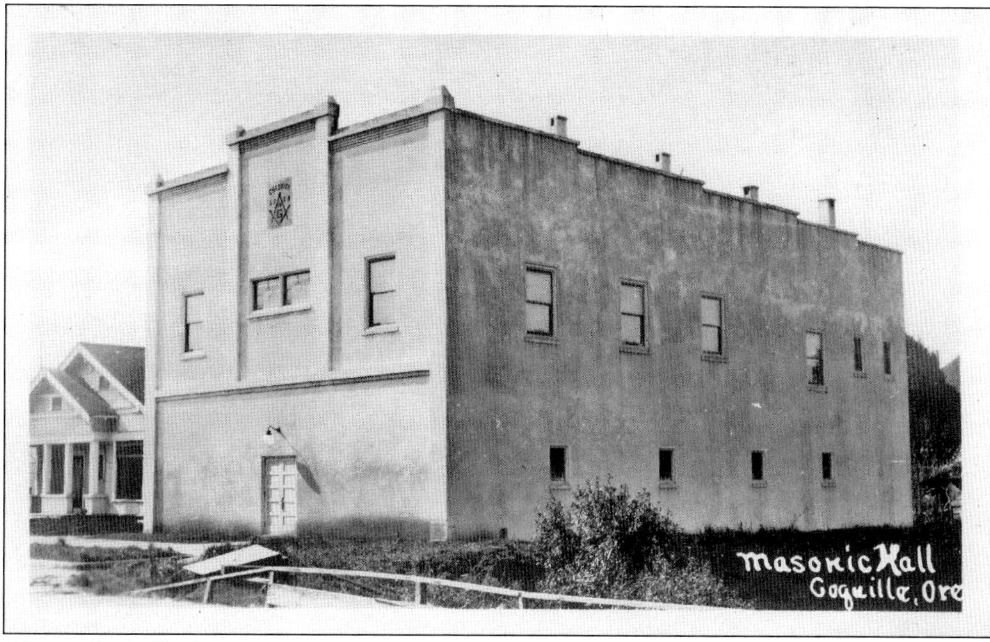

This is the hall of the Chadwick Lodge No. 68 of the Masons, built in 1923 after the loss of their original hall in the fire of 1918. The first hall was built in 1887 by Tom Willard at the west end of First Street and became known as the Masonic Opera Hall, as the first floor was used by traveling stage shows. (CHM 995.D66.)

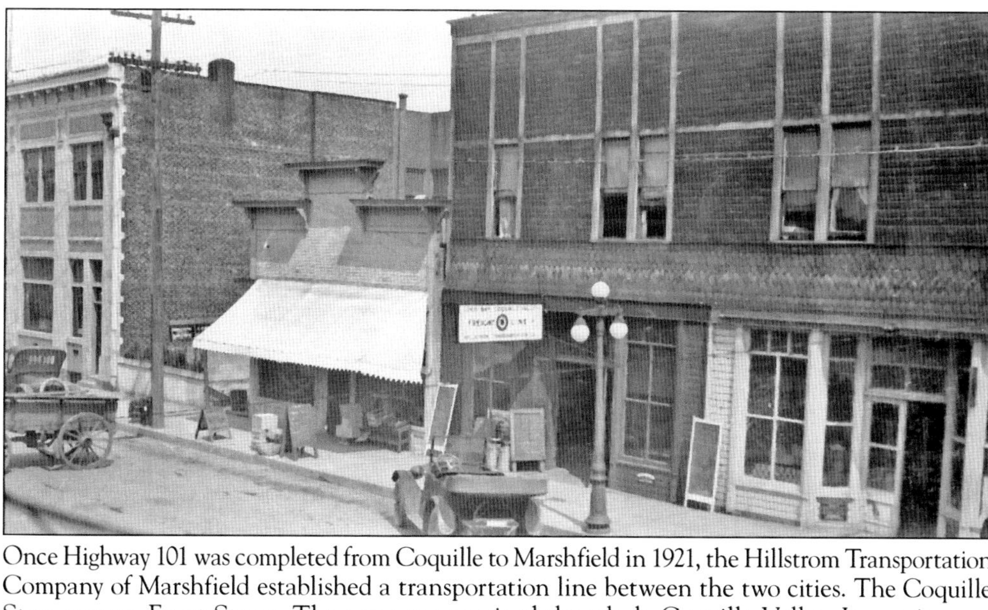

Once Highway 101 was completed from Coquille to Marshfield in 1921, the Hillstrom Transportation Company of Marshfield established a transportation line between the two cities. The Coquille Store was on Front Street. The company serviced the whole Coquille Valley. Its service was cheaper than shipments by rail, with no intermediate handling. (CVM.)

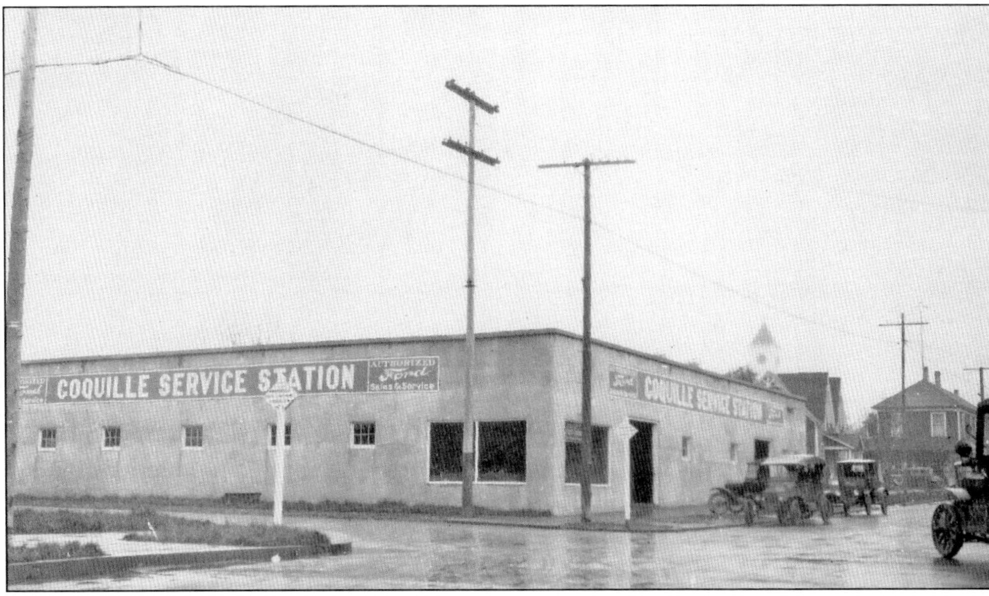

Coquille Service Station, shown around 1920, was one of several early businesses in this building at Second Street and Central Boulevard providing Ford sales and service. Other businesses included Coquille Motors and Walker's Ford Garage, where Model Ts were partially assembled. Later, a gas station by the same name was established across the street. The building is now occupied by Farr's True Value Hardware. (CVM.)

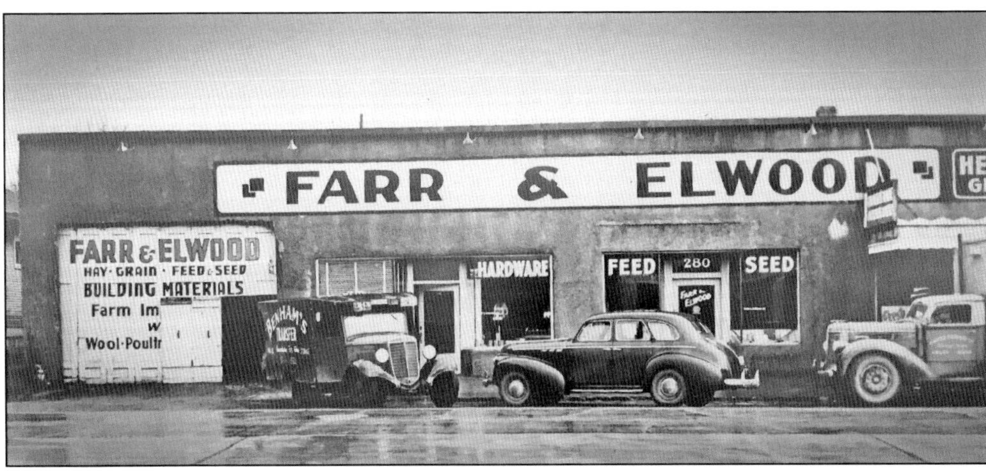

Chester Farr and Cecil Elwood established a hardware and farm supply business at Second Street and Central Boulevard. The building was formerly home to businesses providing Ford sales and service. The Farr & Elwood partnership began as a freight and warehouse business in the former Collier Warehouse between the river and the railroad depot but grew to include hardware stores in Coquille and Marshfield. (JF.)

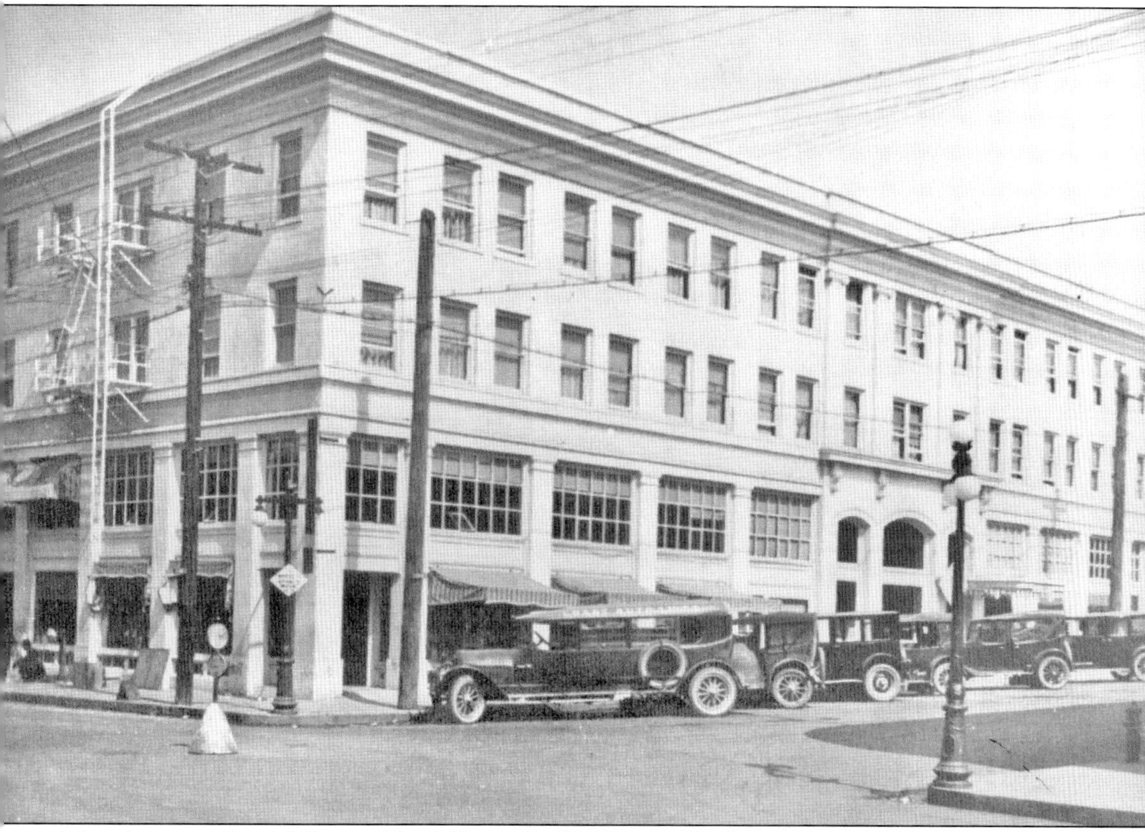

After the wood-framed Baxter Hotel (formerly Hotel Coquille) burned in 1922, an impressive new three-story concrete Hotel Coquille was built in 1923. It was strategically located at the intersection of Central Boulevard and Front Street, which was also the junction of Highway 101 and Highway 42. The building became the landmark of the city and included a restaurant and commercial spaces. It also served as the depot for auto stages, predecessors to buses. Several years after construction of this building, an annex was built in the same style, and together, they were a block long from Front Street to First Street. On August 27, 1985, the building was gutted by a fire that was believed to have started in the Chenango Café and Lounge. The building was then demolished, with the empty area providing parking for nearby businesses. (CVM.)

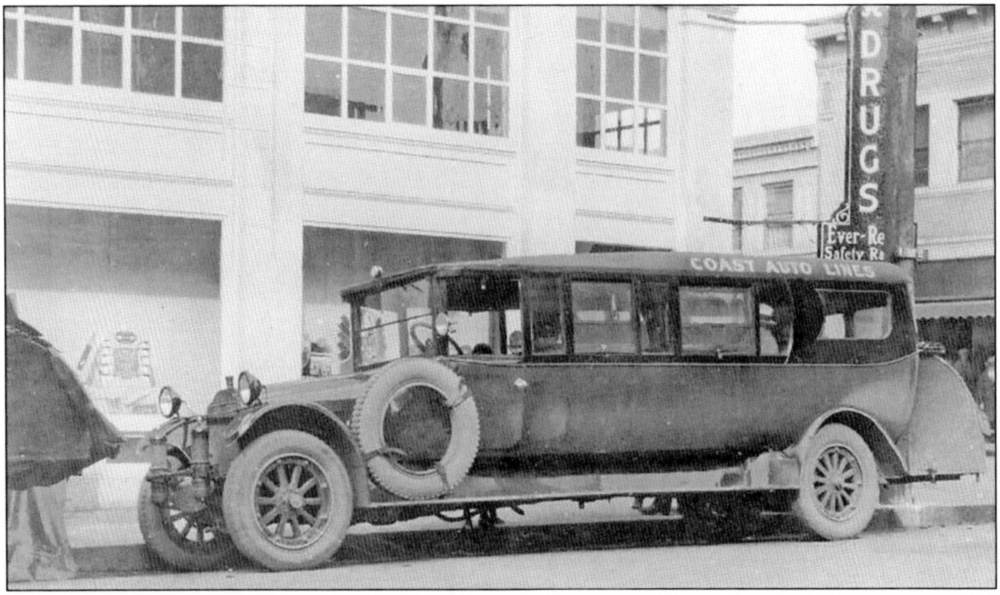

In 1924, George W. Bryant directed the Coast Auto Line Stage, headquartered in Marshfield. The Coquille depot was at the Hotel Coquille and provided service to Myrtle Point, Roseburg, and Bandon. Fare to Myrtle Point was 50¢, to Roseburg was $4.25, and to Bandon was $1. During the winter months, the Coos Bay–Roseburg Wagon Road was in such poor condition that service was discontinued to Roseburg for the season. (CVM.)

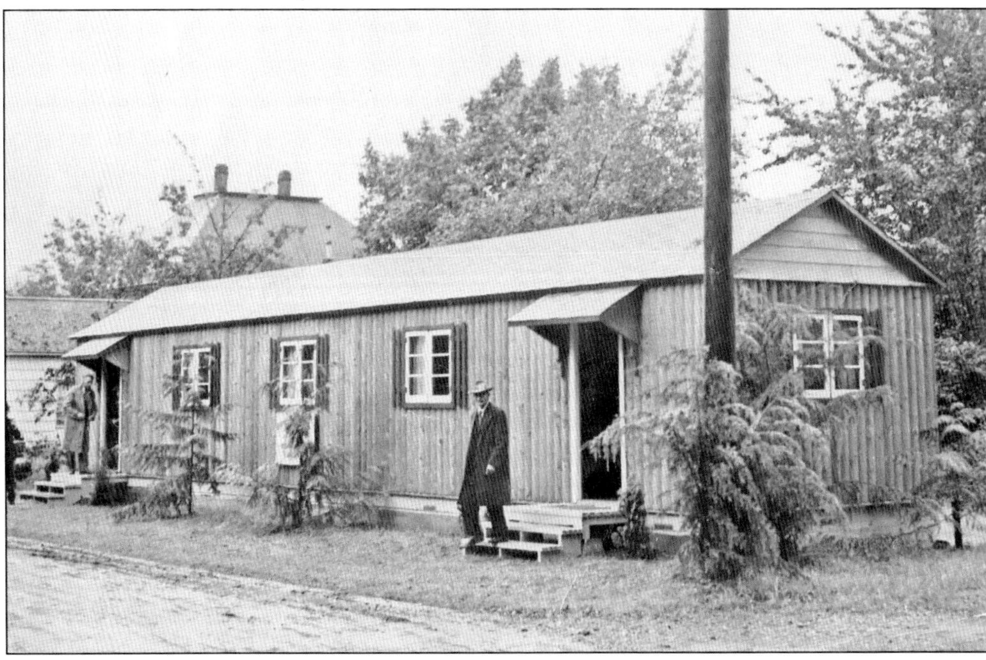

The Pioneer Museum was established in 1947 in Coquille by the Coos-Curry Pioneer Association. The museum was behind the community building, and the exterior was finished with log siding to resemble a log cabin. A new museum was opened in Simpson Park in North Bend in 1958. Today's Coos History Museum was completed in Coos Bay in 2015 by the Coos County Historical Society. (CHM 958.396.)

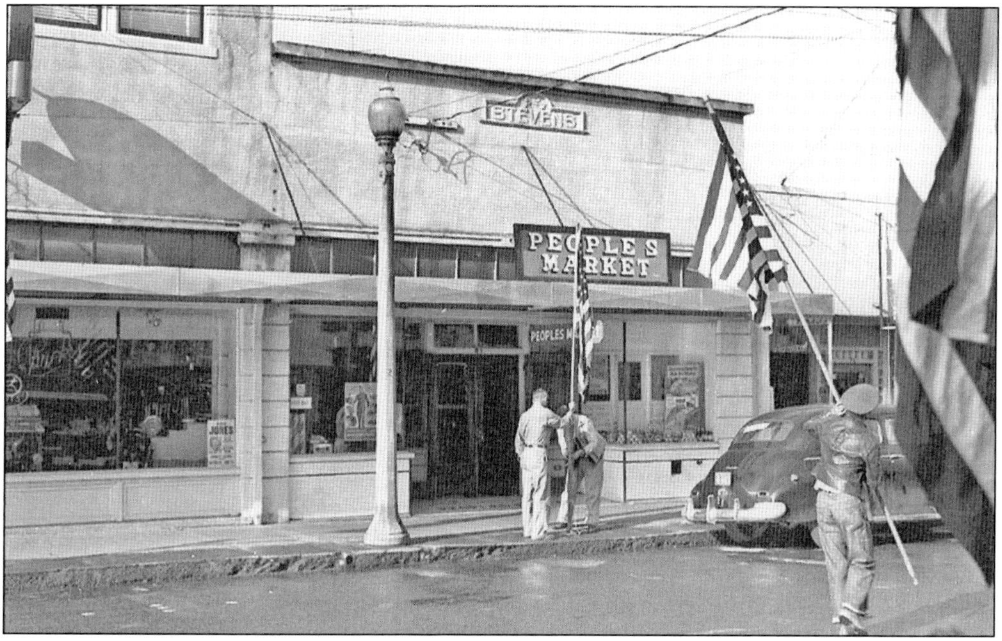

A meat cutter by trade, James L. Stevens moved to Coquille in 1921 and purchased half interest in the Peoples Market. After becoming sole owner, Stevens built the Stevens Building in 1924 and operated the new Peoples Market with his son, Tom, who took over the meat market when James retired. The slogan for the store was "your ideal meating place." (CVM.)

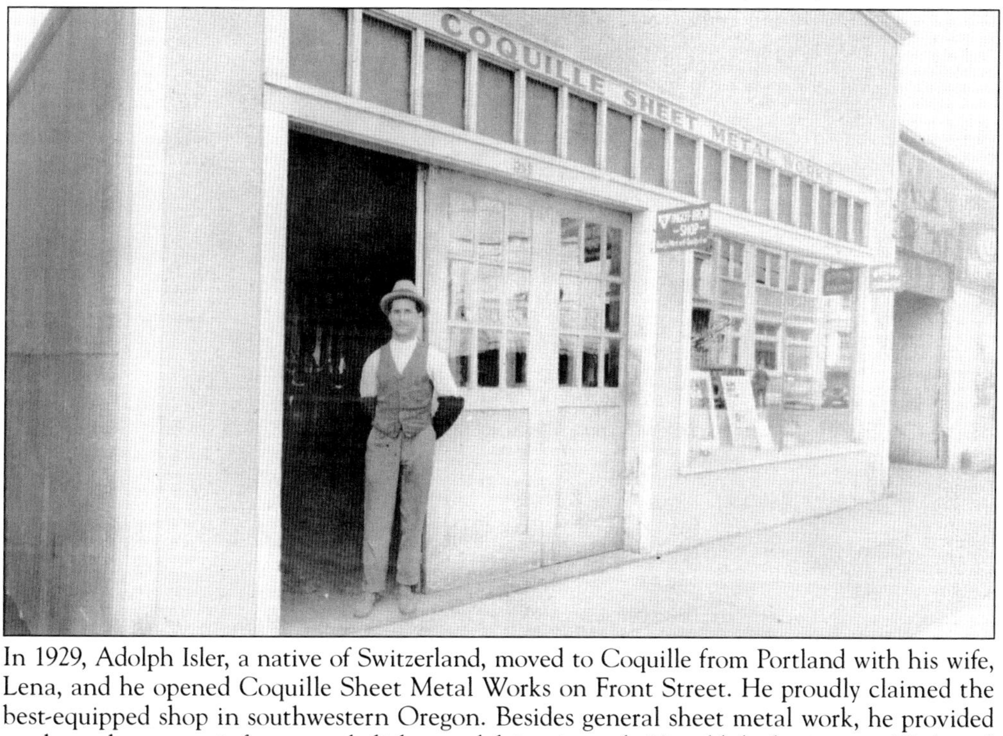

In 1929, Adolph Isler, a native of Switzerland, moved to Coquille from Portland with his wife, Lena, and he opened Coquille Sheet Metal Works on Front Street. He proudly claimed the best-equipped shop in southwestern Oregon. Besides general sheet metal work, he provided smokestacks, warm air furnaces, skylights, and dairy tin work. He sold the business to Clyde and Lonnie Clark in 1958. (CVM.)

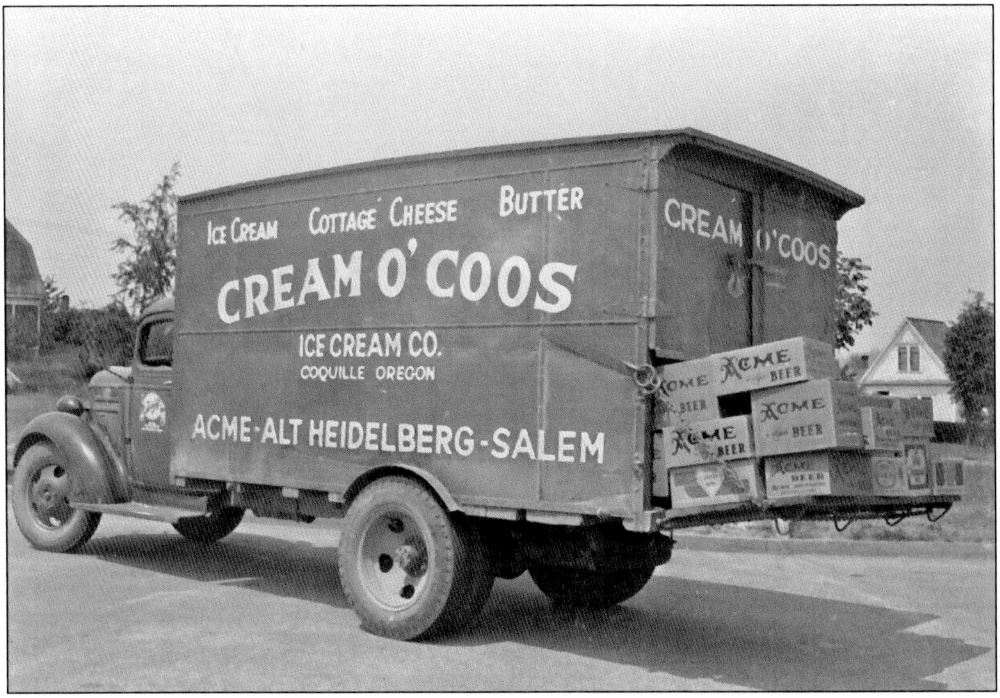

Starting in the 1920s, Cream O' Coos operated an ice and ice-cream plant on the river below the west end of Front Street where O.K. Creamery had earlier been. In addition to ice cream and other dairy products, it also distributed beer. The original owner, Theodore R. Johnson, boasted that his ice cream was the "best in the world." (CHM 986.N846.)

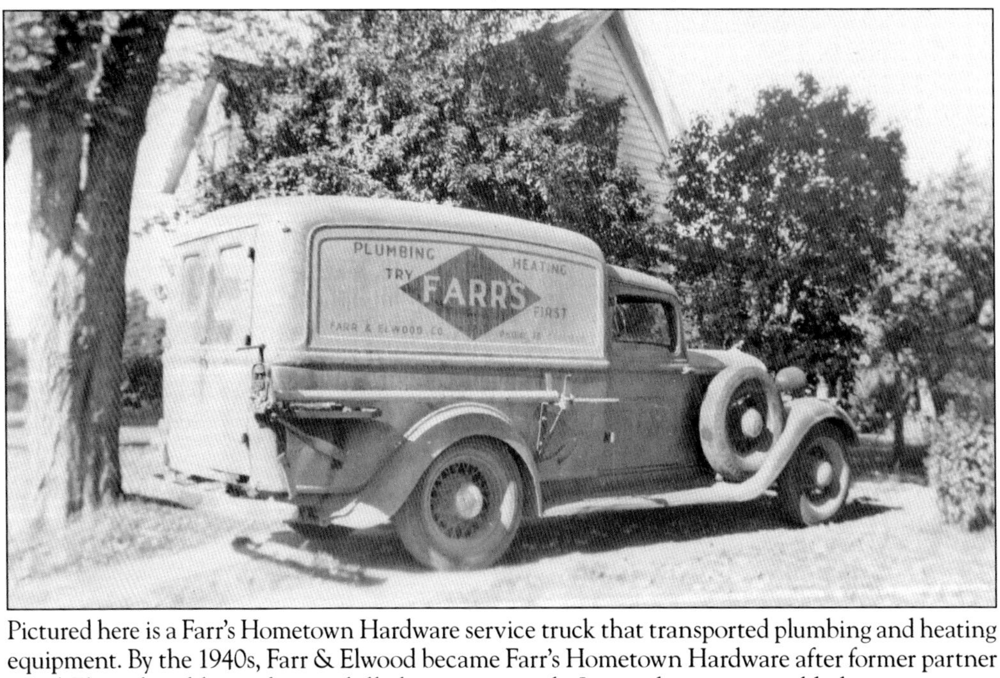

Pictured here is a Farr's Hometown Hardware service truck that transported plumbing and heating equipment. By the 1940s, Farr & Elwood became Farr's Hometown Hardware after former partner Cecil Elwood and his wife were killed in a car wreck. Later, the name would change again to Farr's True Value Hardware. (JF.)

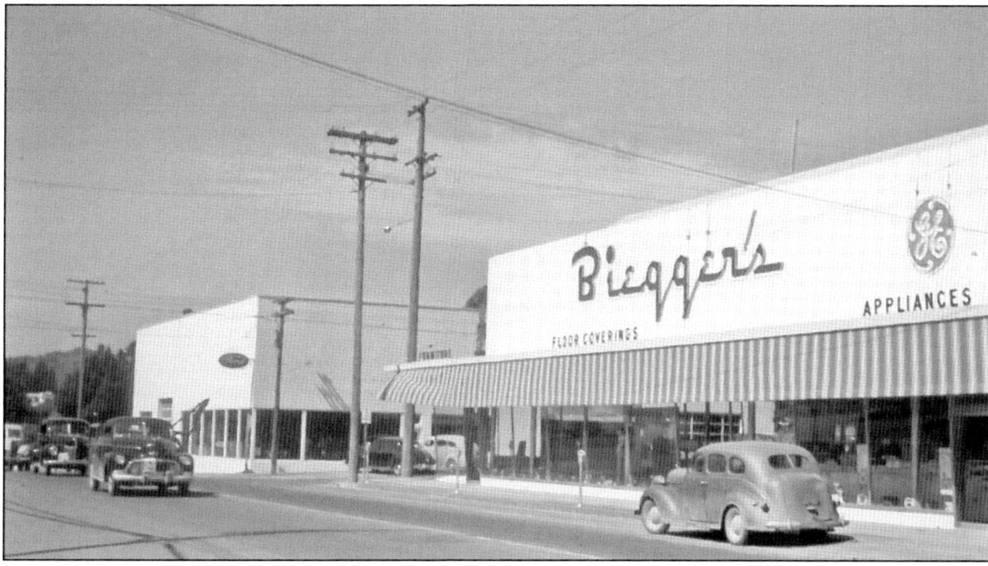

David A. Biegger opened his first furniture and appliance store on Front Street. A new building was constructed at Third Street and Central Boulevard in 1948 for $50,000. The building would later be used as a county annex. In the background is the building that housed the Lounsbury Ford car dealership. (CVM.)

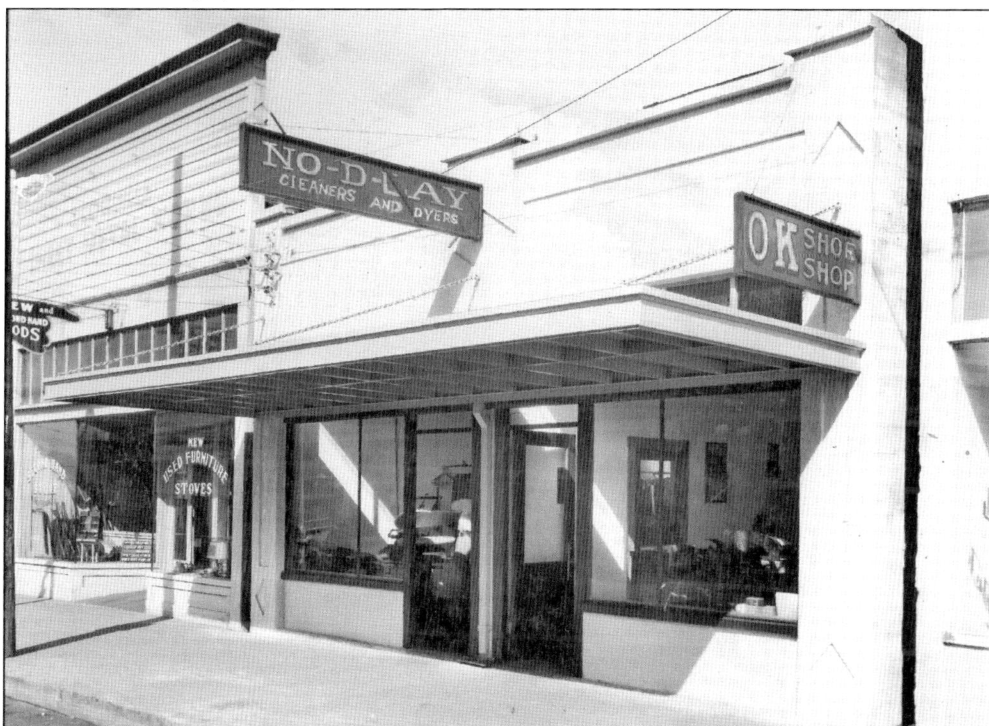

Located on Front Street, NO-D-LAY Cleaners was managed by Clifford and Ernestine Bissett. NO-D-LAY advertised superior service by utilizing the most modern scientific methods of chemical cleaning. It further advertised that its progressive growth since establishment was a direct result of the quality of its work and superior service. (CVM.)

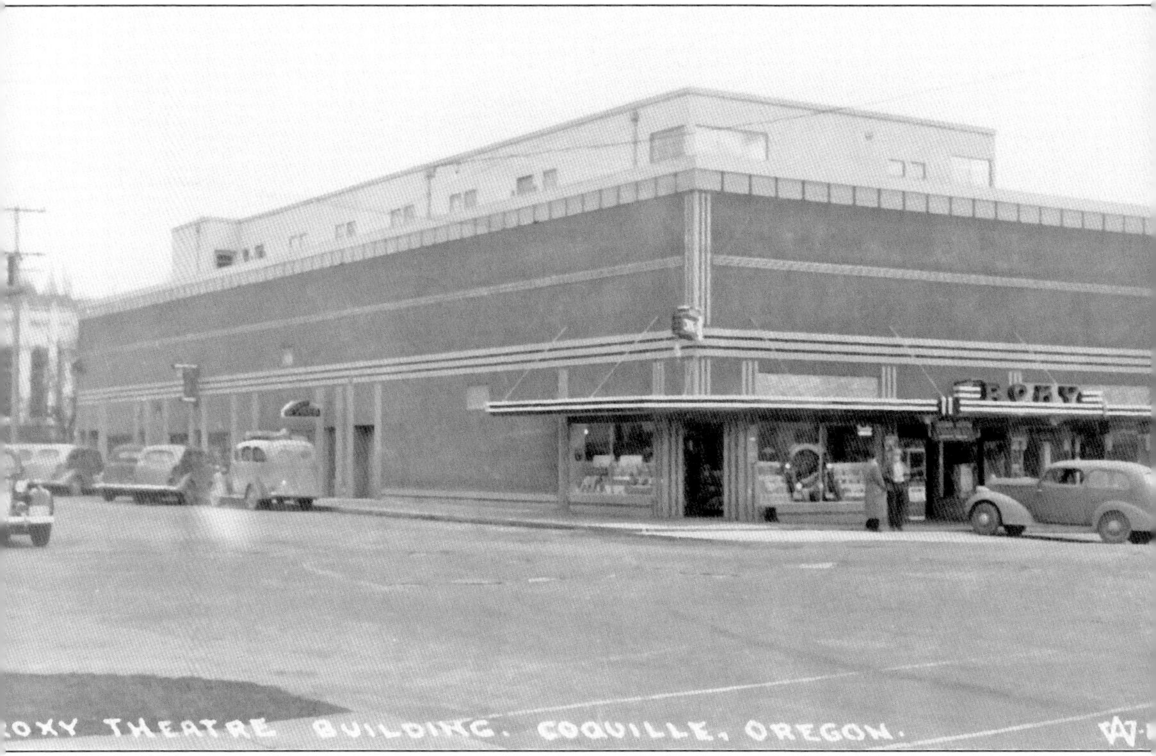

This is the original Roxy Theatre, at the southeast corner of Second Street and Adams Street, around 1940. In 1937, it was opened by Lloyd Claver and Orville Wood while their older Liberty Theatre continued to operate. The building housed a restaurant, barbershop, and two large penthouse apartments. The theater operated until about 1966. It was later used by the Sawdust Theatre Company until it was destroyed by fire in 1994. (CVM.)

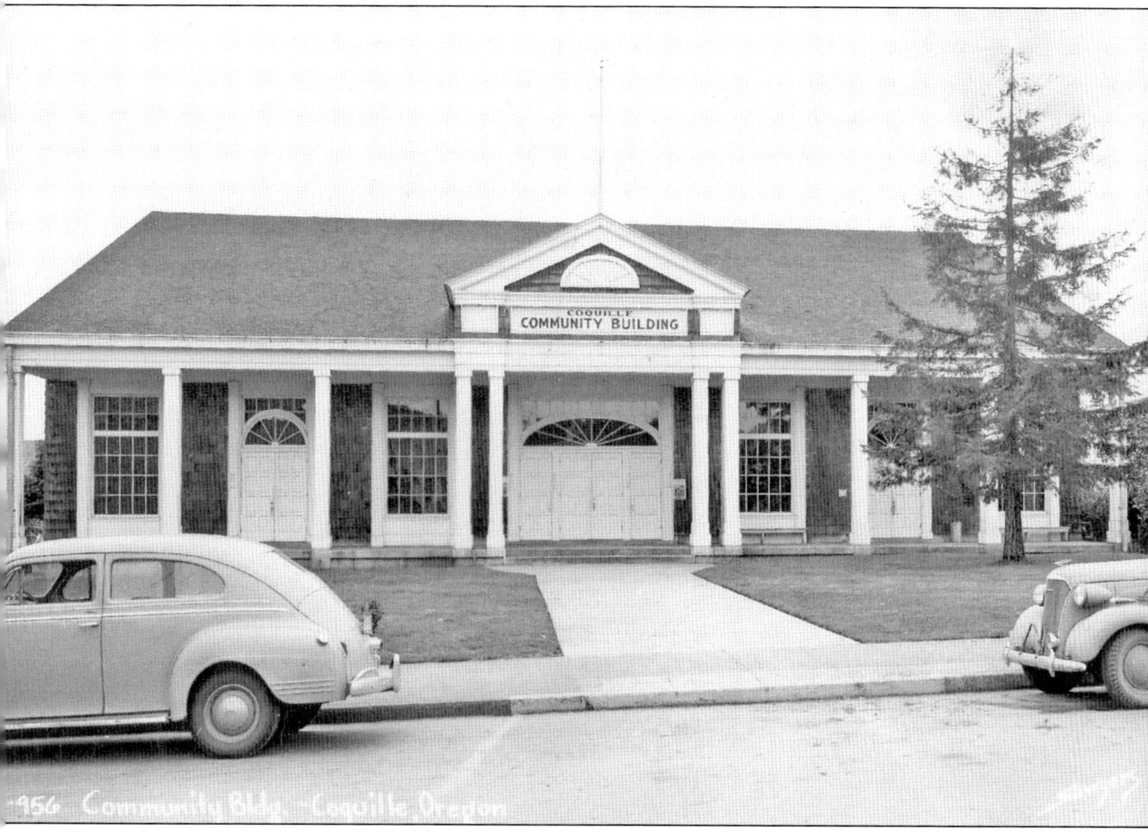

This is the original community building, erected in 1942 with the aid of the Smith-Wood Products company and George A. Ulett. In 1952, the building burned to the ground. Within six months, the citizens of Coquille rallied to plan and construct a new building. The present community building has a similar appearance and includes a library with a public pool adjoining. (CVM.)

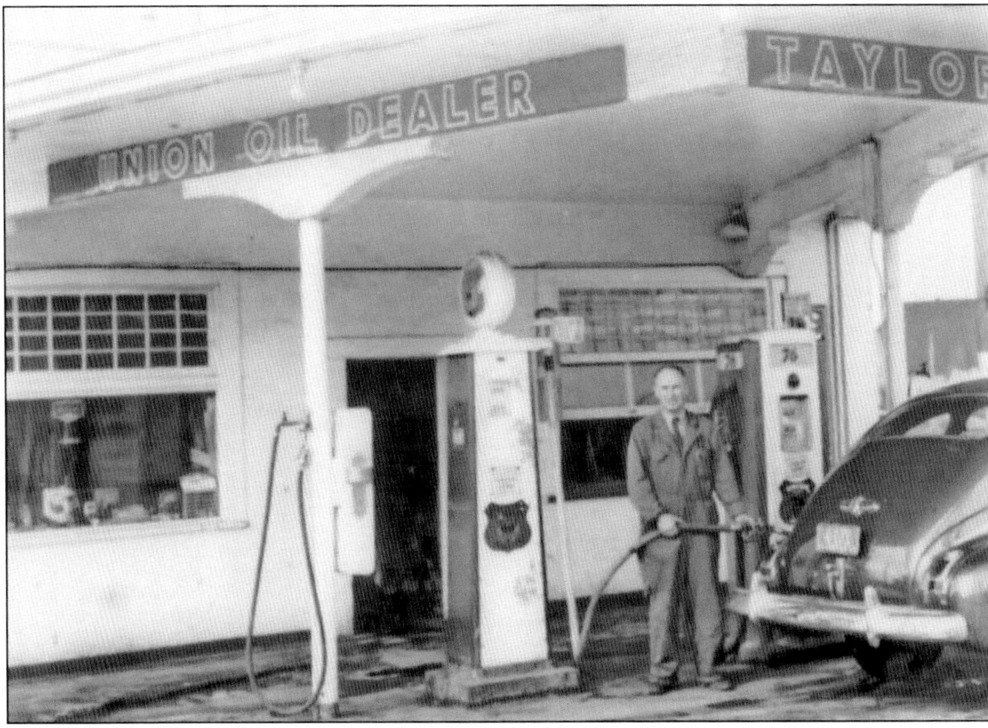

This is Taylor's Gas Station around 1950 at the southwest corner of Second Street and Central Boulevard. George Taylor is pumping gas. At one time, this intersection had three gas stations. The intersection was in the center of town and carried all the traffic on Highway 101, which went through town on Central Boulevard. The building later held Taylor's Sport Shop and is currently the home of the Coquille Valley Museum. (CVM.)

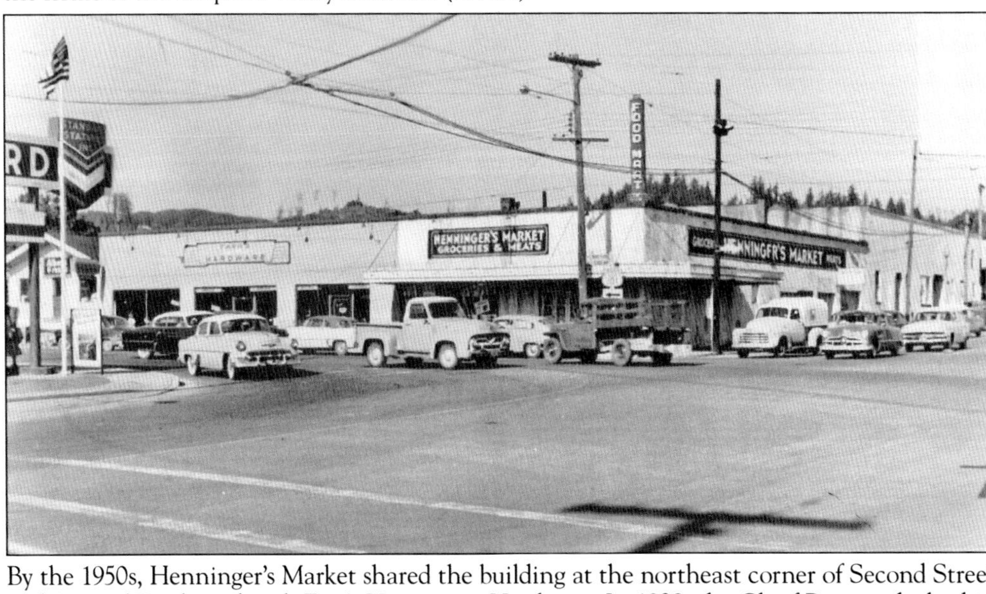

By the 1950s, Henninger's Market shared the building at the northeast corner of Second Street and Central Boulevard with Farr's Hometown Hardware. In 1938, the Chief Pontiac dealership opened a showroom in the building. Later, Wilson-Dunn Glass occupied the same space. Today, Farr's True Value Hardware uses the entire building. (CVM.)

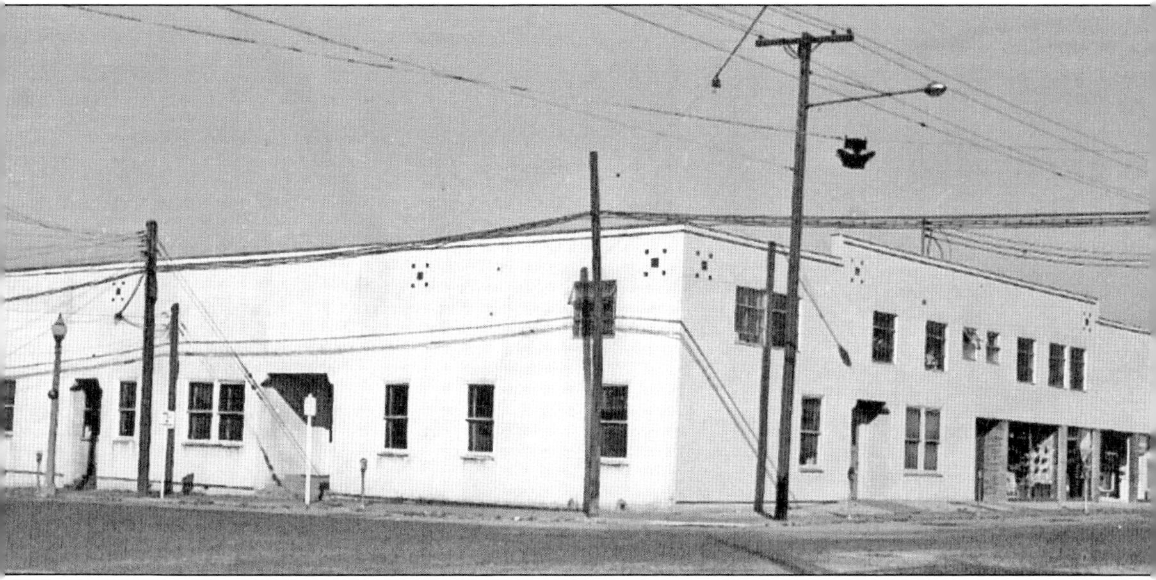

In the 1950s, this building at the northwest corner of Second Street and Adams Street served as the Coquille Hospital. In 1907, a city hospital was located at the northwest corner of Second Street and Alder Street, while the Western Oregon Hospital occupied the former Adventist Academy building on North Dean Street. Around 1911, the Richmond Hospital was established near the southwest corner of Second Street and Folsom Street. It was later renamed the Grayce Hospital, then the Belle Knife Hospital. In 1913, the county hospital was established at the county poor farm two miles from town on Fairview Road. In the 1930s, the Belle Knife Hospital was relocated to the second floor of the Richmond-Barker Building at Front Street and Central Boulevard. It was later renamed the Falk Hospital. Thereafter, Coquille was served by the Mast Hospital in Myrtle Point. Finally, the Coquille Valley Hospital was built in Coquille and opened in 1971. (CVM.)

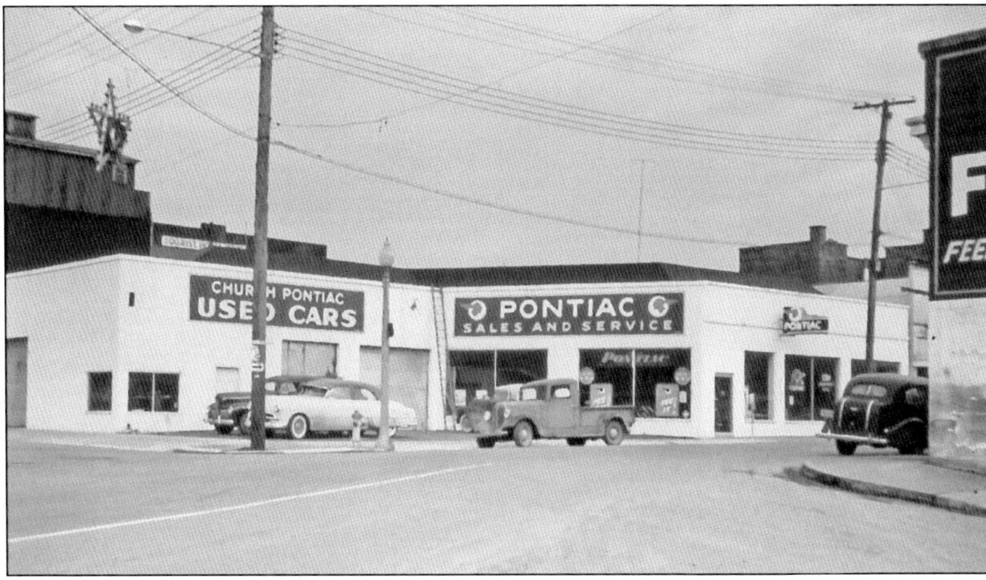

In 1940, the Church Pontiac dealership relocated from the Gilmore gas station at the southwest corner of Front Street and Birch Street to the east end of Front Street. By 1950, the dealership moved to the northeast corner of Front Street and Birch Street. Over time, the dealership sold Oldsmobile, GMC, Jeep, and Volvo vehicles. (CVM.)

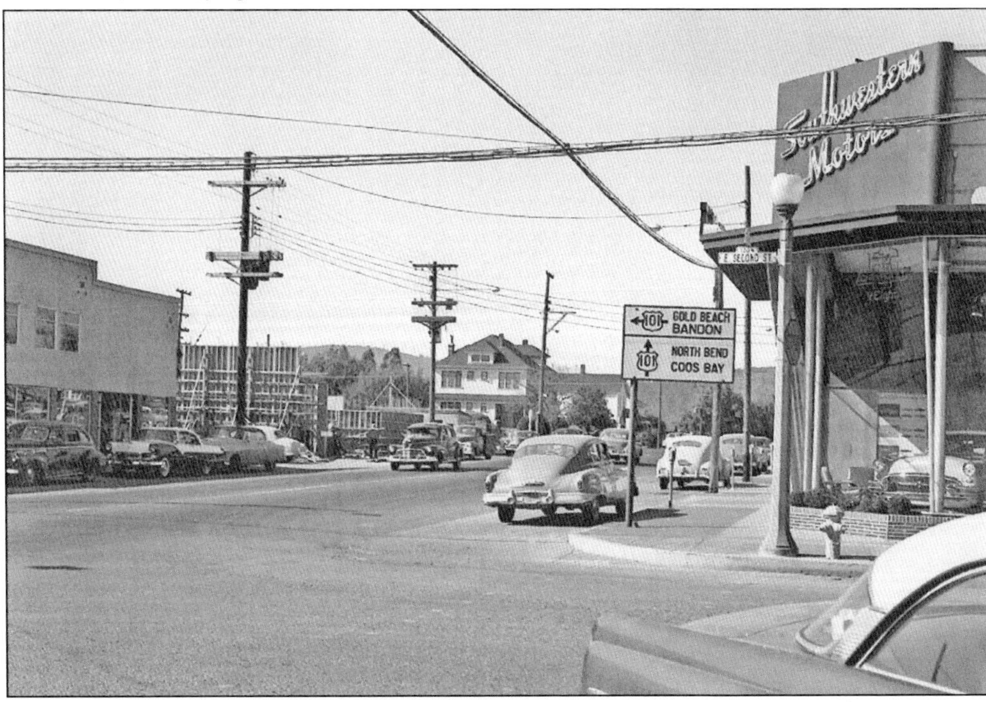

This is Southwestern Motors in their second location at Second Street and Adams Street in the 1950s. The dealership had been located near the west end of First Street. The dealership originally sold Buick, Chevrolet, Oldsmobile, and Pontiac. Owners throughout the years included Marvin Lamphere, Elgie Sparks, and Jim Vick. The third First National Bank building is under construction in the background. (CVM.)

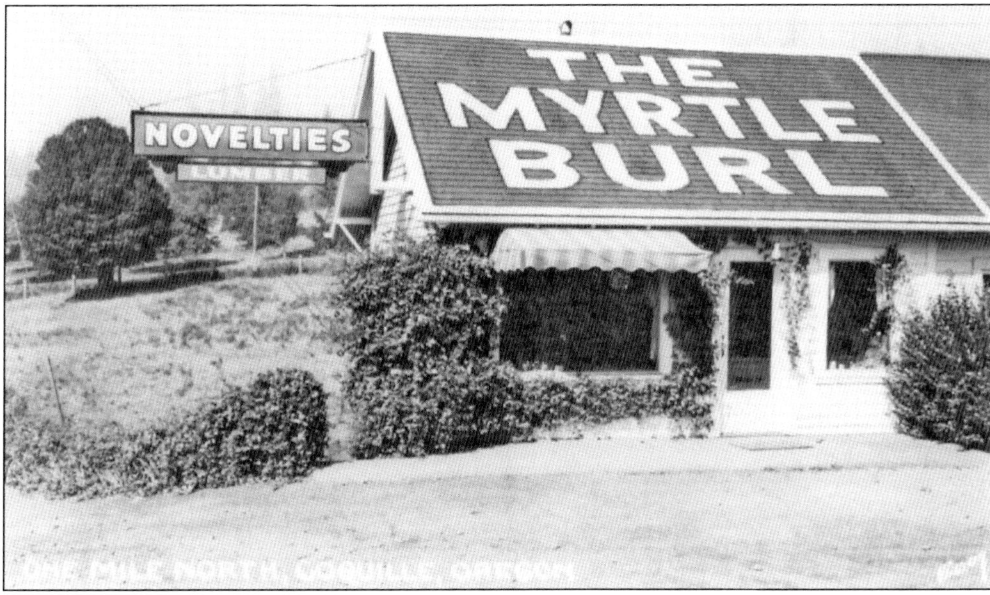

The Myrtle Burl was on Central Boulevard near the current high school. The Oerding family produced handcrafted myrtle wood giftware beginning 1907. John H. Oerding and sons built their original myrtle wood sawmill, planing mill, and furniture factory on the downtown waterfront. After continuous operation since 1907, the fourth generation of Oerdings discontinued the retail business in 1989. (CVM.)

The KWRO AM 630 radio station has operated in Coquille since 1949. Its office and broadcast studio were on the north side of the city for decades. The station originally broadcast a varied format including music under a daytime license. It currently broadcasts talk radio and sports but no music. (CVM.)

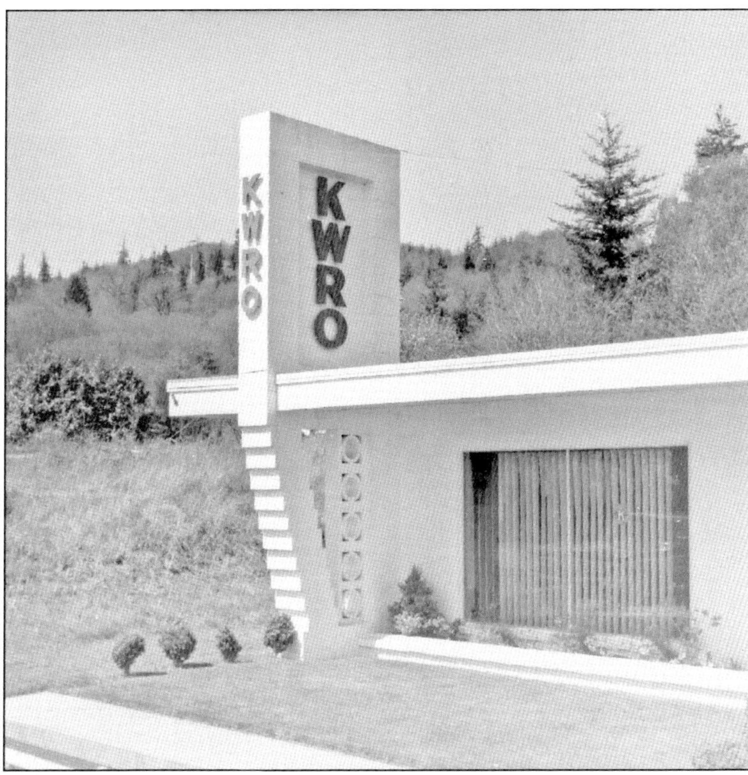

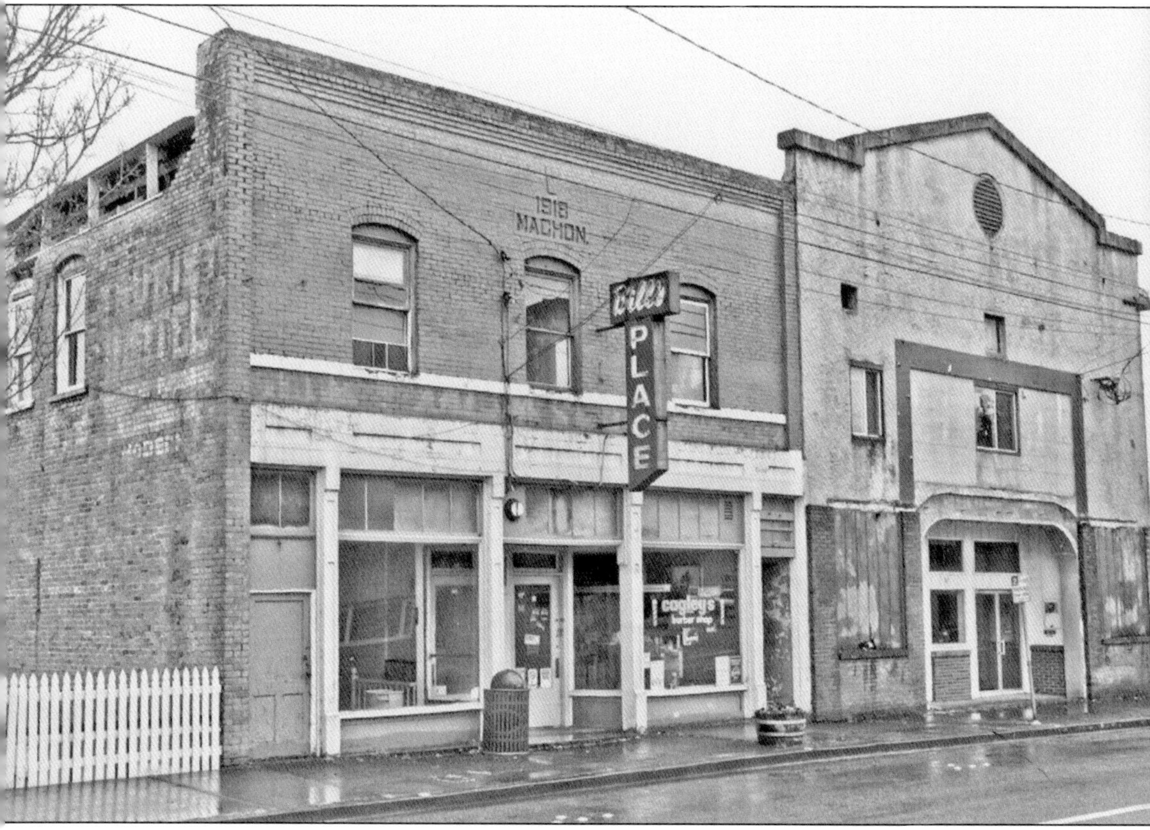

W.H. "Bill" Fortier, a well-known baseball player and retired manager of the Coquille Loggers, was the owner Bill's Place near the west end of First Street. The building and adjoining theater building next door were built in 1918 by Charles Machon. The original business in the location was the Club Billiards. Fortier established his business in 1928, and it was the local bar for a beer and a game of snooker for many years. It served as the after-hours meeting place for lumberjacks and mill workers. There were apartments upstairs called the Tourist Hotel and Cagley's Barber Shop next door. Donna Marie Roberts was the first woman bartender. Bill's Place was reported to be the last "stand up bar" in Oregon, as there were no stools, only a brass foot rail along the bar with spittoons. There were pool tables, billiard tables, and a snooker table. All used 1.5-inch slate that was reportedly brought around the Horn. Eventually, the building deteriorated beyond repair, and the owner demolished the building in 2014. (LN.)

Five

Street Scenes

Coquille developed a compact and dense downtown anchored on the south by the waterfront. Activity was concentrated on Front Street initially and later First Street, bounded by Adams Street on the east and Birch Street on the west. Central Boulevard went north from Front Street through the middle of the downtown and was part of Highway 101, which routed traffic and commerce to Coquille.

The city was initially built entirely of wood, with wooden planks on the streets to manage the mud in the winter and the dust in the summer. As the city expanded past the small plateau where the town started, the wood-plank streets were built on bridges or trestles over low areas. Both the west and east ends of Front Street were elevated wood planking. In 1914, according to the *Oregonian* newspaper, Coquille paved 10 city streets and 35 blocks with "hard surface pavement."

Framing lumber became available around 1880; hence, new homes and businesses were built in the wood-frame style. Commercial businesses were built with false fronts. Later, after devastating fires, brick and concrete became a material choice for buildings. In 1909–1910, the First National Bank, the Richmond-Barker, and the Laird Buildings were constructed using brick or concrete. Some of the bricks used in local buildings were produced in a brickyard in Arago.

When the railroad arrived, the depot was placed at the east end of Front Street, with the rail line running along Front Street. Later, the railroad was routed along the waterfront, and a new depot was built on the west side of the downtown.

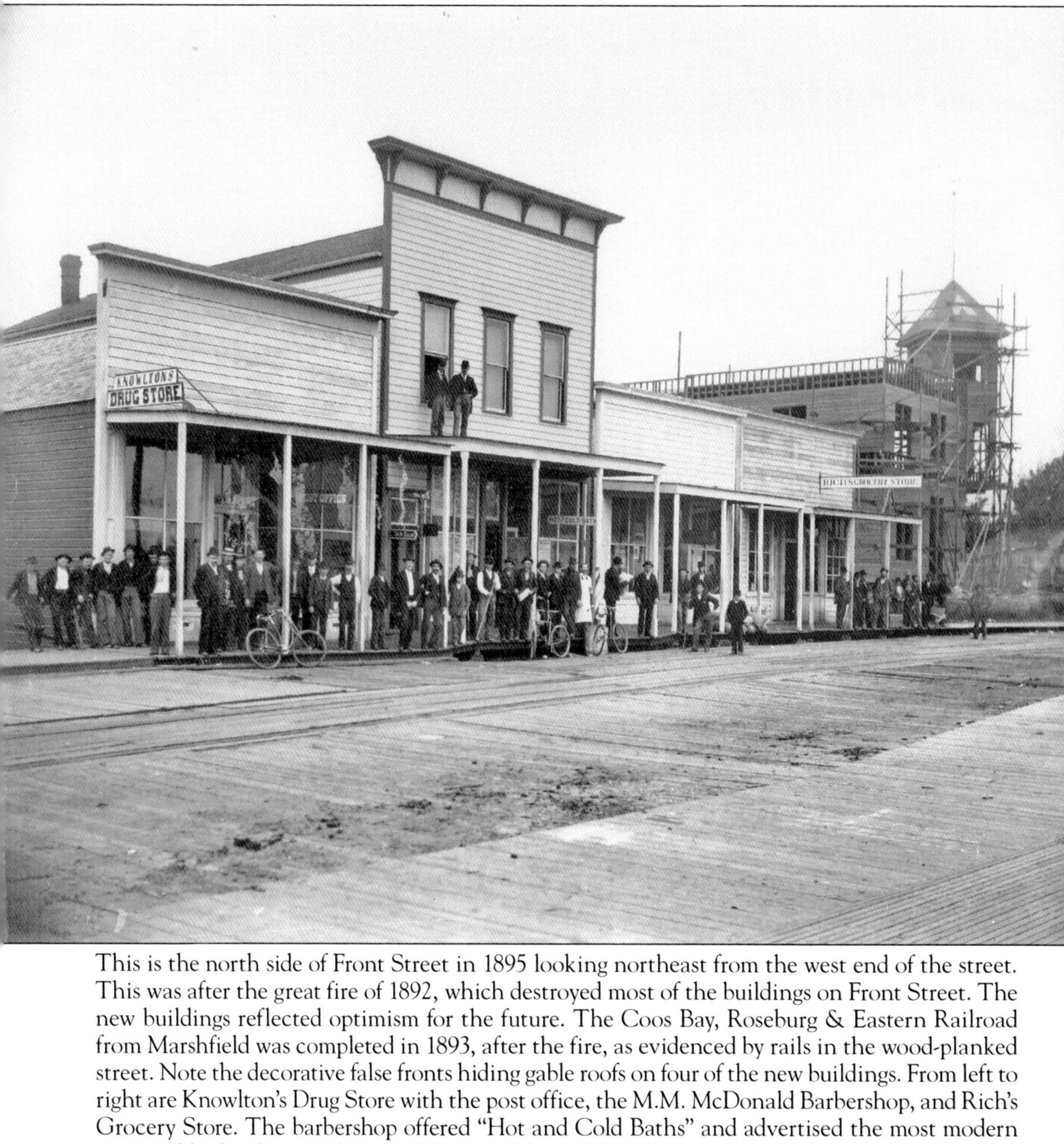

This is the north side of Front Street in 1895 looking northeast from the west end of the street. This was after the great fire of 1892, which destroyed most of the buildings on Front Street. The new buildings reflected optimism for the future. The Coos Bay, Roseburg & Eastern Railroad from Marshfield was completed in 1893, after the fire, as evidenced by rails in the wood-planked street. Note the decorative false fronts hiding gable roofs on four of the new buildings. From left to right are Knowlton's Drug Store with the post office, the M.M. McDonald Barbershop, and Rich's Grocery Store. The barbershop offered "Hot and Cold Baths" and advertised the most modern arranged barbershop in the area. The wood-framed Hotel Coquille, under construction on the right, was a source of community pride and would anchor the new downtown. (CVM.)

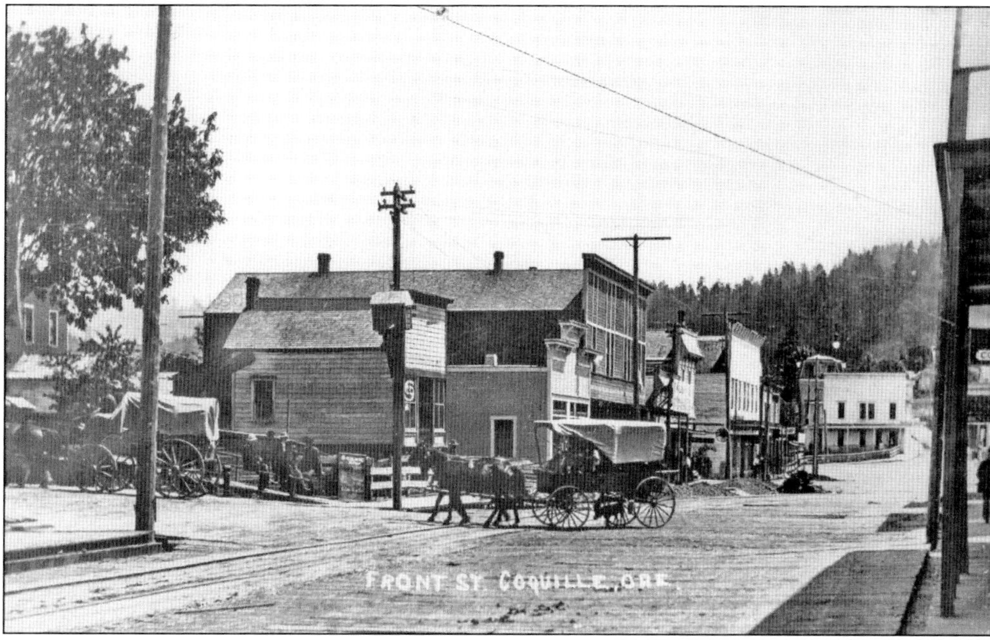

This is the intersection of Front Street and Central Boulevard looking east around 1900, before the arrival of the automobile. The Nasburg Saloon is at the northeast corner, beyond the wagons. Front Street was home to many taverns over time. Early saloon keepers included John Nasburg, V.N. Perry, S.E. Stewart, John Jinkens, Capt. M. Olson, C.O. Gilkey, James Burch, and E.A. Beckett. (CVM.)

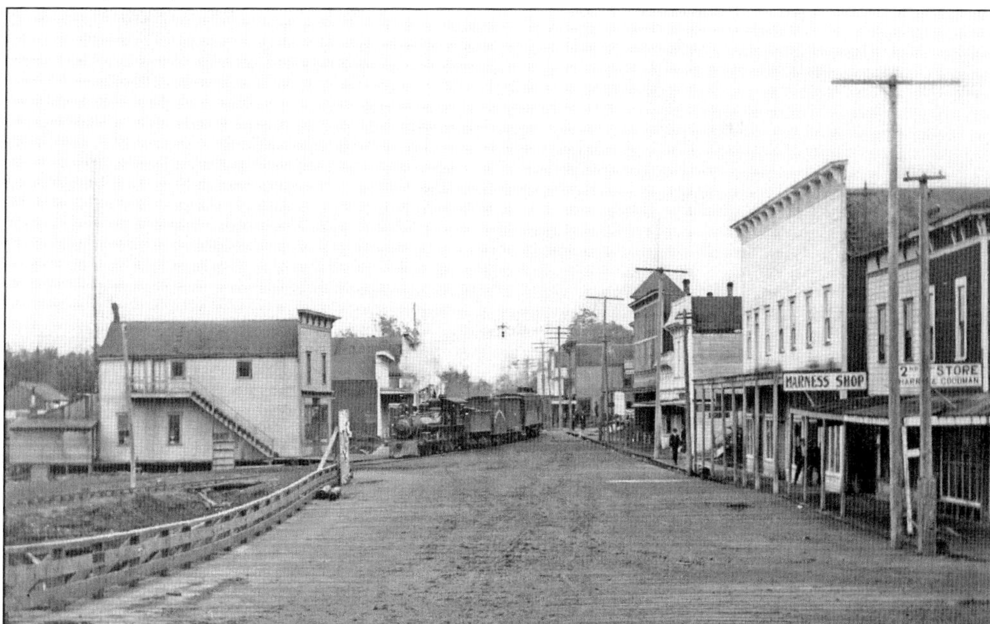

This is Front Street looking west from the east end around 1900. Dominating the scene is the Coos Bay, Roseburg & Eastern Railroad train coming down the street. The street is elevated, as shown by the railing on the left. Visible on the right are the F. Long and Son harness shop and Fox's second-hand store. The harness shop was advertised as the largest in the state. (RG.)

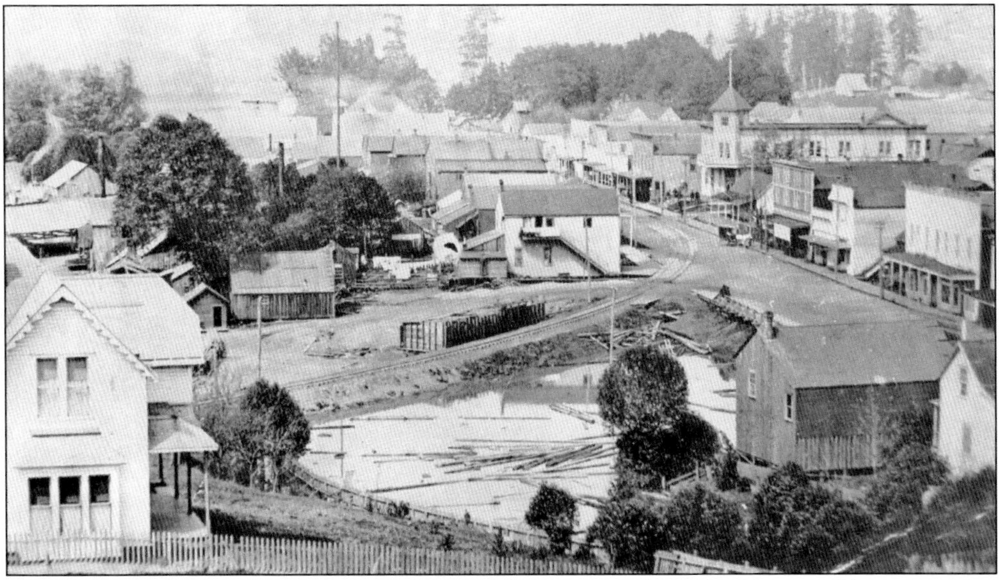

This is the east end of Front Street around 1900 looking west from the Sherwood house at Main and Collier Streets. The Mehl house is on the left, and behind it is the waterfront sawmill, partly obscured by trees. Railroad tracks are visible on Front Street. The Hotel Coquille tower is visible in the upper right. (CVM.)

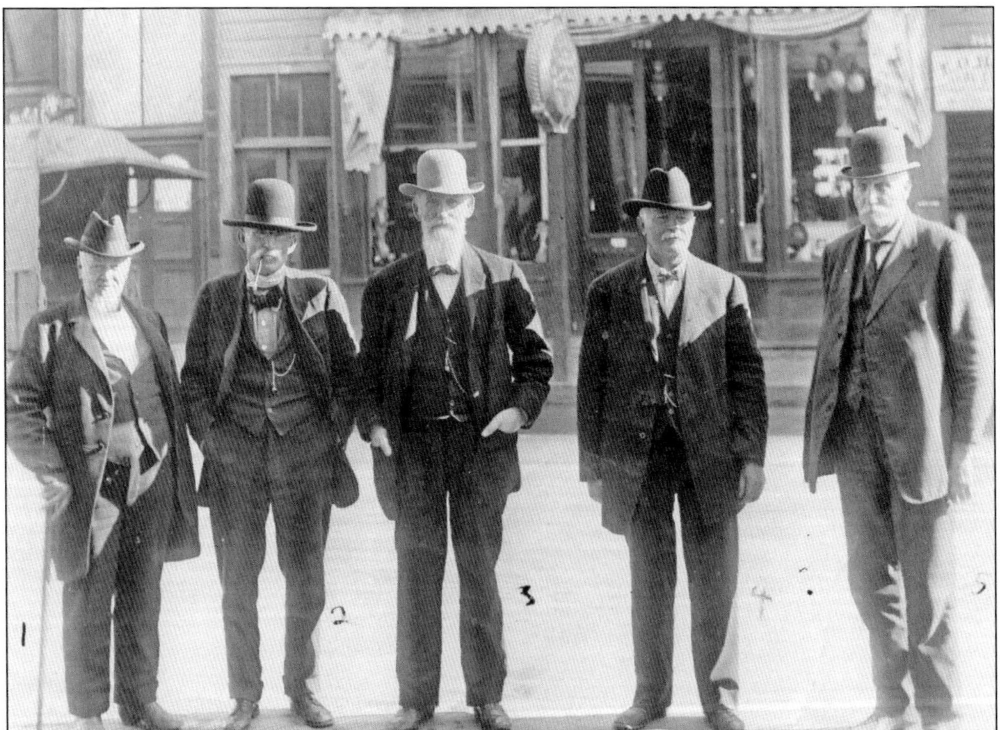

Five men in business attire are pictured on Front Street around 1910. From left to right are David Lowry Watson, Liman Noble, Capt. James R. Lightner, John Cordeiro, and E.O. Hall. In the background are a sign for E.O. Hall Real Estate and a clock that is visible in many early pictures. (CVM.)

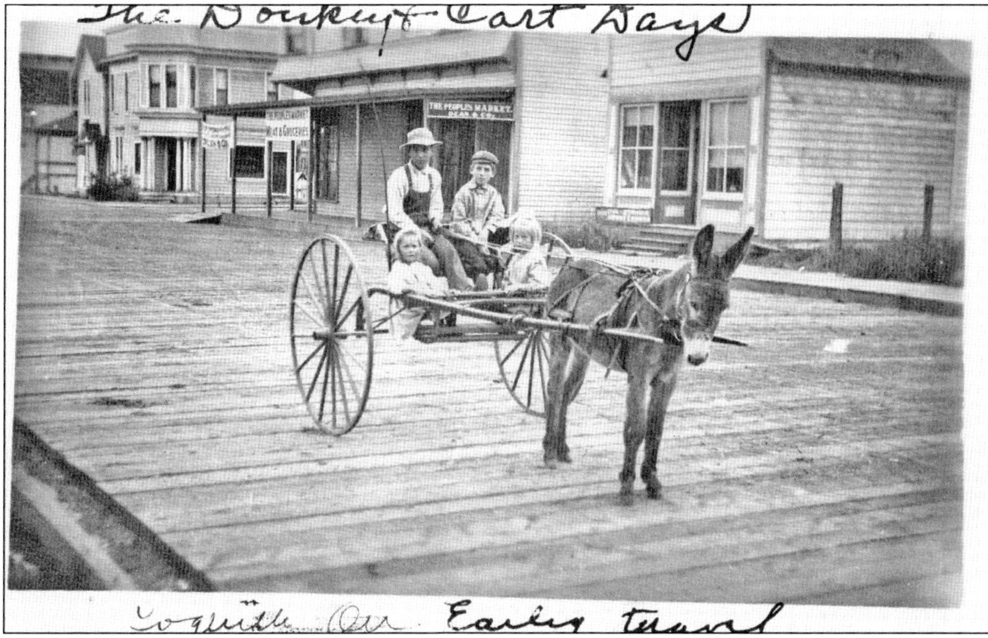

This is First Street looking northwest around 1900 with a cart filled with children pulled by a donkey. From left to right in the background are the original wood-framed First National Bank, the People's Market, and Dean and Company. To the right is an office for a civil, hydraulic, and mining engineer. The street surface is clearly wood-planked. (CHM 982-241.)

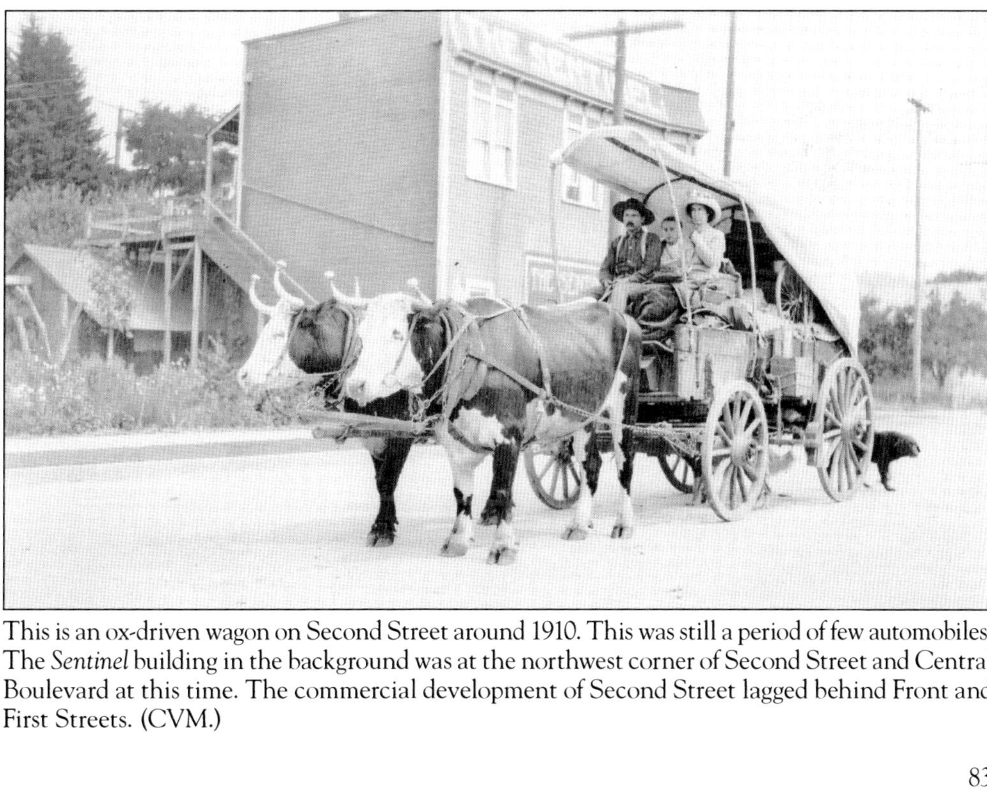
This is an ox-driven wagon on Second Street around 1910. This was still a period of few automobiles. The *Sentinel* building in the background was at the northwest corner of Second Street and Central Boulevard at this time. The commercial development of Second Street lagged behind Front and First Streets. (CVM.)

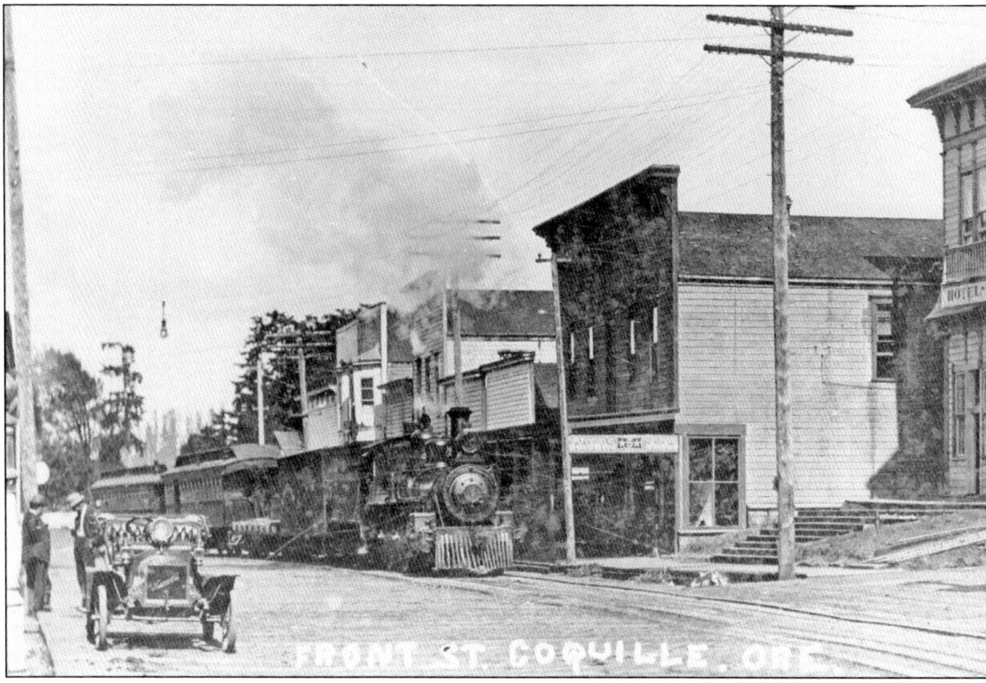

This is Front Street looking west from the intersection with Central Boulevard around 1910. On the left is an early Maxwell automobile. Prominent in the center is Engine No. 3 and cars of the Coos Bay, Roseburg & Eastern Railroad. Brown's Shoes and the Hotel Coquille are on the right. Sidewalks were wooden, streets were wood-planked, and there were no good roads to neighboring towns. (CVM.)

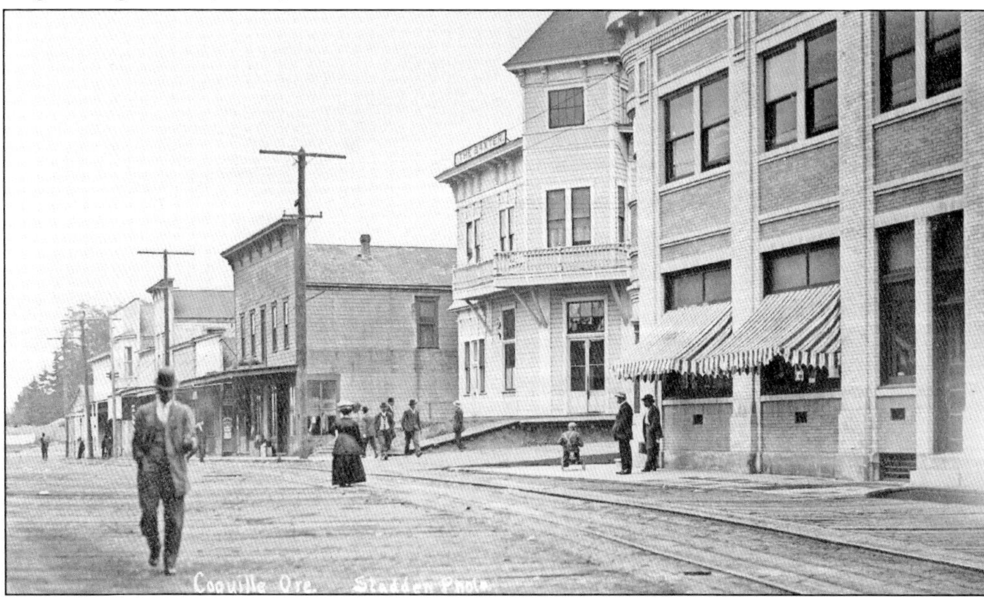

This is another view of Front Street looking west around 1910. The building in the middle is the Baxter Hotel, formerly the Hotel Coquille. The Richmond-Barker Building on the right, built in 1909, has the Farmers & Merchants Bank on the ground floor. The railroad tracks are still in the street, and the surface is still wood-planked. (RG.)

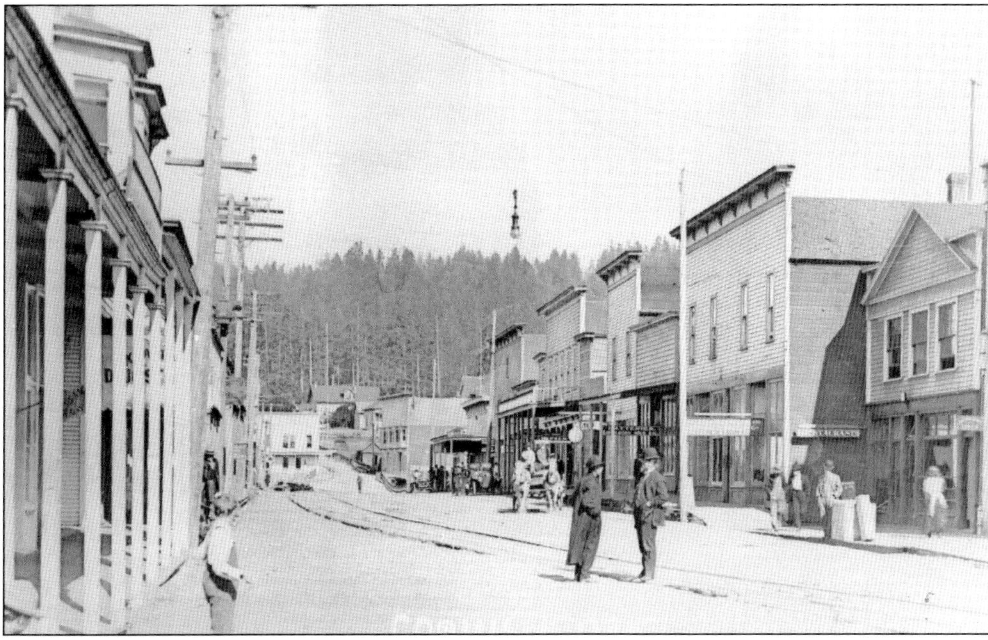

This is a view of Front Street around 1910 looking east from the west end of the street. From left to right on the right side of the street are the Palm; a business offering "Batteries, Lubricating Oil, Etc."; Mrs. M. Nosler's Uptown, offering "Board & Lodging"; a restaurant; and Wells Fargo & Company Express. The railroad would soon be moved to the waterfront. (CVM.)

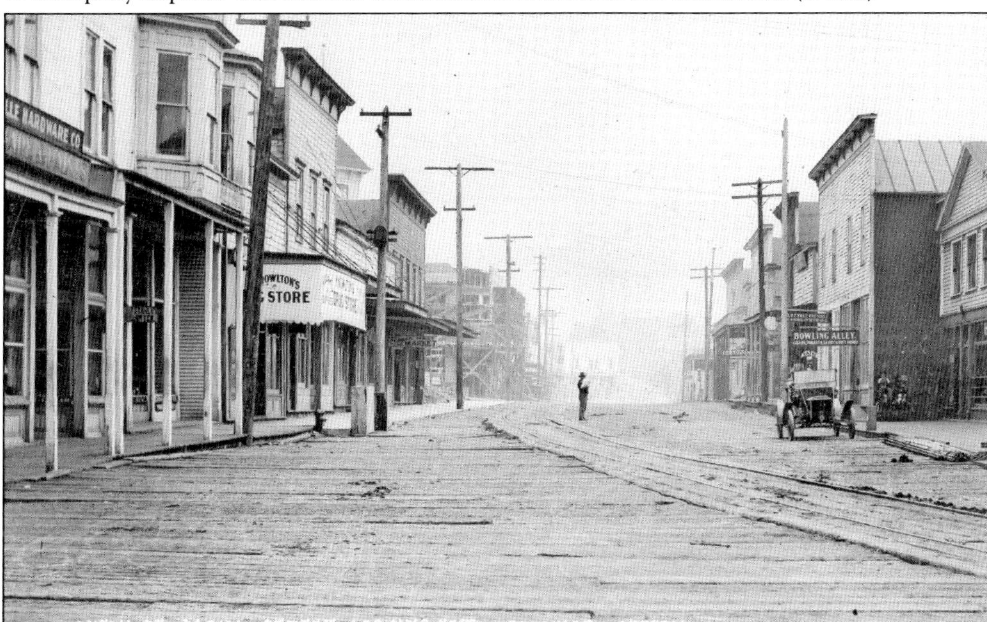

This is Front Street in 1909 looking east from the west end. From left to right are Coquille Hardware, the J.J. Stanley law office, Knowlton's Drug Store, Pioneer Meat Market, and the Richmond-Barker Building under construction. On the other side is the public reading room, a business offering "Electric Fixtures, Lighting and Wiring," Oerding's Bowling Alley, a shoe-shine stand, and Wells Fargo & Company Express. (CVM.)

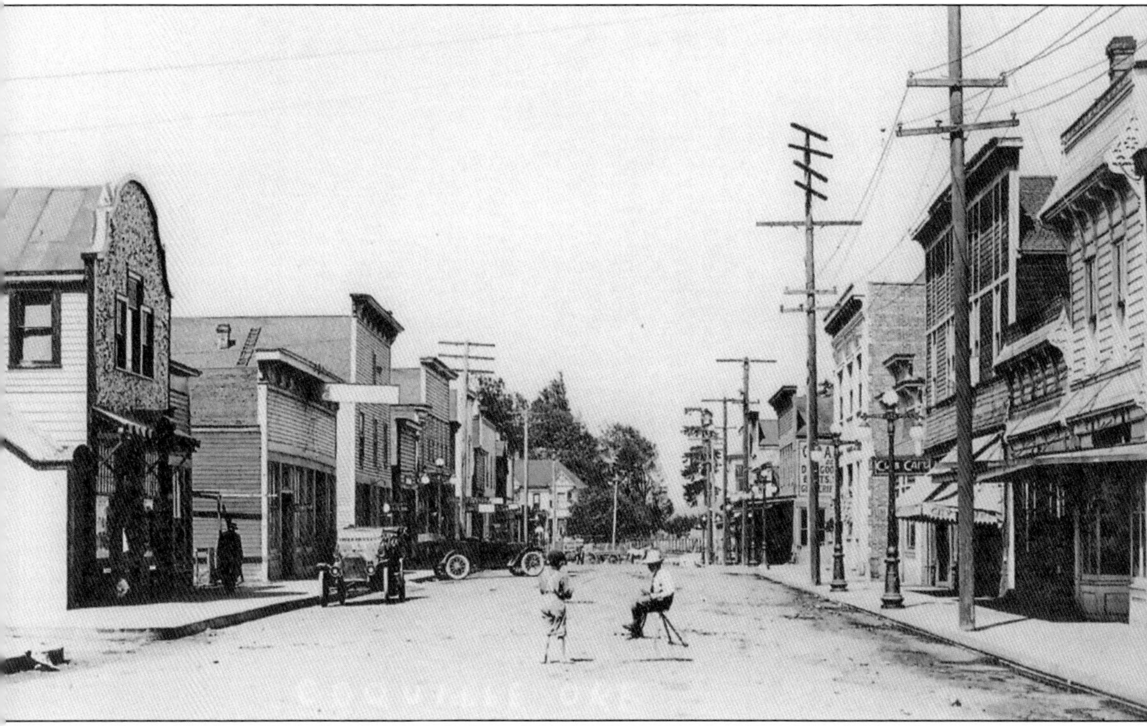

This view is looking west from the east end of Front Street around 1915. The city has clearly matured. Automobiles, power lines, streetlights, and concrete sidewalks have arrived. The street appears to be paved, with an absence of wood planking. The railroad has been moved to the waterfront, and tracks are no longer in the street. An electric power plant has been built at the sawmill behind the buildings on the left. On the left are signs for tailor Fred Slagle, a millinery and dress-making shop, a confectionery, and shoes. The Collier house is visible at the end of the street. On the right is the George A. Robinson general store, the Richmond-Barker Building, Club Café, and City Bakery. At this time, the Grand Theater, offering motion pictures and burlesque shows, would have been located to the right of this scene. The theater and the adjoining Skookum Restaurant were destroyed by a fire in 1915. (CVM.)

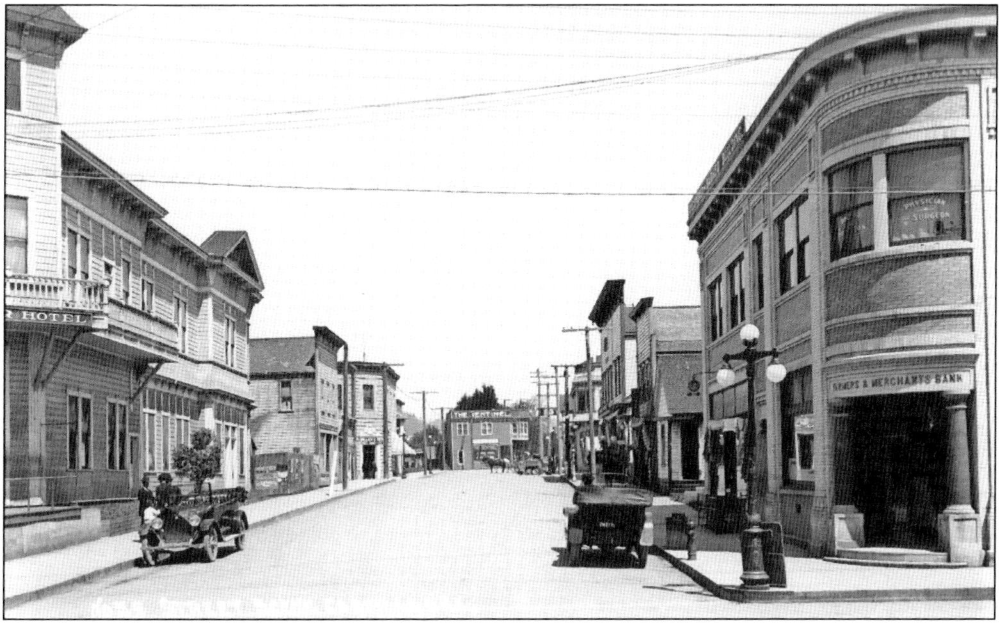

This is looking north on Central Boulevard from Front Street around 1915. On the left are the Baxter Hotel, Miller's Sanitary Market, and the First National Bank. At the end is the *Sentinel* building. On the right are the Workmen of the World and Odd Fellows buildings and the Richmond-Barker Building, home of the Farmers & Merchants Bank. Paved streets and sidewalks were completed in the period 1912–1914. (RG.)

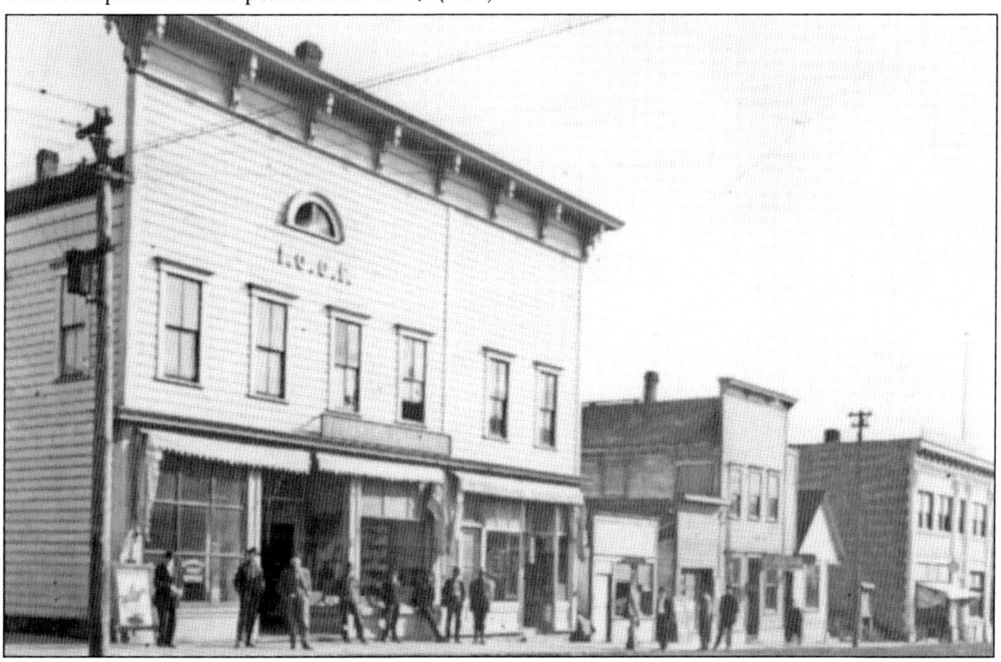

This view is looking south on Central Boulevard from First Street around 1915. On the left is the original wood-framed Odd Fellows building, containing Fuhrman's Pharmacy, the post office, and the McDonald Barbershop. On the far right is the Richmond-Barker Building with four smaller buildings in between. Note the power lines overhead. (CVM.)

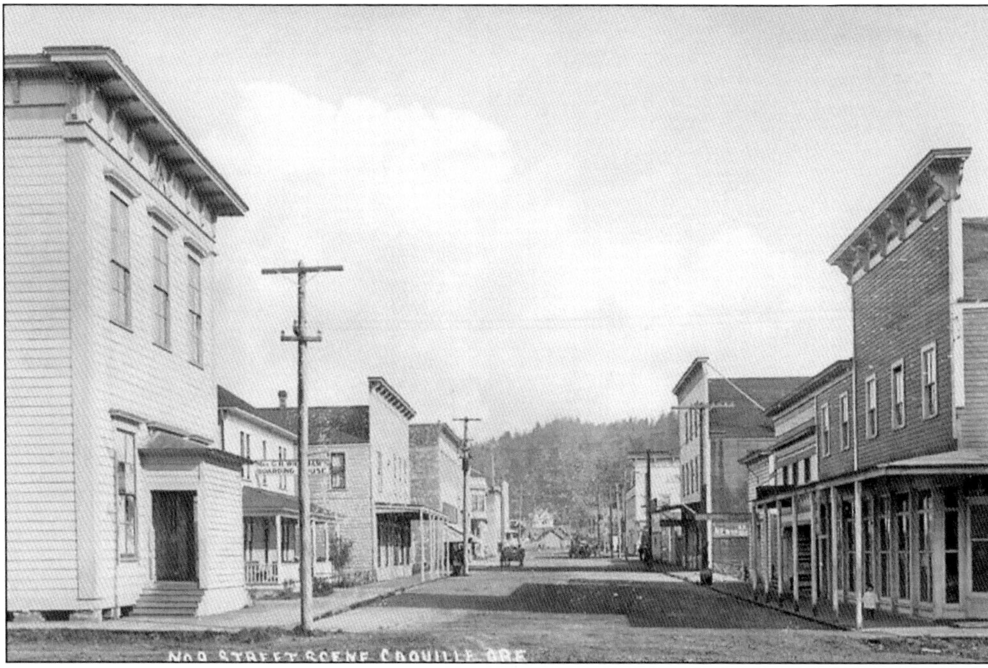

This scene is looking east down First Street around 1915 from the perspective of today's community building. From left to right are the Masonic Opera Hall, the Wickham Boarding House, the Leach Building, and the First National Bank. On the right is a three-story building, the telegraph office, the Scenic Theatre, and the J.E. Quick Second Hand Store. Most of these buildings were destroyed in the fire of 1918. (CVM.)

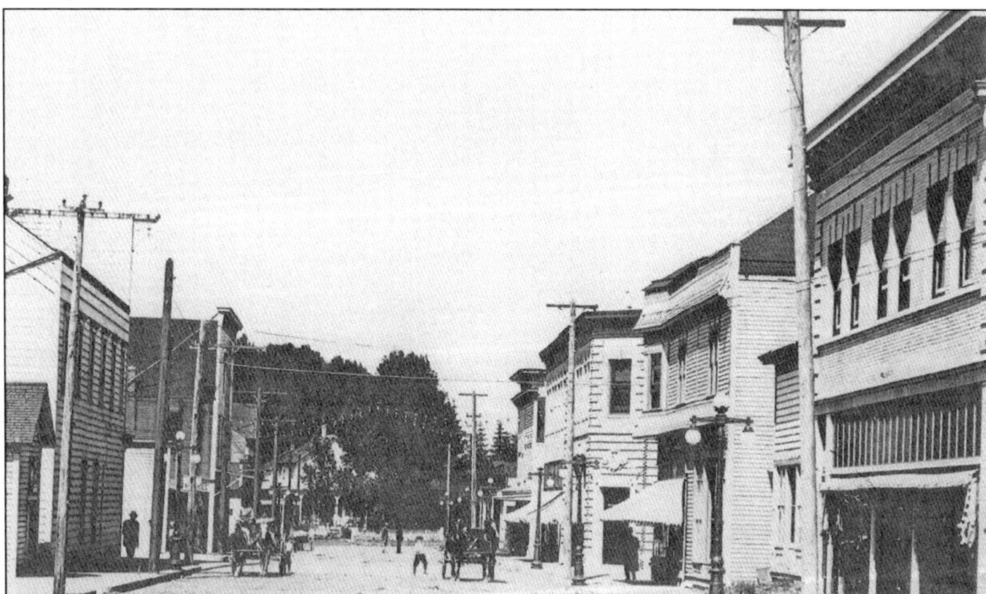

This scene is the developing First Street looking west around 1915. On the left is the original wood-framed Odd Fellows building. From left to right on the right are the First National Bank, the Woodmen of the World, and the Laird Building. The First National Bank and the Laird Building were both constructed in 1910 using masonry or concrete materials. (CVM.)

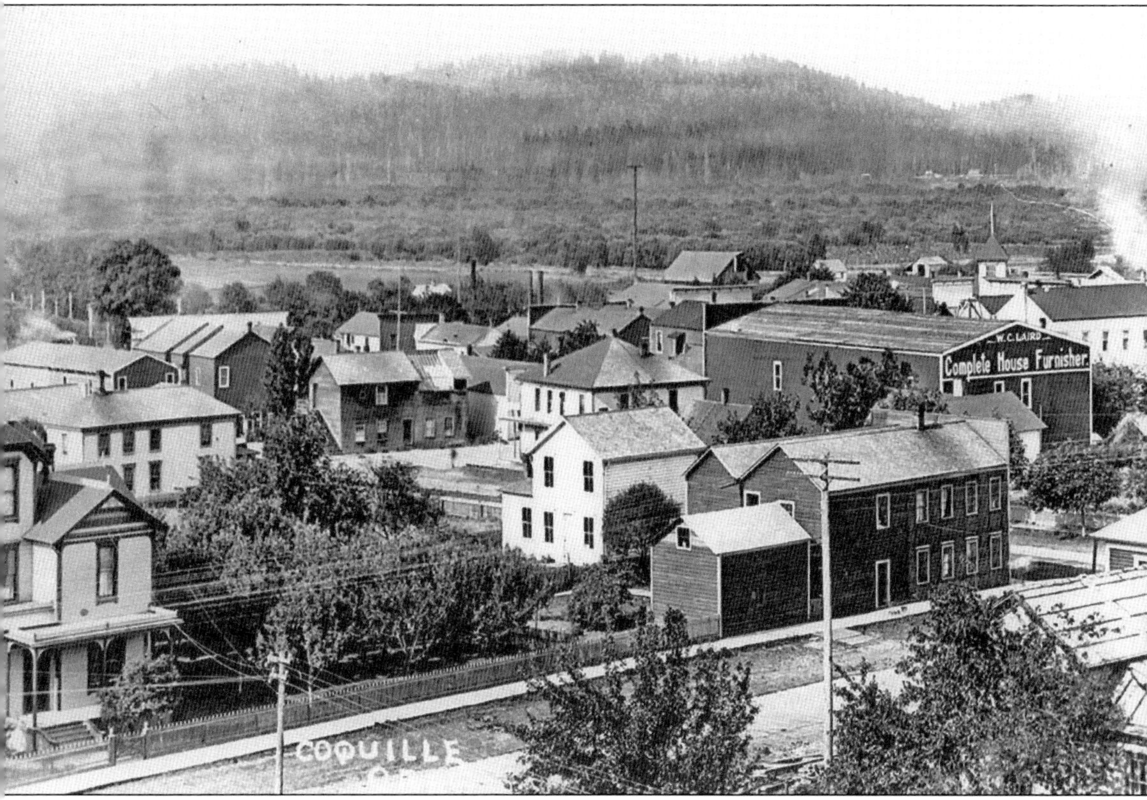

This is a southwest view of the city around 1910 from the courthouse tower. Second Street is in the foreground, and in the background is the valley floor, with the Fat Elk hills beyond. In the center is the back side of W.C. Laird's large Complete Home Furnisher building on First Street, where J.C. Penney's was later located. Laird opened his store in 1908 offering a wide variety of household goods. His motto was "the house that is pleased when you are pleased." To the left and on the northwest corner of First Street and Adams Street is the Little Hotel, which was owned and operated by T.J. Little. The hotel is best known as the residence of M.D. Landis, realty partner of newspaperman John Dean. In 1901, Landis disappeared after being accused of a murder near Cedar Point. To the left is the residence and studio of early photographer Charles Wilkins on the southwest corner of First Street and Adams Street. In addition to this studio, Wilkins operated a "floating studio," taking his equipment to other communities. (CVM.)

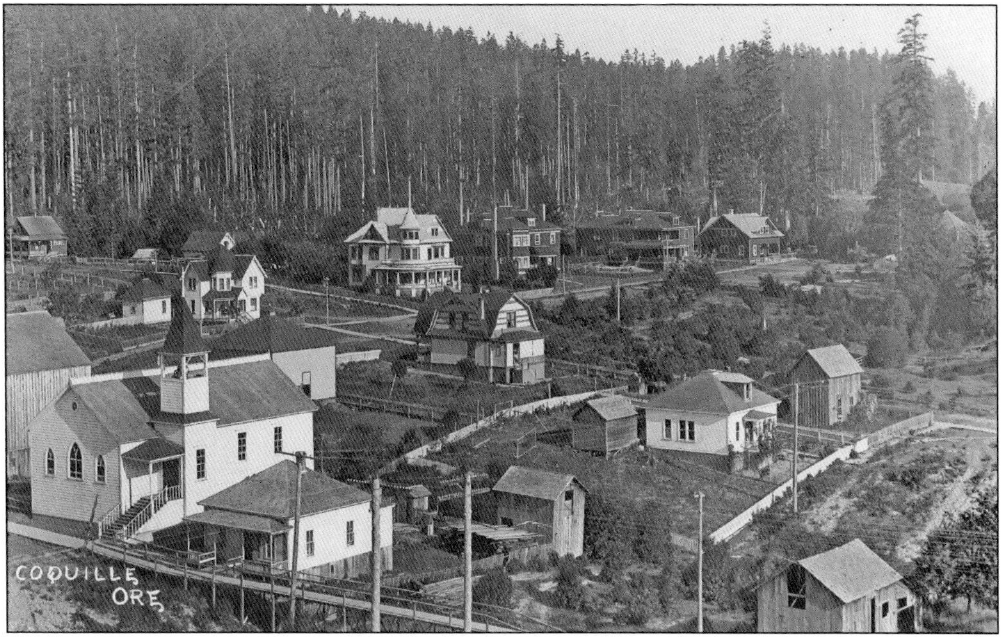

This is a southeast view from the courthouse tower around 1910. On the left is the Methodist Episcopal church, North. From left to right above it are the homes of jeweler William Schroeder and sawmill owners John Paulson and Fred Belloni. This neighborhood was home to many fine homes. (CVM.)

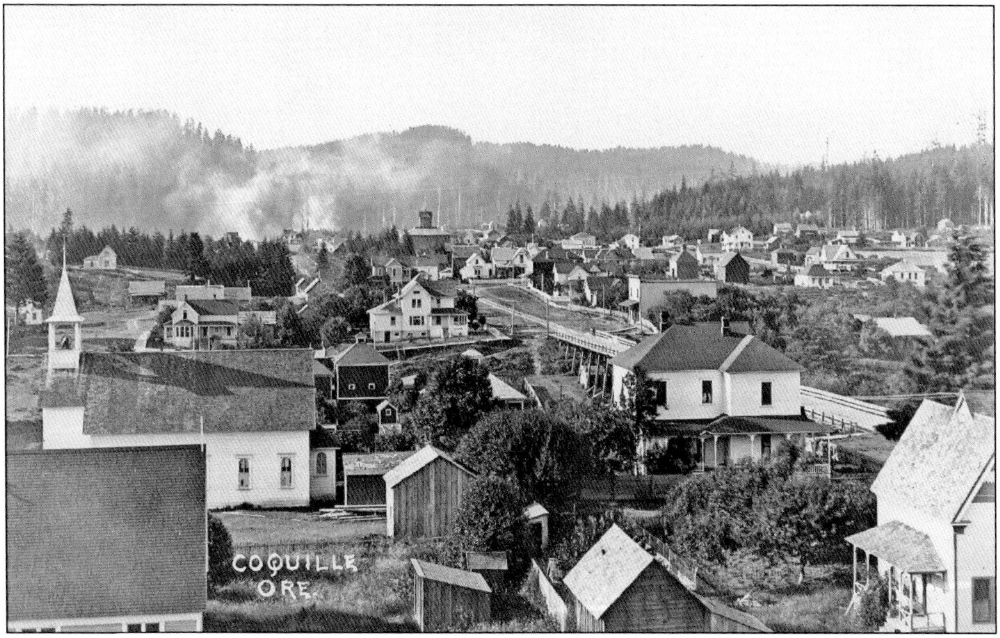

This is a view looking north from the courthouse tower around 1910. On the left are the St. James Episcopal Church and the First Presbyterian Church. In the center background in the distance is the Adventist Academy with its tower. At the right is the Henry Street Bridge, with the North Coquille Store (later Dieu's Market) at the far end of the bridge. (RG.)

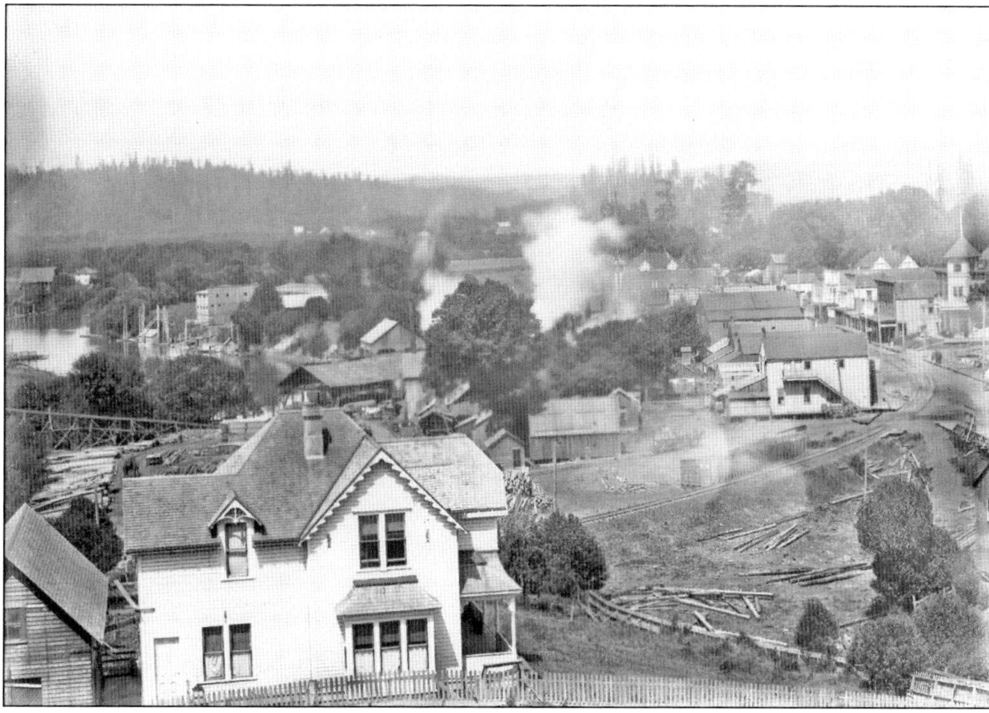

This is a view of the Mehl home looking west from the Sherwood home about 1910 with the sawmill, waterfront, and Front Street in the background. In 1874, Gottleib Mehl arrived in Coquille and established the City Brewery. He sold land to Bunch, Bennett & Company for the sawmill in the background. In 1889, the brewery burned and was immediately rebuilt. (CVM.)

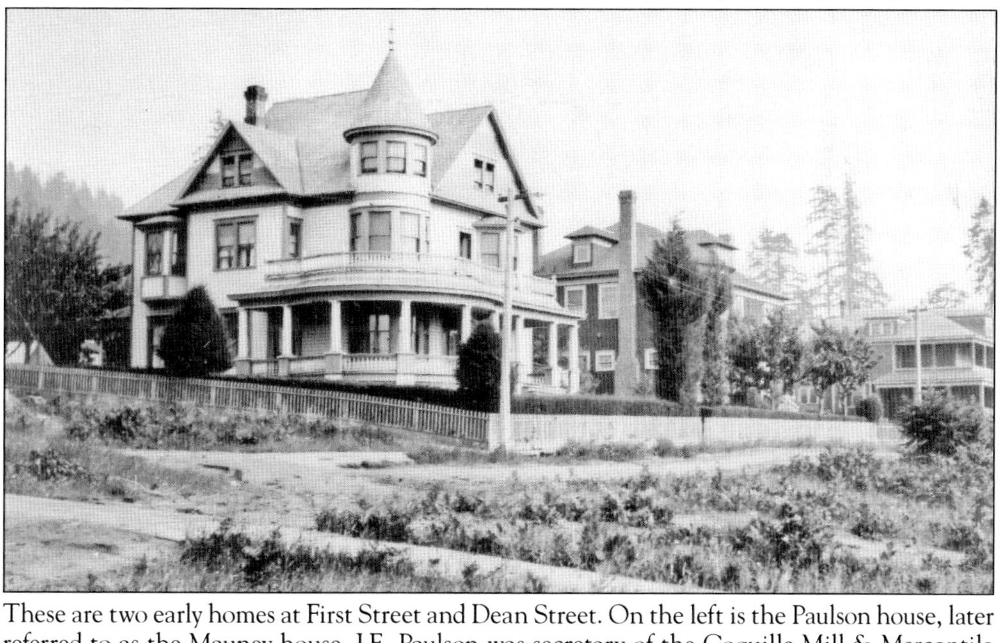

These are two early homes at First Street and Dean Street. On the left is the Paulson house, later referred to as the Mauney house. J.E. Paulson was secretary of the Coquille Mill & Mercantile Company. The dark house to the right is the Belloni or Nye house. Fred Belloni was vice president and nephew J.M. Nye was president of the Coquille Mill & Mercantile Company. (CVM.)

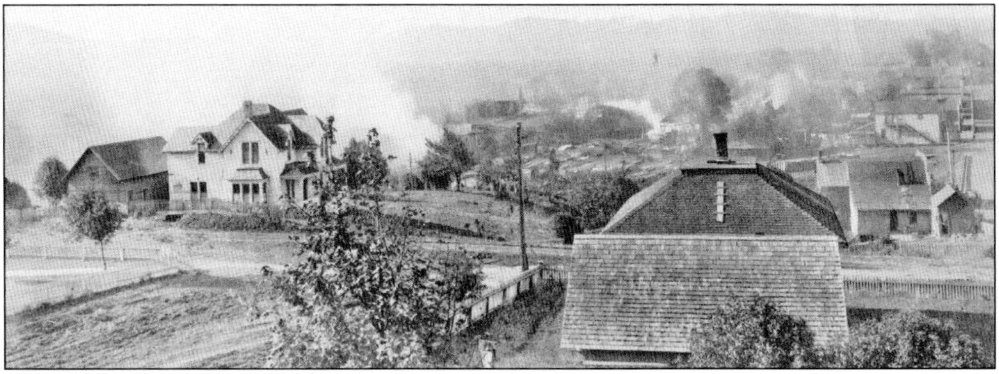

This is the first pane of a panorama, looking west from about Main Street and Collier Street around 1910. From left to right are the Mehl house, the downtown waterfront sawmill, and Front Street. On Front Street, the tower of the Hotel Coquille is visible in the background, and the white Tuttle Hotel is in the foreground. (CVM.)

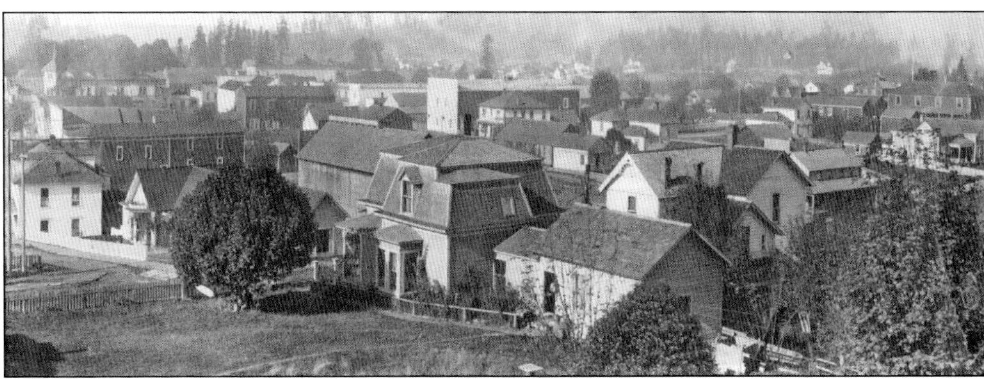

This is the second pane of the panorama, looking northwest from Main Street and Collier Street around 1910. From left to right are the white Tuttle Hotel in the foreground, the Hotel Coquille tower beyond, the Farmers Barn livery, W.C. Laird Complete Home Furnisher (skating rink), Little Hotel, the Methodist Episcopal Church South building, and the First Street bridge. (CVM.)

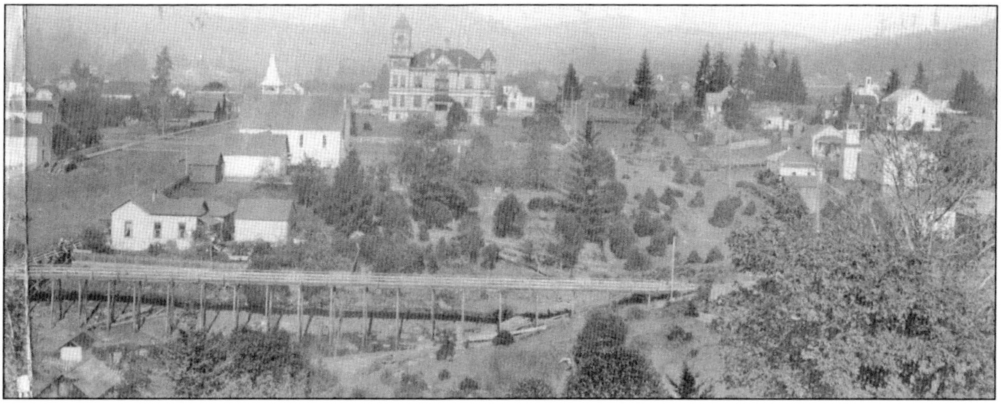

This is the third pane of the panorama, looking north from about Main Street and Collier Street around 1910. From left to right are the Methodist Episcopal Church South building, the courthouse, the Adventist Academy tower faintly visible in the background, and the Methodist Episcopal Church North building. The First Street bridge is in the foreground. (CVM.)

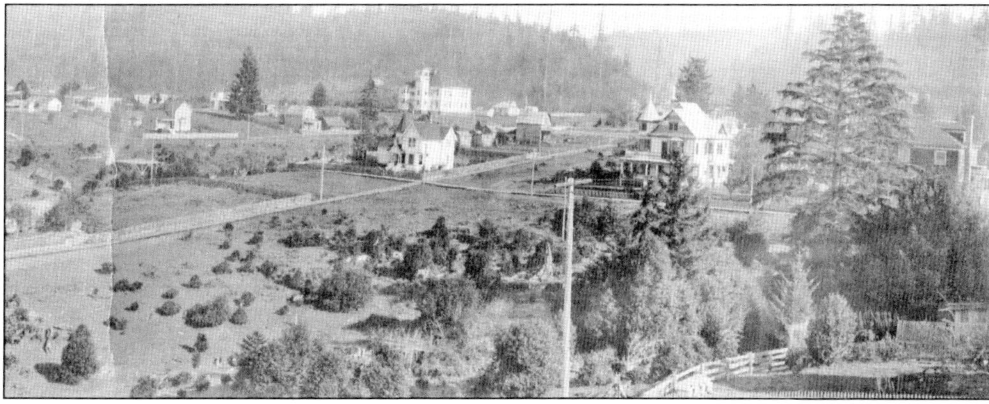

This is the fourth pane of the panorama, looking northeast from about Main Street and Collier Street around 1910. Visible from the center from left to right are the wooden sidewalks of First Street, the William Schroeder home with the Coquille Public School behind, the John Paulson home, and the Fred Belloni home. (CVM.)

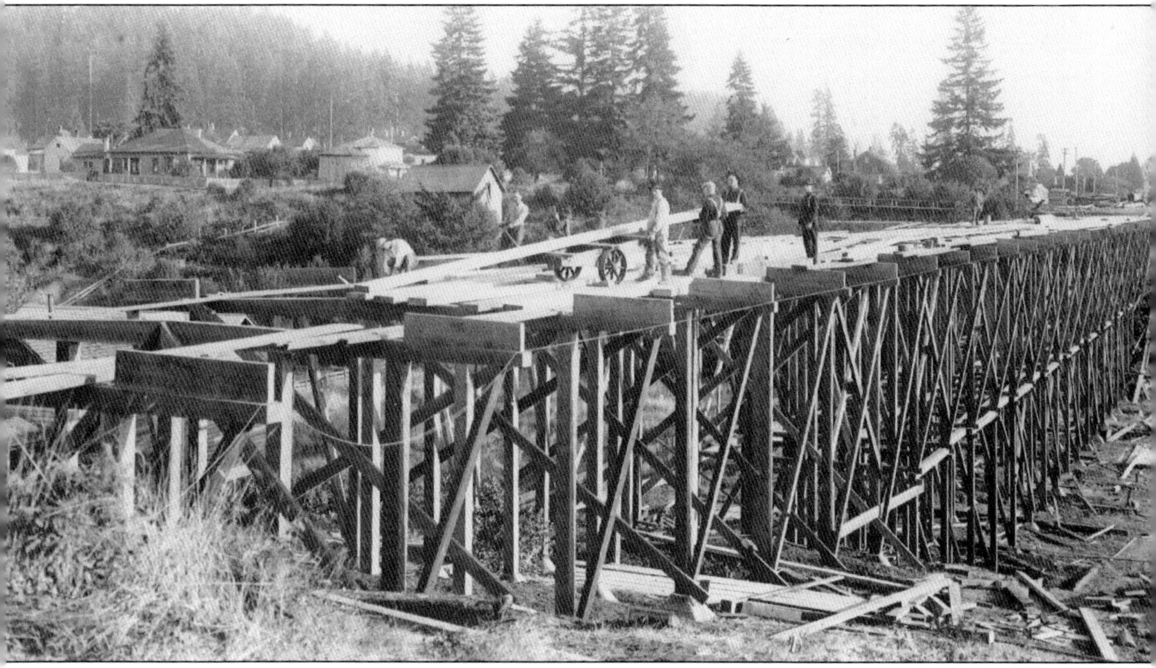

Author and historian Boyd Stone referred to Coquille as the "city of bridges" due to the number of bridges that once dotted the community on First Street, Fourth Street, and Henry Street. The Henry Street (now Collier Street) bridge was perhaps the most widely used bridge in town connecting downtown with points north. It was so popular that in December 1904, a petition was circulated to rock and gravel a portion of the Cunningham Creek Road beginning at the north end of the bridge. In 1906, the North Coquille Store, operated by Mrs. M.C. Boyrie, was located at the north end of the Henry Street bridge. Family residences were also near the north end of the bridge. Pictured is the July 1907 replanking of the bridge. J.W. Briggs replanked the bridge and installed new railing. First used by pedestrians, horses and buggies, and wagons, it was eventually used by automobiles well into the late 1940s. It was not uncommon for people to live under the bridge. (RG.)

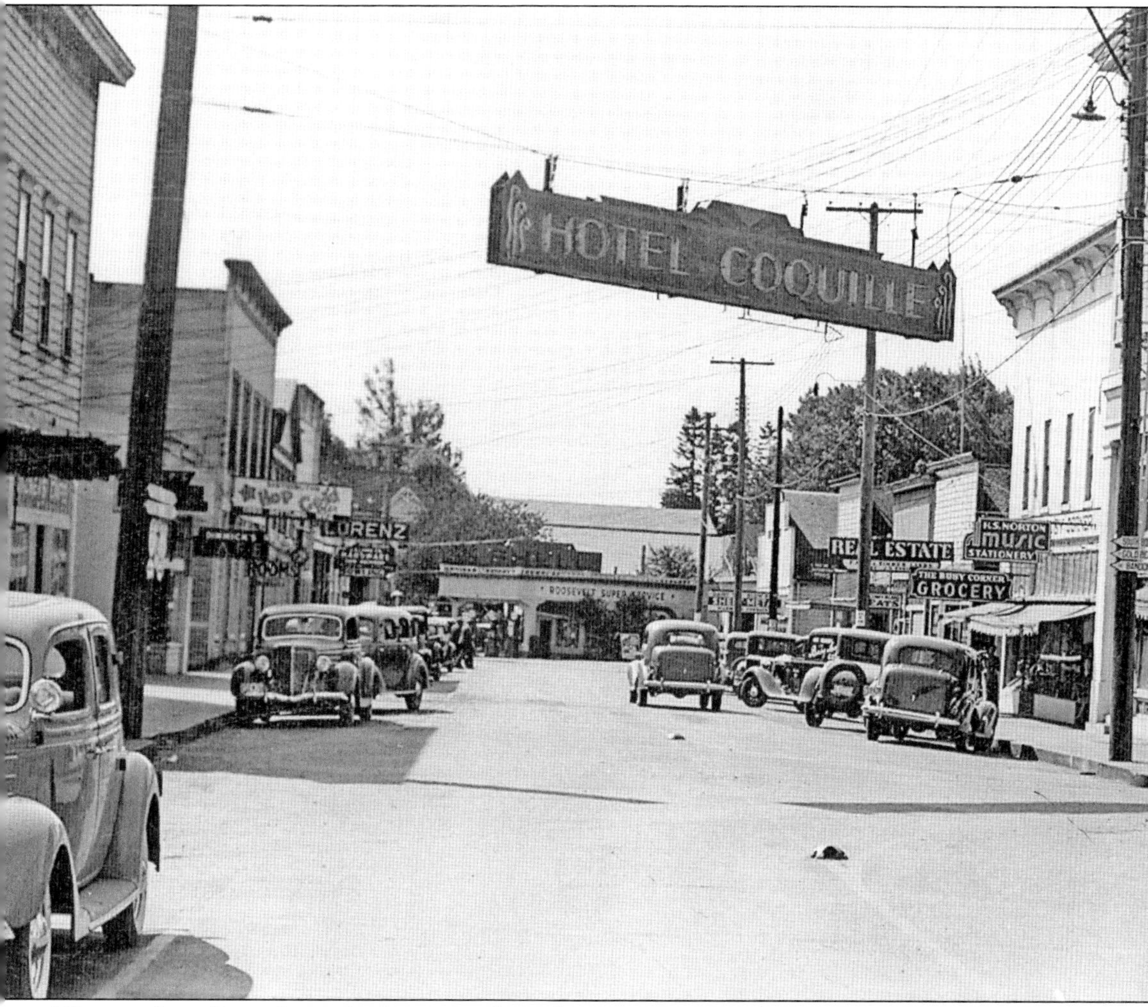

This is a busy Front Street looking west from the intersection with Central Boulevard in the 1930s. This is where Highway 101 met Highway 42, creating substantial traffic and commercial activity. South coastal residents and business traffic had to come through Coquille to reach Marshfield and vice versa. Tourists exploring the Oregon coast came through Coquille. Looming over the street is the sign for the substantial Hotel Coquille on the right, built in 1923. The street contained cafés, taverns, a bowling alley, and hardware and other stores. Of note are the West Hill Rooms and Lorenz store in the distance on the left and the Busy Corner Grocery store on the right. At the end of the street is the Roosevelt Super Service station, with the state highway shops behind. Later, buildings remaining on the left (south) side of this street would be demolished for a Highway 42 realignment. (RG.)

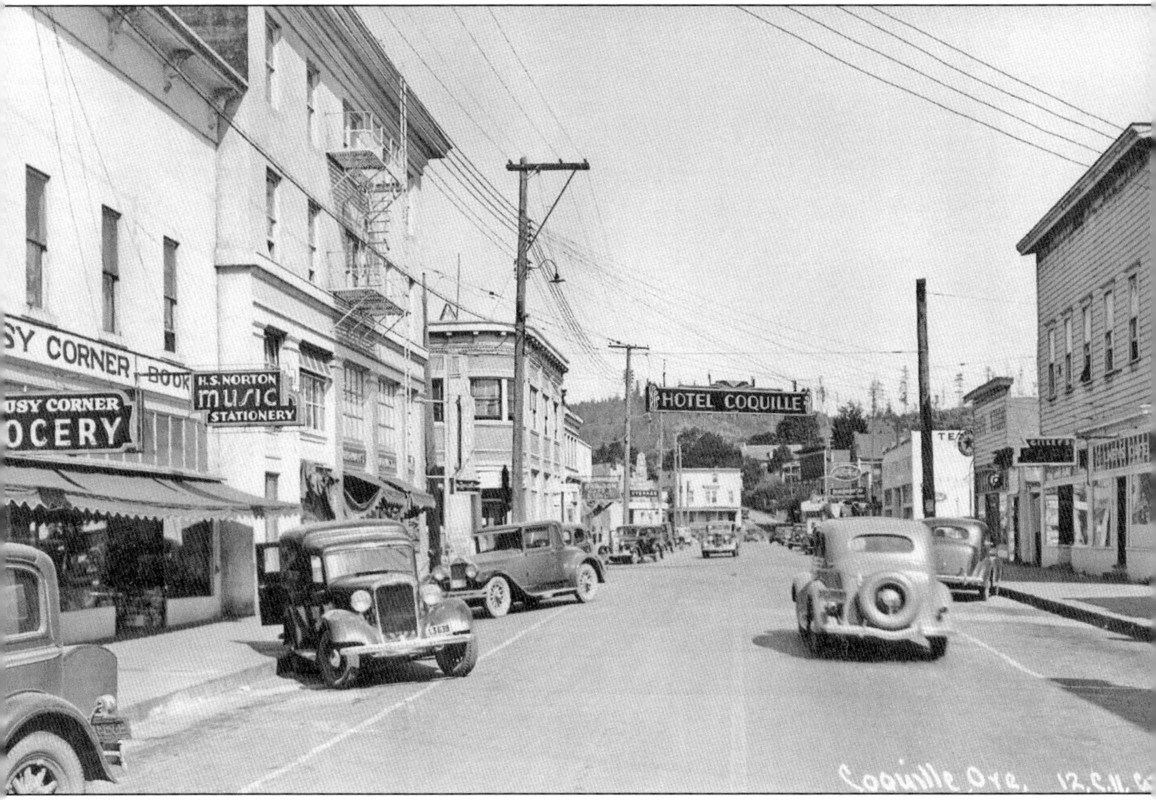

This is the busy Front Street looking east in the 1930s. The buildings are a mix of newer brick and concrete construction and older wood-frame structures with false fronts. Busy Corner Grocery is on the left, along with H.S. Norton Stationery. The Hotel Coquille is just beyond, with Fuhrman's Pharmacy on the ground floor at the corner. The Richmond-Barker Building, which had previously housed Farmers & Merchants Bank, is across Central Boulevard on the corner. In the distance on the left are Sunset Café and a Dodge and Plymouth dealer. At the end of the street is a white building that was once the Tuttle Hotel. On the right in the distance are a Ford dealer and Texaco station. Closer on the right is Gilkey's Café. Front Street would fall into decline when Highway 101 bypassed Coquille. Later, the buildings remaining on the right side were demolished for the Highway 42 realignment. (RG.)

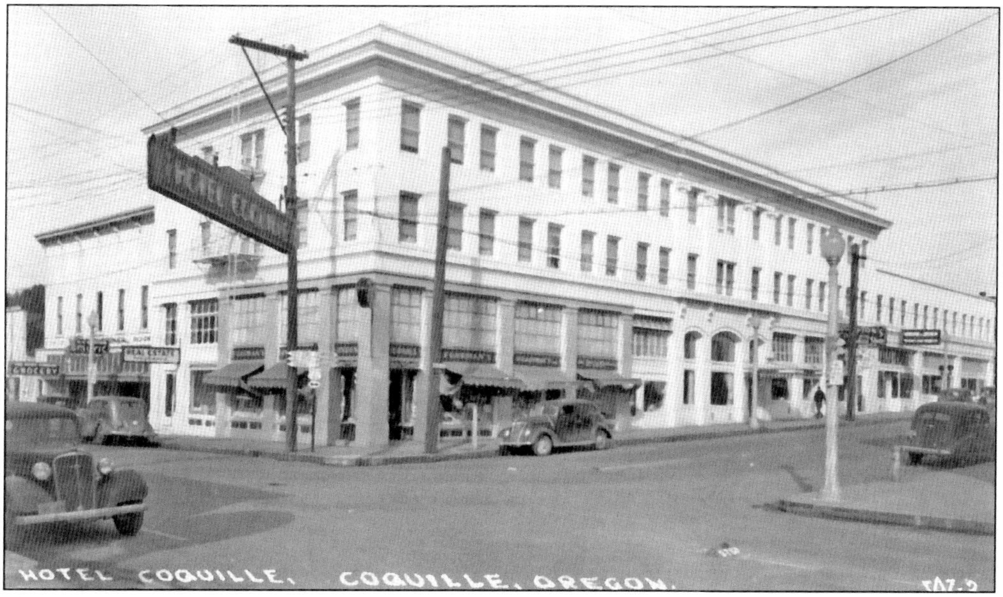

This is the Hotel Coquille at the intersection of Front Street and Central Boulevard in the 1930s. To the left are the Busy Corner Grocery, Norton Stationery, and a real estate and insurance office. Fuhrman's Pharmacy is on the corner, and Compton's Coffee Shop is to the right of the entrance. Greene & Jensen Western Auto Supply is in the hotel annex to the right. (CVM.)

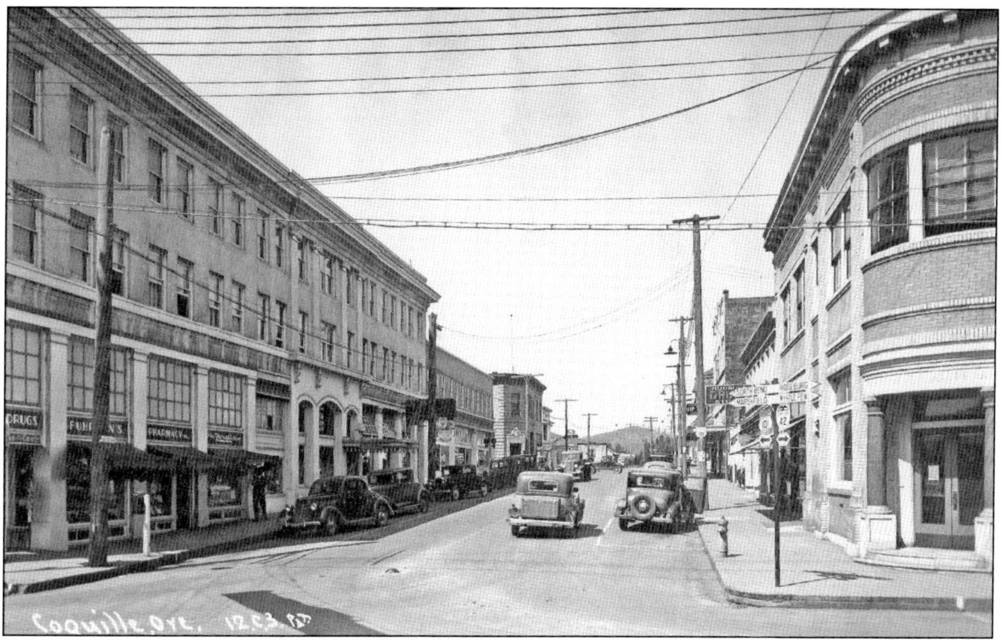

This is a view looking north up Central Boulevard in the 1930s. On the left is the Hotel Coquille, and beyond is the hotel annex. Further on is the First National Bank. On the right is the Richmond-Barker Building, with a recently vacated Farmers & Merchants Bank on the corner. Beyond are the Hudson Drug Store and the Tip Top Fountain. (RG.)

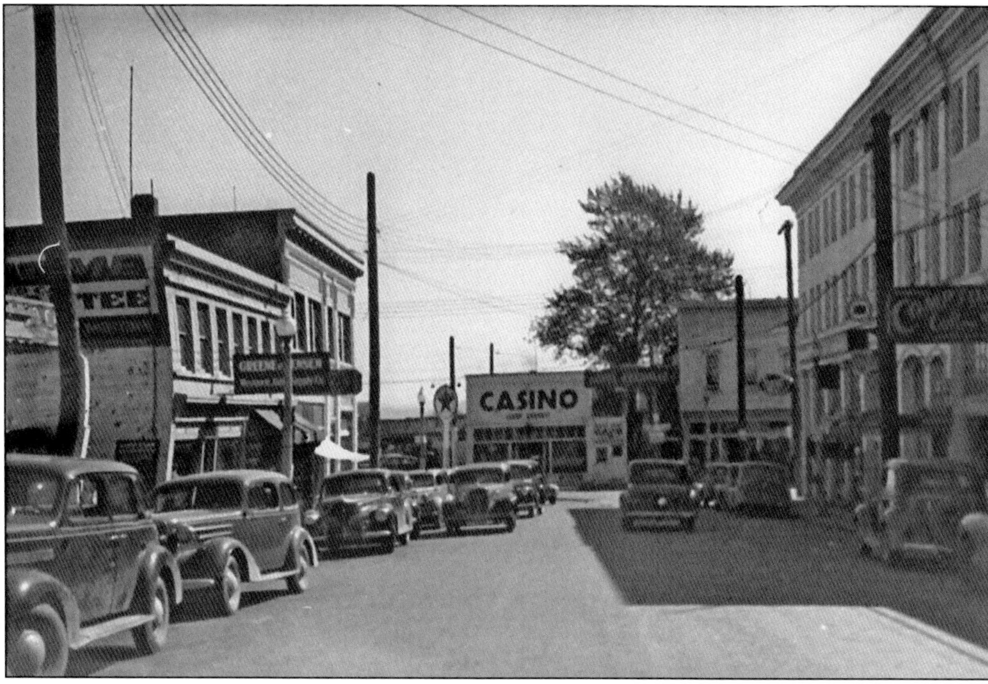

This is a view looking south on Central Boulevard around 1940. From left to right are the Southwestern Motors used car lot, Greene & Jensen Western Auto Supply, and Hudson Drugs. A Texaco gas station and the Casino Tavern are in the center, and the Hotel Coquille and Compton's Coffee Shop are on the right. (CVM.)

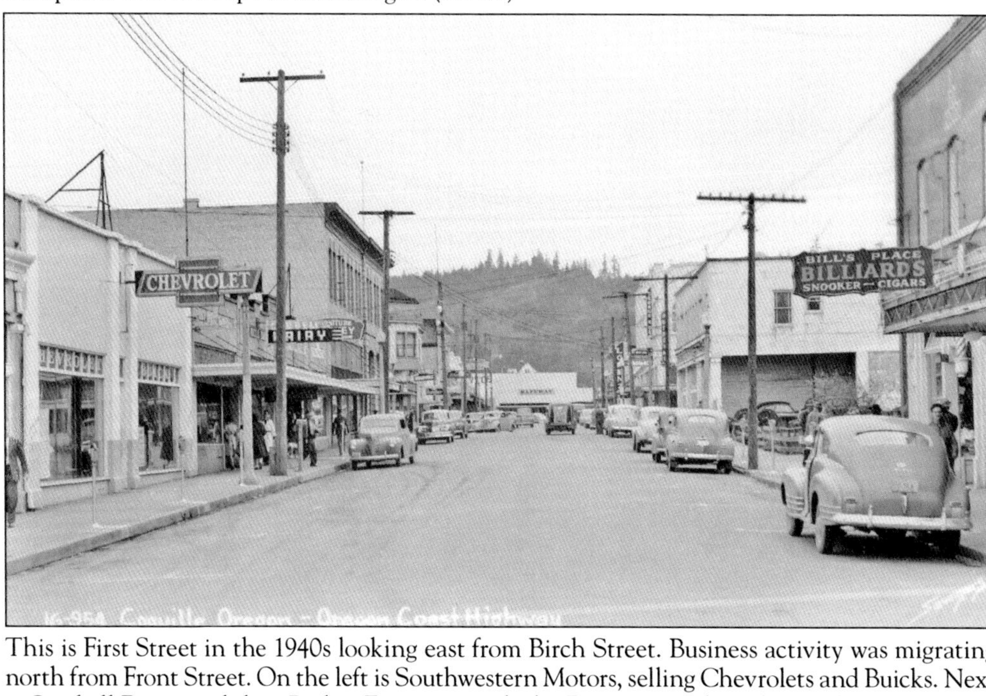

This is First Street in the 1940s looking east from Birch Street. Business activity was migrating north from Front Street. On the left is Southwestern Motors, selling Chevrolets and Buicks. Next is Cowbell Dairy, and then Purkey Furniture with the First National Bank. On the right is Bill's Place, with rooms upstairs to rent. The Liberty Theatre would be just to the right. (BM 51725.)

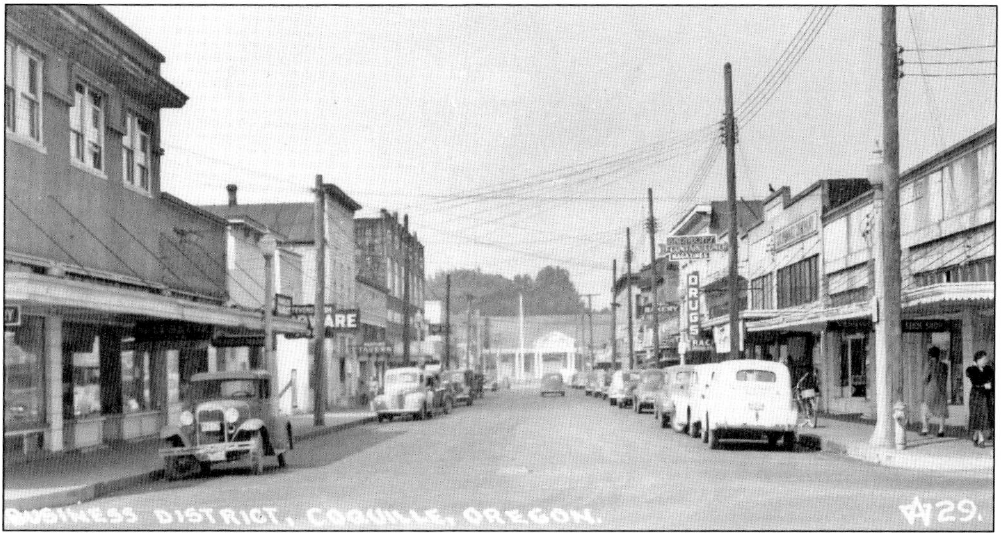

This is First Street looking west from Adams Street in the 1940s. From left to right are Gant's Grocery, People's Market, Steven's Cash Hardware, Pastime Tavern, Tip Top Café, the community building, Ideal Bakery, Rackleff Drugs, Brandon's Fountain Lunch and J.C. Penney's, V.R. Wilson Optometry, and a shoe shop; to the right is the Coquille Bakery. (CVM.)

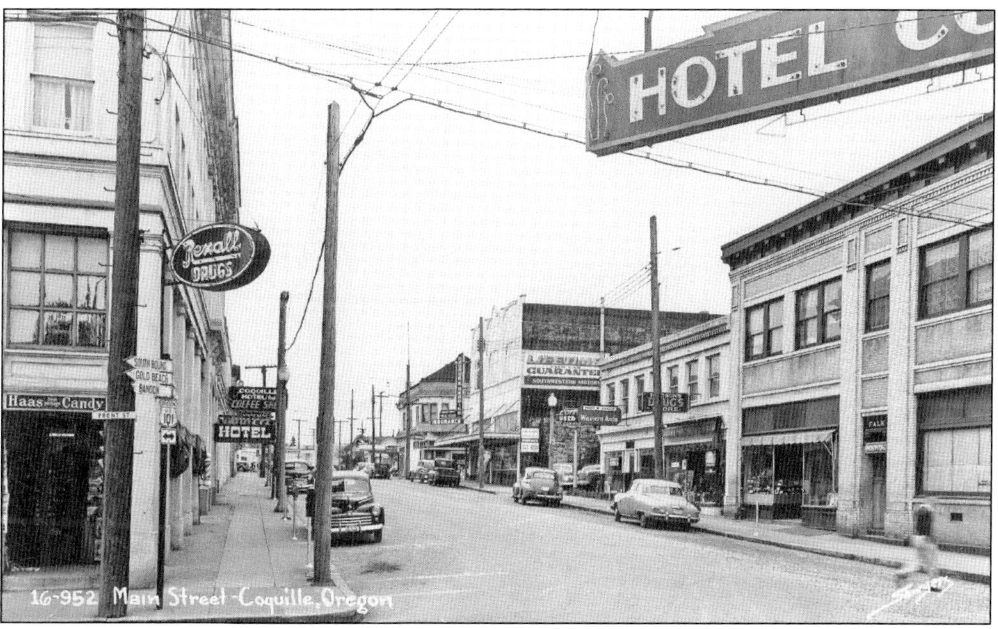

This view was taken looking north on Central Boulevard from Front Street around 1950. Fuhrman's Pharmacy is in the corner of the Hotel Coquille building. On the right are George Oerding Insurance in the Odd Fellows building and the Southwestern Motors used car lot. Harry M. Johnson Western Auto and Hudson's Drugs are in the Ellingson Building. The Falk Hospital is upstairs in the Richmond-Barker Building. (RG.)

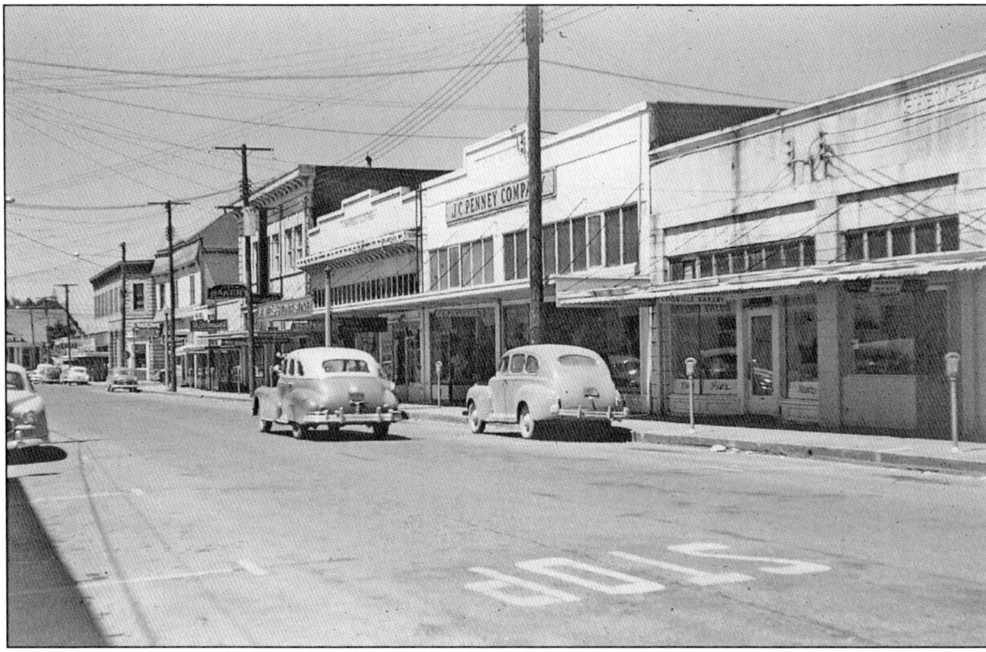

This is the north side of First Street looking west from Adams Street around 1950. From left to right are the First National Bank, Rackleff Insurance, the Bootery, Herman's Men's Store, Ideal Bakery, Slater's Five & Dime, Brandon's Fountain, J.C. Penney's, Coquille Bakery, and Johnny's Music. Note that J.C. Penney's was in the Gould Building, and the bakery and music store were in the Shelley Building. (CVM.)

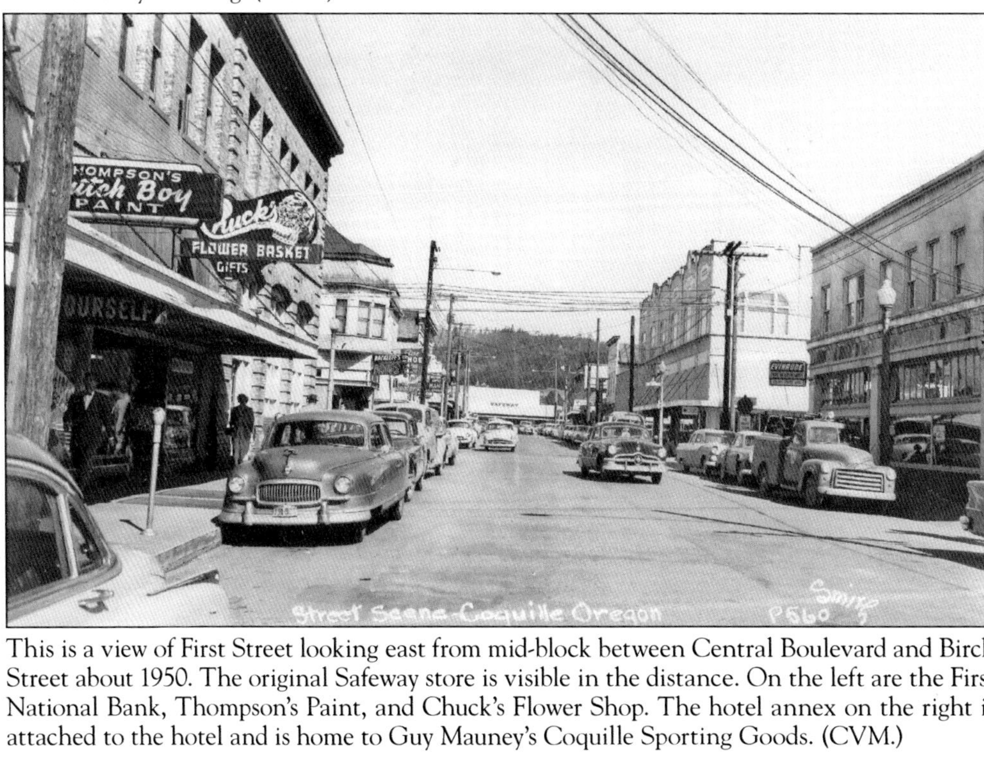

This is a view of First Street looking east from mid-block between Central Boulevard and Birch Street about 1950. The original Safeway store is visible in the distance. On the left are the First National Bank, Thompson's Paint, and Chuck's Flower Shop. The hotel annex on the right is attached to the hotel and is home to Guy Mauney's Coquille Sporting Goods. (CVM.)

Six

Roads, Railroads, and Highways

Coquille was established on the river and depended on it for many years. While the river provided transportation for the lower valley, wagon roads, railroads, and highways provided expanded routes and supported growth. In 1884, the first major improvement was the construction of a wagon road from Marshfield. Prior to this, the trip was arduous, especially through Beaver Slough. In 1893, the railroad was completed from Marshfield to Coquille and Myrtle Point, providing further improved routes for transportation.

The railroad provided better passenger and freight service. Businessmen in Roseburg and Marshfield formed a corporation they called the Coos Bay, Roseburg & Eastern Railroad and Navigation Company. Organizers included J.W. Bennett of Marshfield and T.R. Sheridan of Roseburg. They were joined by contractor R.A. Graham of California, who led the construction of the railroad and the development of the Beaver Hill coal mine. The line was intended to reach Roseburg but proved too expensive. The railroad and coal mine were mostly financed by John D. Spreckels & Company of California, which assumed control when Graham was unable to repay loans.

Better roads were desired with the introduction of automobiles. In 1921, a paved highway was completed between Marshfield and Coquille as part of the Roosevelt Coast Military Highway (later called US Highway 101). The highway replaced the wagon road built in the 1880s. This provided another transportation route, leading to the construction of a steel bridge across the river in 1922 and the development of a new road to Bandon. The road to Myrtle Point and Roseburg (later Oregon Highway 42) was vastly improved. All of these developments led to another economic boost to the city, resulting in new buildings and businesses.

Coquille benefitted from expanded commerce with residents of towns along the south coast. Merchants sold merchandise including cars, furniture, and clothing. Residents benefitted from expanded businesses and a selection of consumer goods. When Highway 101 bypassed Coquille in 1954, directly connecting Bandon and other south coast communities with Coos Bay, the community suffered, as commercial activity declined.

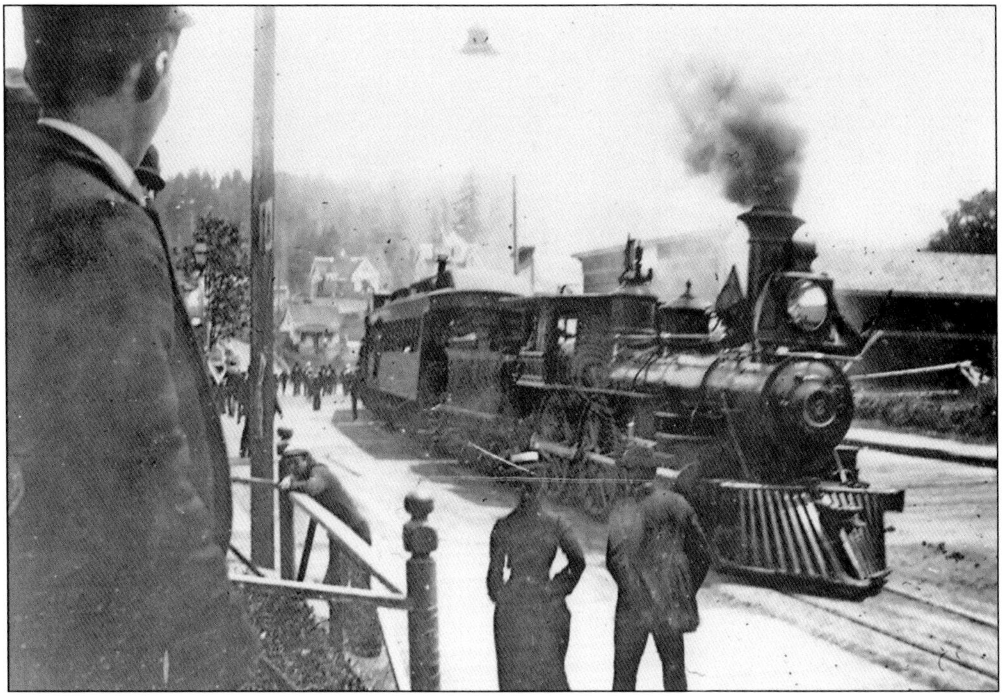

Steam engine no. 2 and cars of the Coos Bay, Roseburg & Eastern Railroad are headed west on Front Street about 1900. Tracks ran on Front Street from 1893 until about 1910, when they were moved to the waterfront. The picture was taken from the porch of the Hotel Coquille. (DCM N11394.)

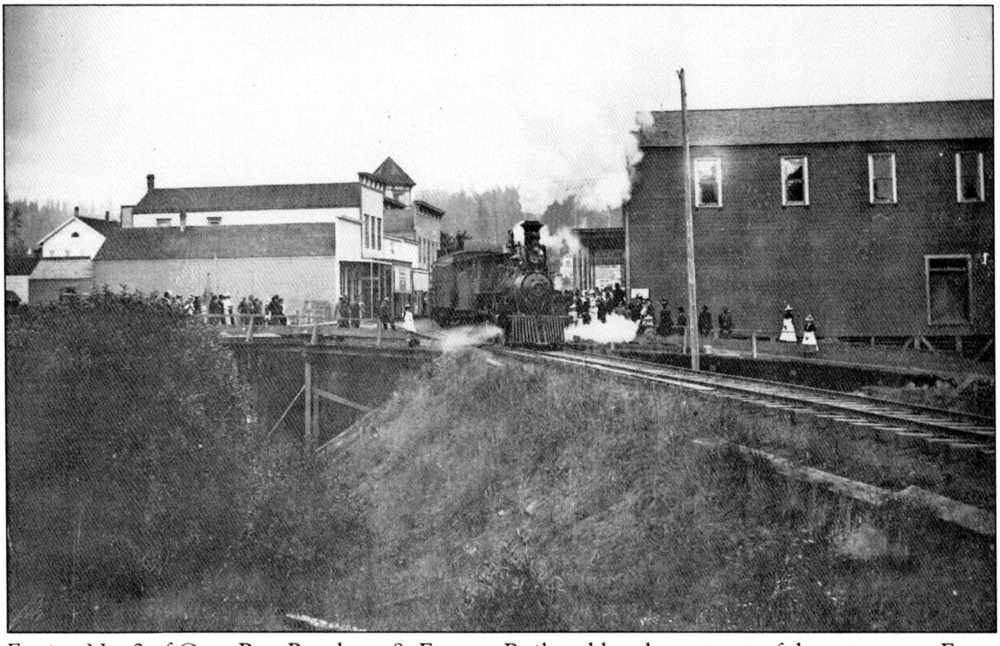

Engine No. 2 of Coos Bay, Roseburg & Eastern Railroad heads west out of downtown on Front Street around 1900. The railroad grade required a cut on Front Street and fill at both ends. Note the raised and planked streets on either side of the tracks. The tower of Hotel Coquille is visible above other buildings. (DCM N11389.)

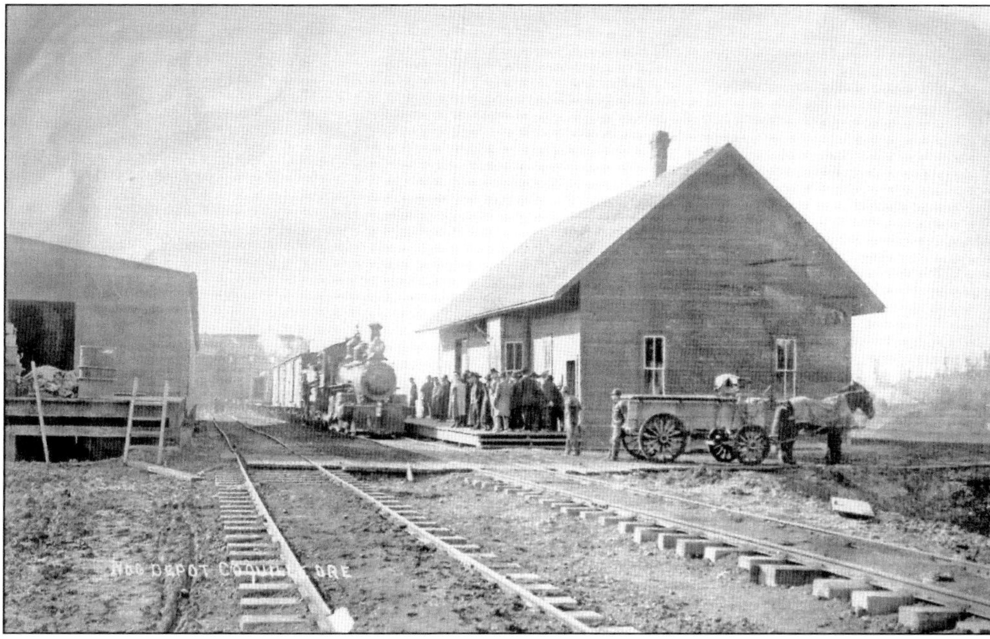

In this view looking west, a Coos Bay, Roseburg & Eastern train arrives at the depot around 1910. The Joseph A. Collier Warehouse is on the left, and the Coquille Valley Creamery is in the background. Beyond the creamery is where the Coquille Lumber sawmill was built in 1912; it would later be known as the Sitka Spruce Mill. (CVM.)

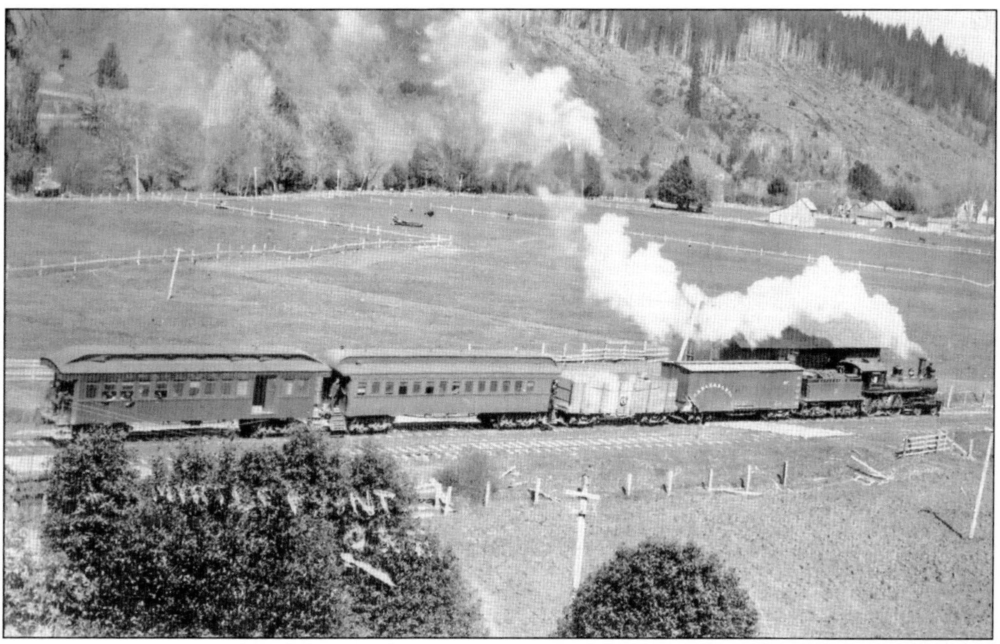

A Coos Bay, Roseburg & Eastern Railroad train is pictured between Coquille and Myrtle Point around 1900. Myrtle Point was the southernmost point on the railroad until 1916, when the railroad was extended from Myrtle Point to the Powers area in order to transport logs from the timberlands of the South Fork drainage of the Coquille River. (CVM.)

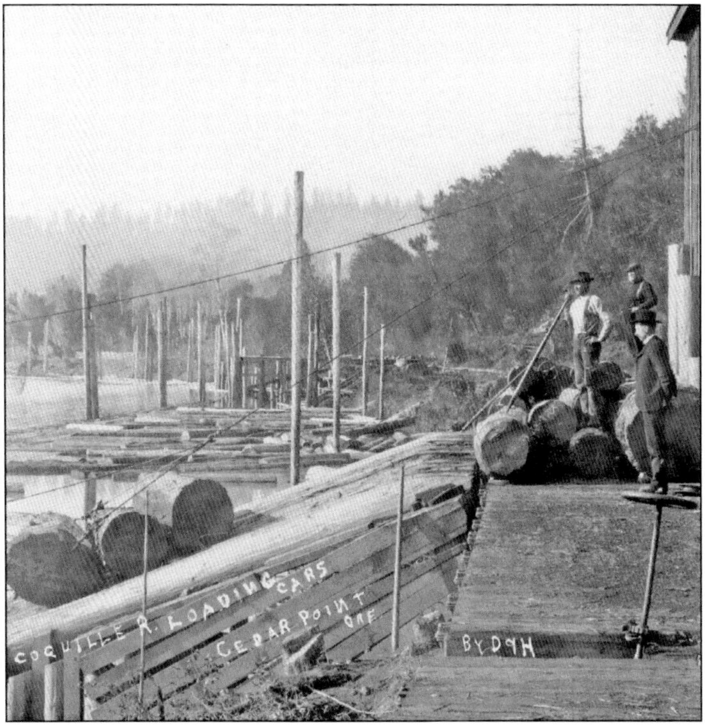

This c. 1910 scene shows the transfer of logs from the river to the railroad at Cedar Point. Mooring rights to store logs along the river were bought and sold. The logs were from logging camps along the river and were destined for Marshfield sawmills. Later, the Coquille Plywood Mill was built at the same location. (BM 28577.)

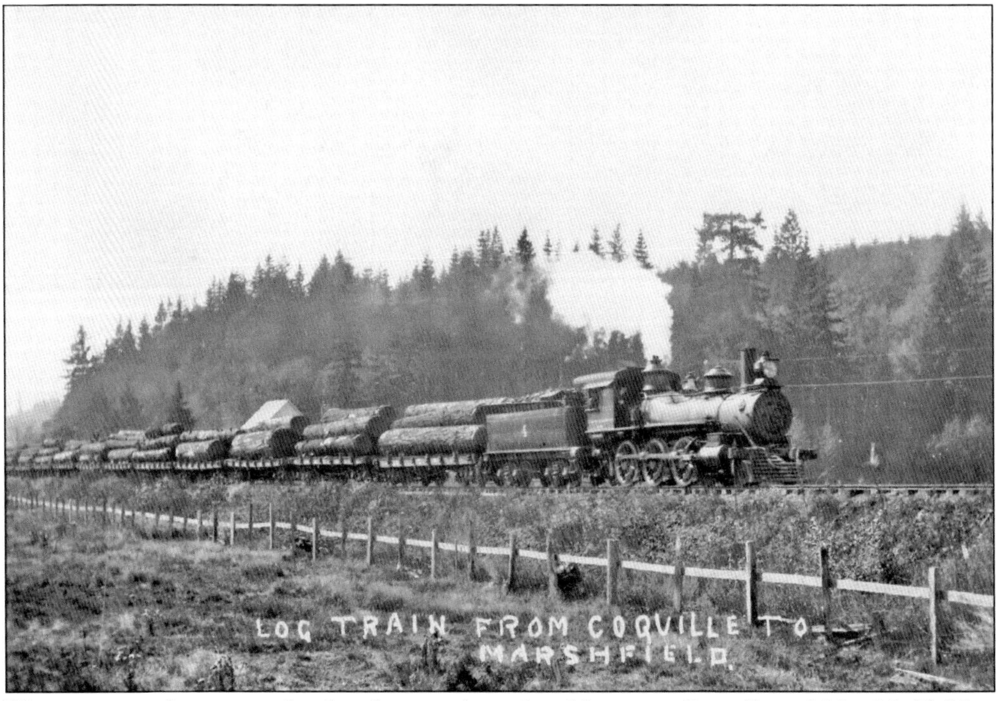

This is a steam locomotive hauling logs on the railroad between Coquille and Marshfield. This railroad from Marshfield to Myrtle Point, completed in 1893, made the harvest of vast tracts of timber on the Coquille River system available to the Marshfield sawmills. The railroad closely followed the route established earlier by the wagon road. (CVM.)

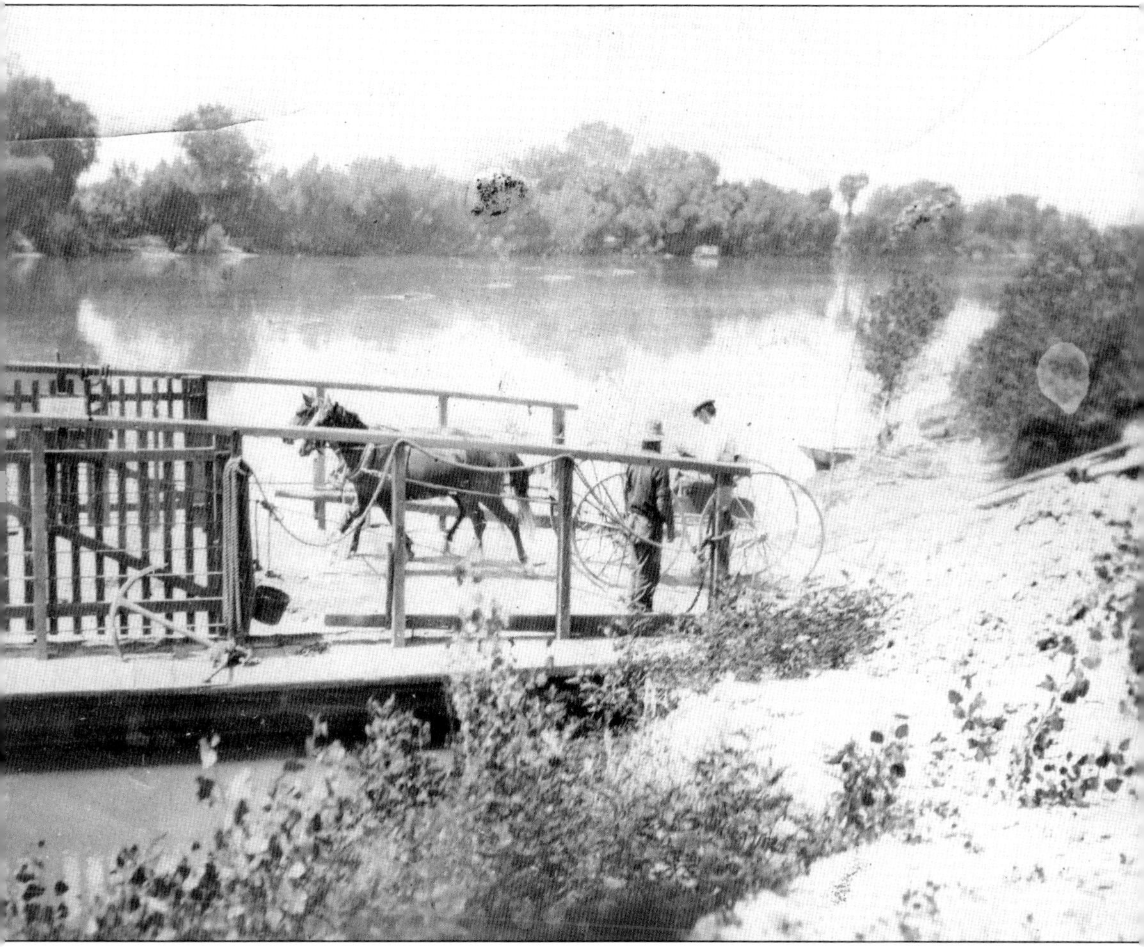

In 1905, Coos County authorized the installation of a ferry from the west-end extension of Front Street across the Coquille River to the county road on the opposite side. Deemed a public necessity, the ferry was free to use. This ferry provided access to Fishtrap, Fat Elk, Arago, Riverton, and Bandon. Prosper shipbuilder Emil Heuckendorff received the contract to build the ferry boat for $250. Simon Whetstone received the bid to operate and attend the ferry for one year with the salary of $20 per month. The ferry was in operation daily from 6:00 a.m. until 9:00 p.m. In 1906, C.H. Simpson received the contract to operate the ferry. In 1911, J.H. McNair was the ferryman. On Sunday, June 15, 1914, the ferry carried a record 100 cars. The ferry remained in use until a steel bridge was constructed in 1922 in the same location. (CHM 008.1.14)

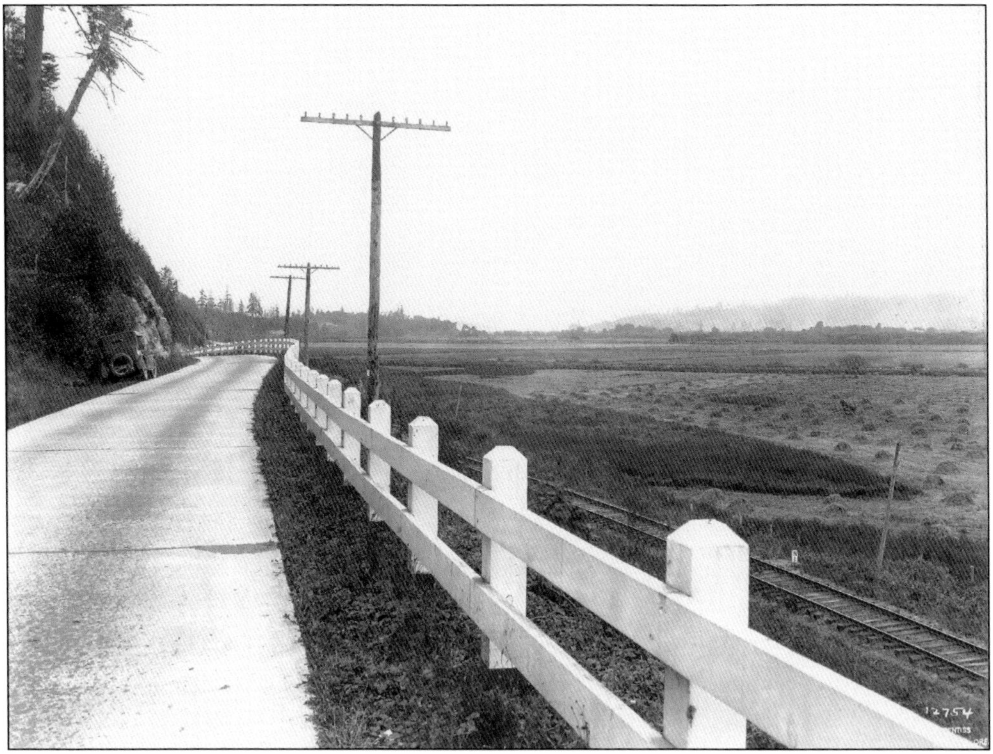

This view of Highway 101 north of town looks south toward Cedar Point in 1923. In 1921, the highway was completed from Marshfield to Coquille for the cost of $400,000, replacing a wagon road built in the 1880s. The pavement was concrete, 16 feet wide and 6 inches thick. Guardrails were made of wood and painted a distinctive white. (ODOT.)

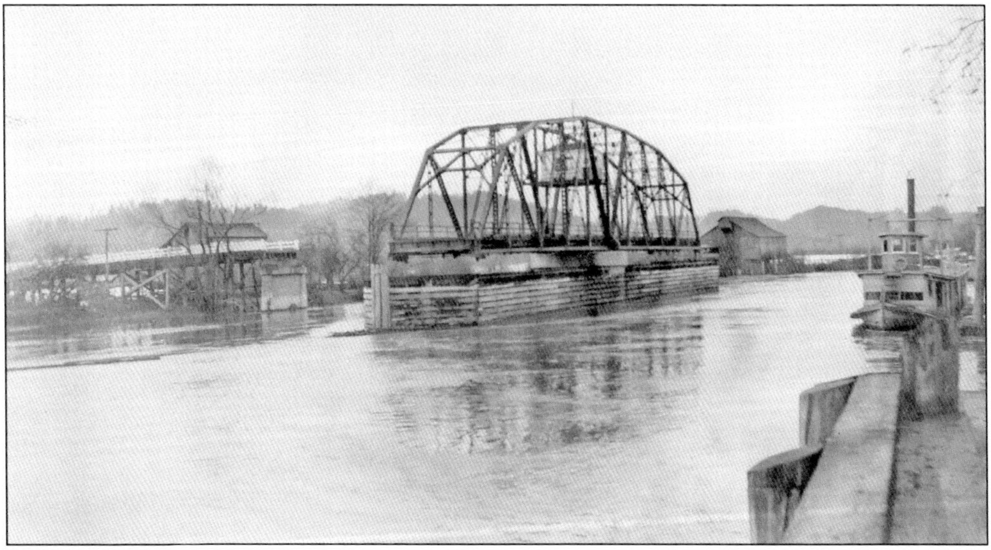

This is the old Coquille River bridge at the west end of downtown in the open position to allow a riverboat to pass. Completed in 1922, It was designed by state bridge engineer Conde B. McCullough. The bridge was on the original route of Highway 101. When it was retired in 1983, it was one of the oldest swing span bridges in Oregon. (BM COQUILL5.)

Seven

Schools and Churches

From the very beginning of the community, education was valued. In the 1860s, the region's first school was established by Evan Cunningham near Cunningham Creek north of the emerging town. This location proved too remote, and a small school was opened within today's downtown area. This building was soon outgrown, and another school was built northeast of downtown.

In 1890, a large private high school and teacher's college called the Adventist Academy was built north of the downtown. In 1900, a large and beautiful public school was constructed east of downtown. Three elementary schools were later established and named for Washington, Lincoln, and Jefferson. In 1922, the first dedicated public high school was built in at Tenth Street and Central Boulevard. In 1953, it became the junior high when the present high school was built further north on Central Boulevard.

As the town expanded, churches were founded, soon growing in size and number. According to historian and author Orval Dodge, the religiously inclined residents had a place of worship in 1877; a modest little church was built by subscription and named the Universalist church. The early Church of Christ congregation shared Cunningham's first schoolhouse until it constructed its own church building around 1891.

By 1915, Coquille contained the following denominations: Baptist, Catholic, Christian, Christian Science, Episcopal, Lutheran, Methodist Episcopal, Seventh-Day Adventist, and Presbyterian. By 1989, Coquille had 19 churches.

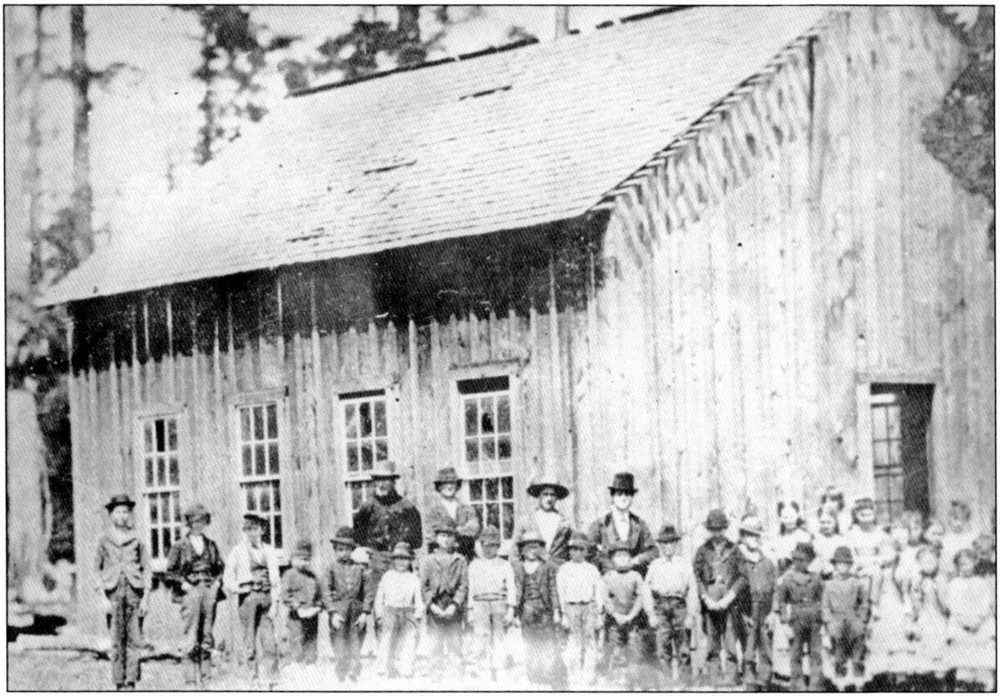

The first public school building inside the city was on the northwest corner of First Street and Central Boulevard, where the First National Bank building is now. A previous school constructed with logs north of town near Cunningham Creek was too far from the small but growing community. Soon this building was outgrown too. (BM 17584.)

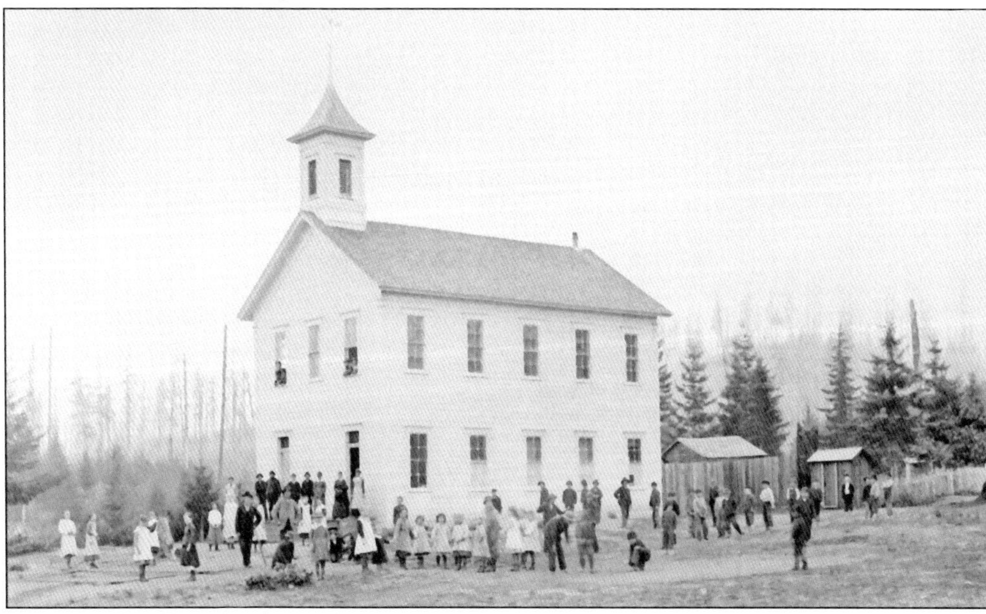

The second public school near the downtown area was built in 1881 and one block north of the courthouse on Baxter Street. When a new and larger school was near completion in 1899, this school was advertised for sale along with a second school building next to it. In the same year, the building was purchased by the First Presbyterian Church. (CHM 989-P143.)

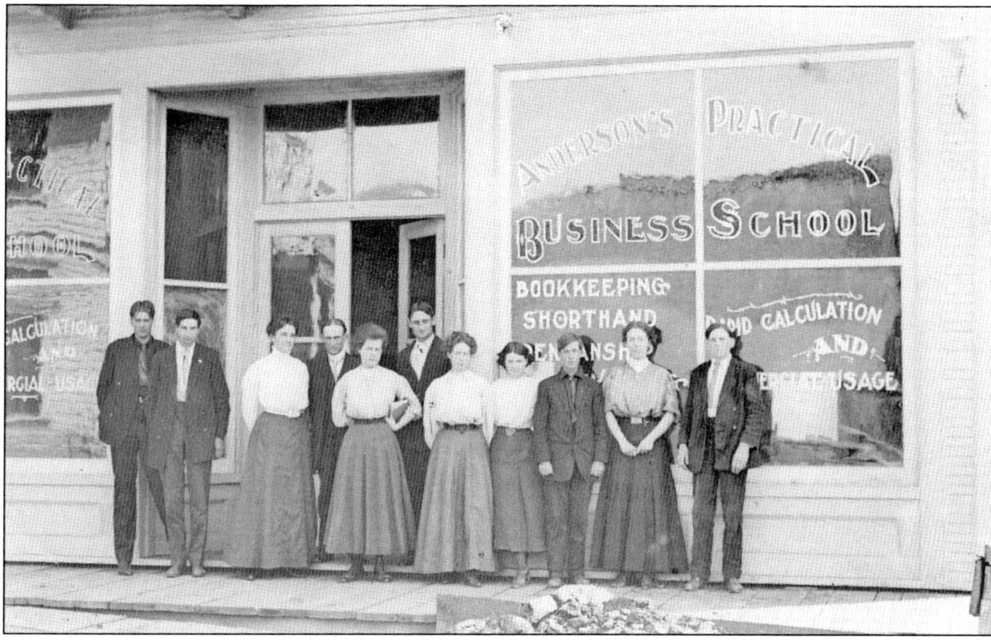

Anderson's Practical Business College was established by Prof. Frank B. Anderson in 1907 at the west end of Front Street. The school taught bookkeeping or shorthand and typewriting for $30 or the combined courses for $50, which included instruction in penmanship and rapid calculation. Individual instruction in bookkeeping, shorthand and typewriting, penmanship, rapid calculation, and commercial usage was also offered. (CHM 975-107f.)

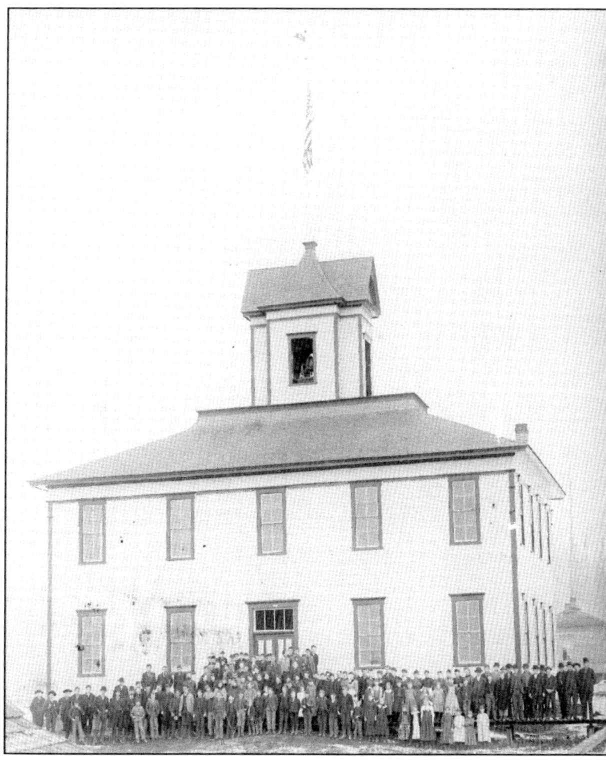

The Adventist Academy was built in 1890 by William H. Bunch and others and was north of downtown on Dean Street. In 1897, it was owned by Rev. J.L. Futrell and named the Coquille Collegiate Institute. In 1907, the building was the Western Oregon Hospital. In 1915, it was a public school. Later, Ben and Belle Knife converted the building into apartments, adding a third floor and porches. (BW.)

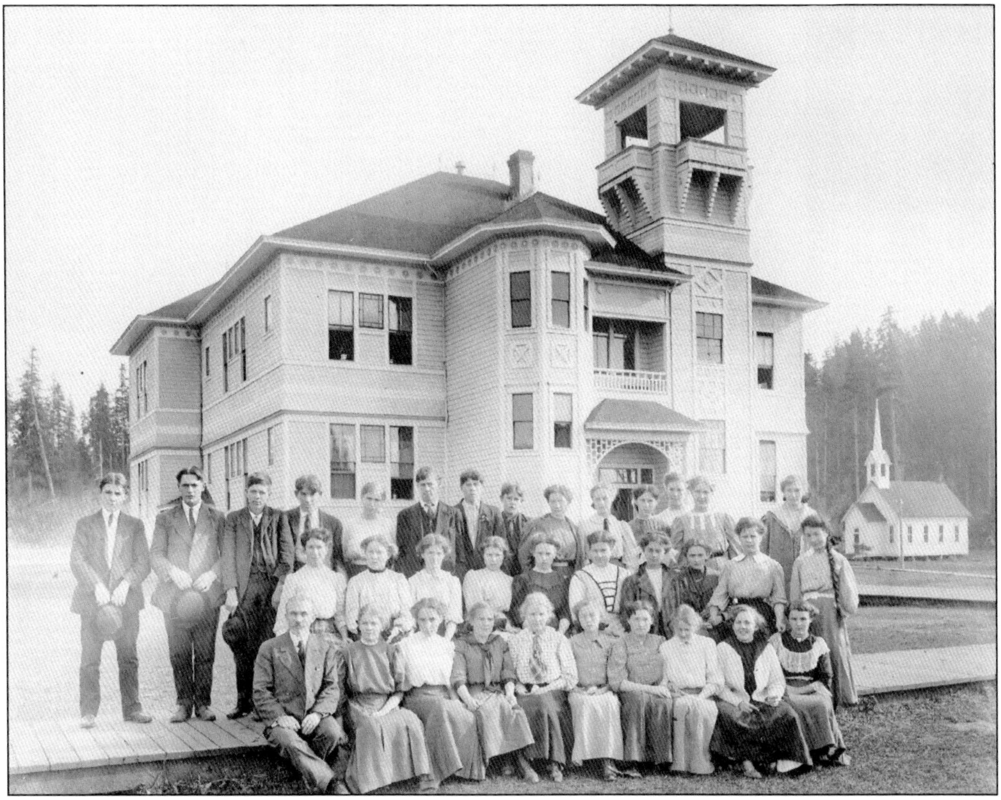

Above is the Coquille Public School building and students in 1907. The Adventist church is in the background. Below is the school's classroom for the ninth and tenth grades for the 1903–1904 school year. The school opened in 1900 at the site of the later Washington Elementary School at Second Street and Folsom Street, a few blocks east of downtown. Advertisements for bids described a building with six classrooms and a capacity for 300 students featuring a basement, brick foundation, and modern heating and ventilating appliances. The school was built to serve the fast-growing community and replaced the school on Baxter Street. The wood-framed school was arguably one of the city's finest buildings. (Both, CVM.)

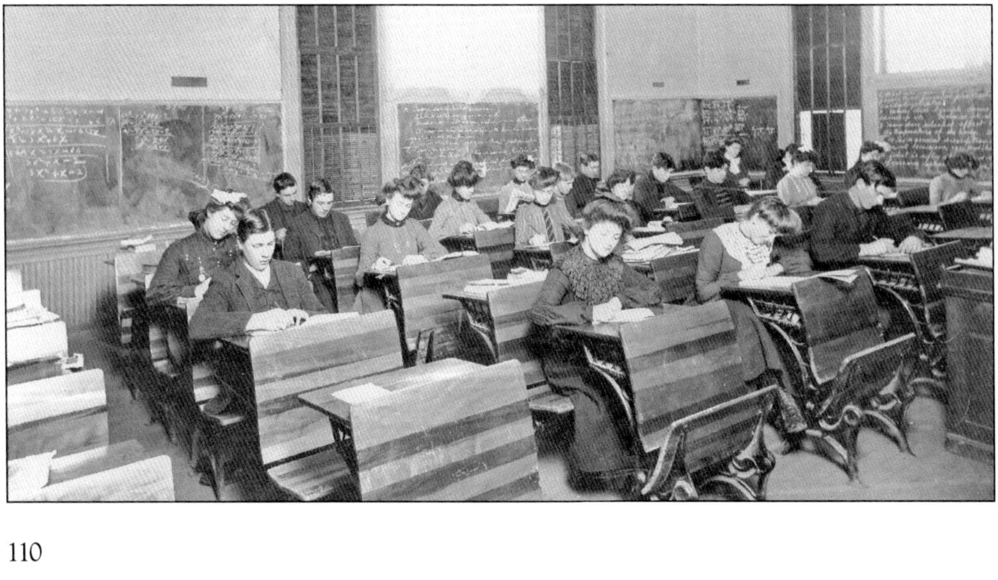

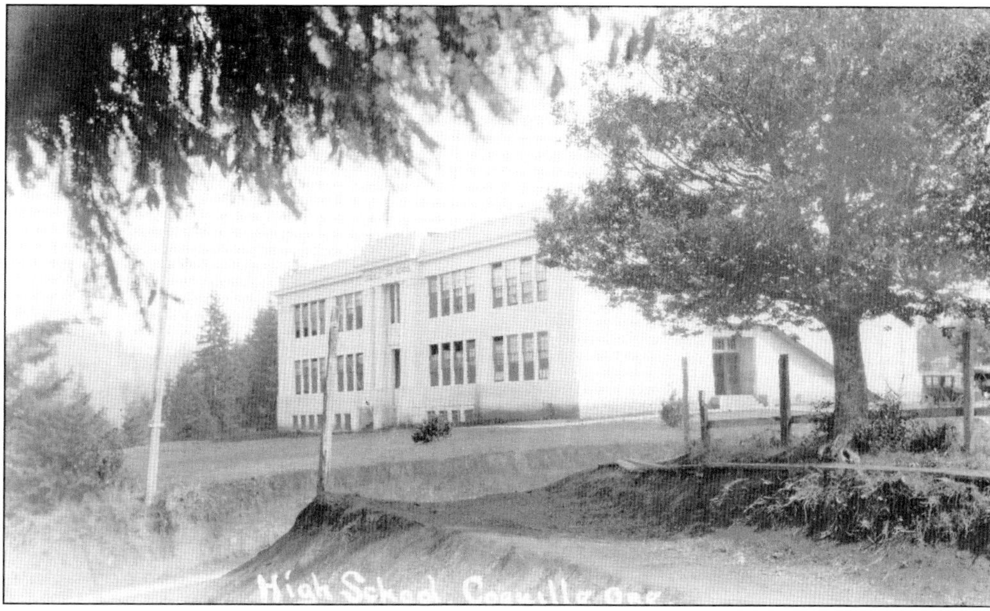

In 1922, the first Coquille High School was built at Tenth Street and Central Boulevard. The building had two floors and a basement. Once the new Coquille High School was built farther north on Central Boulevard in 1953, this building became the Coquille Junior High. The junior high annex next door, originally the first Lincoln School, was built in 1926. (CVM.)

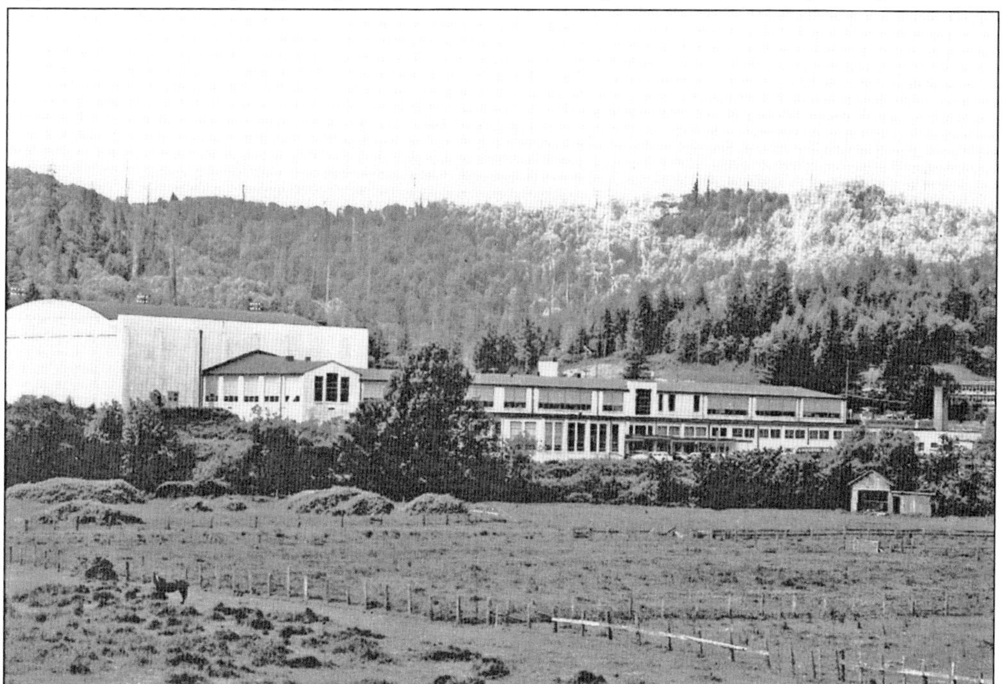

This is the current Coquille High School, built in 1953 north of downtown on Central Boulevard. It replaced the old high school at Tenth Street and Central Boulevard, which became the Coquille Junior High. The new school was much larger and included a library, cafeteria, shops, gymnasium, football field, and track. (CVM.)

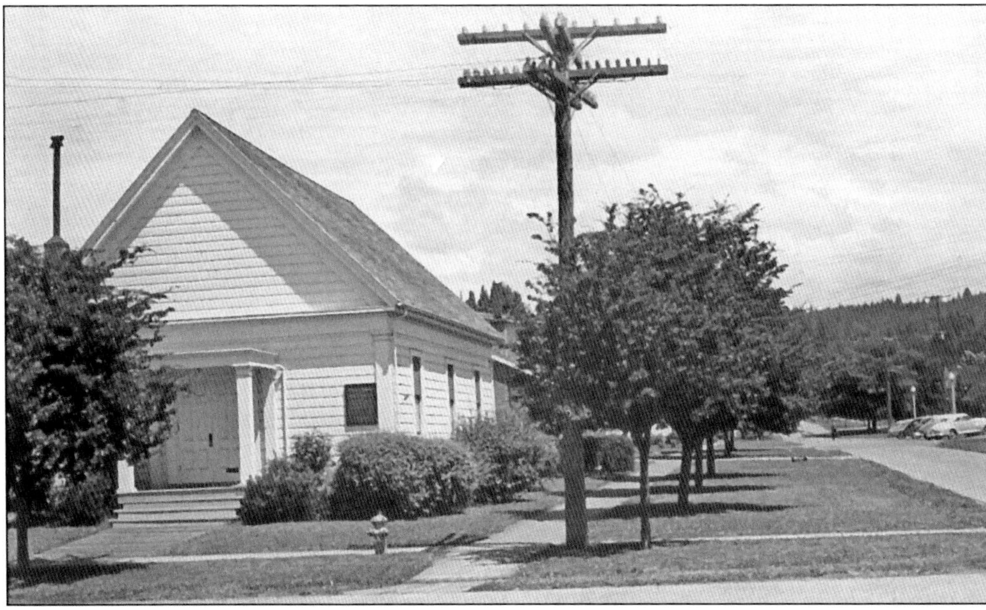

The Christian Science church was located at the northeast corner of Third Street and Adams Street. This building was used by the congregation beginning in 1912 and was originally called the First Church of Christ, Scientist. The building was formerly a Universalist church that allowed use by other denominations and organizations. Built around 1877, the Universalist church was most likely the community's first church building. (CVM.)

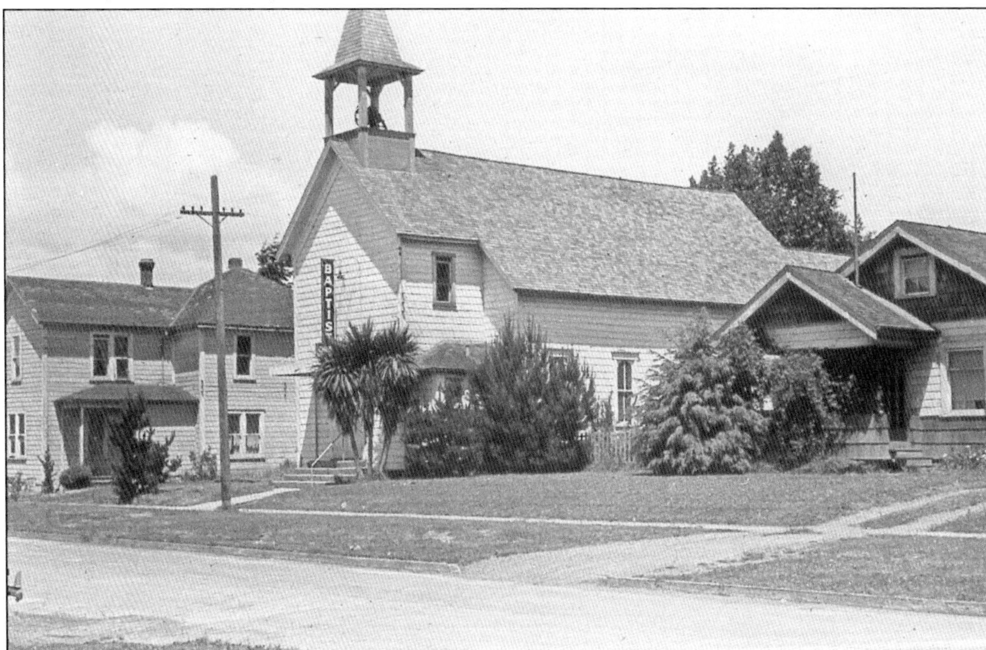

The Emmanuel Baptist Church was formed in 1923–1924 and purchased the First Presbyterian Church building on Baxter Street, which had originally been a public school built in 1881. In the late 1930s, a parsonage was added. The church was used until 1997, when a new church building was purchased on Sixth Street. This building is now a private residence. (CVM.)

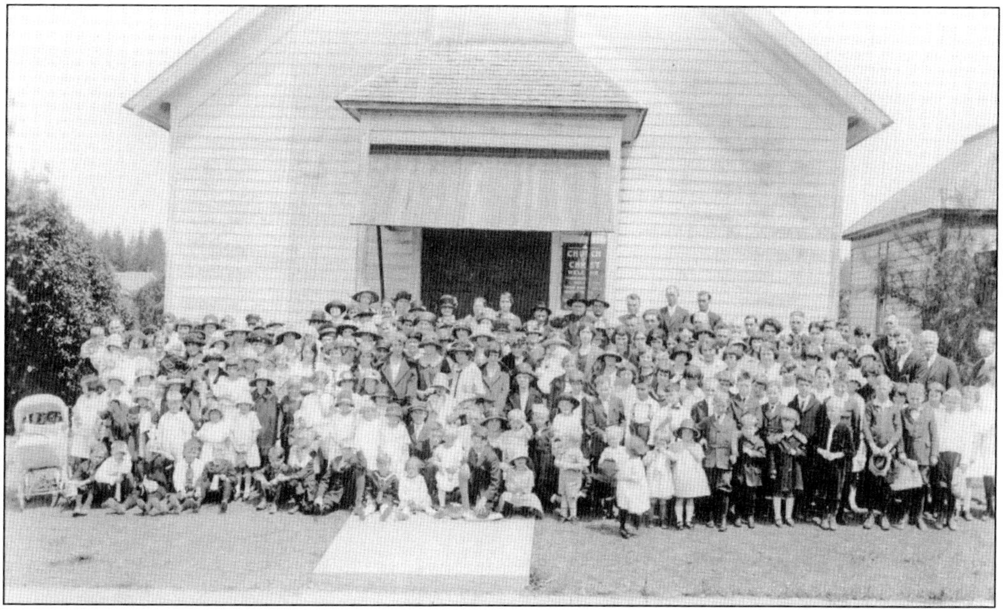

The Church of Christ building near Fourth Street and Dean Street was built in 1892. The structure was 36 feet by 45 feet and included a bell tower. The congregation, numbering 20 people in 1871, was one of the earliest in the area. Before erecting their own church building, they shared the first area school near Cunningham Creek. The building is now a private residence. (CVM.)

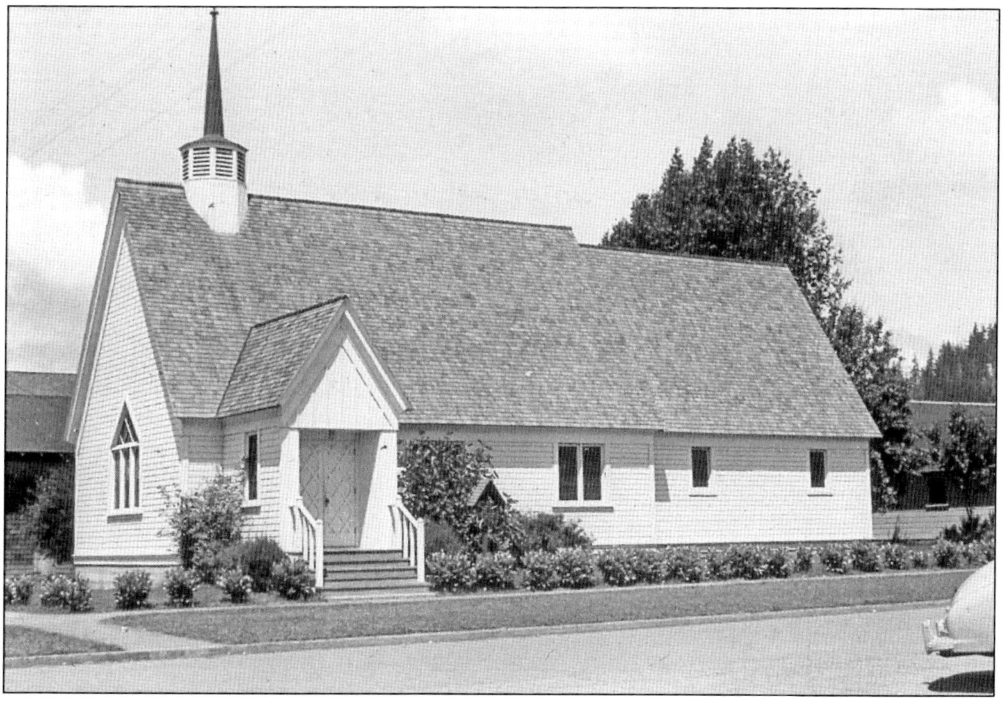

St. James Episcopal Church, on the northeast corner of Baxter Street and Third Street, was built in 1897 with a parish hall added in the 1920s. In 1938, a chapel was added to the sanctuary. The structure is a rare example of Gothic Revival architecture and was added to the National Register of Historic Places in 1992. (CVM.)

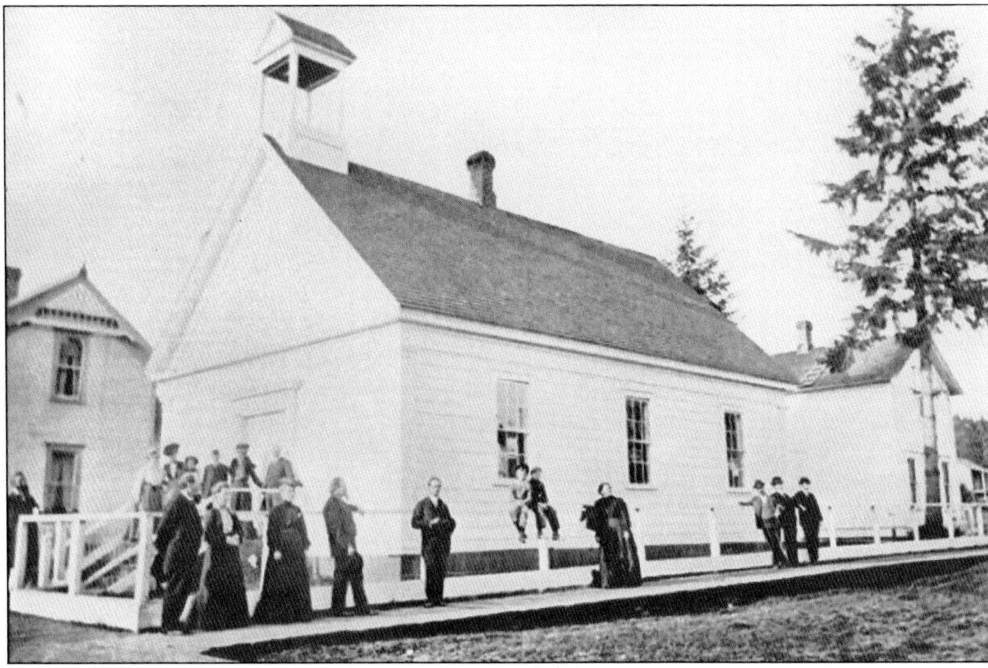

The local Church of Redeemed Israel was incorporated on February 18, 1897, with nine elected trustees: K.V. Millard, R.D. Sanford, C.H. Cecil, G.W. Martin, Samuel M. Nosler, Ada Millard, C.A. Hanson, J.H. James, and W.H. Nosler. They met in the Universalist church at the corner of Third Street and Adams Street. (CVM.)

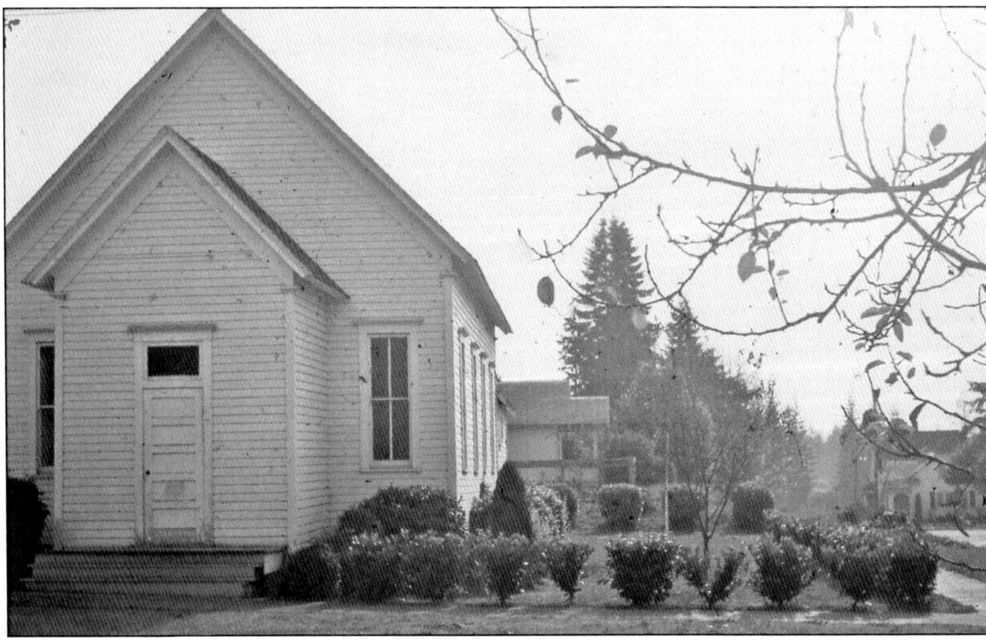

The Seventh-Day Adventist Church was organized by James C. Bunch and others in the late 1870s. This church building was erected at Second Street and Gould Street. The building served the church until 1951, when it was replaced with a new building, which was in turn sold to the Church of Christ around 1989. Afterward, new church buildings were erected at Cedar Point. (CVM.)

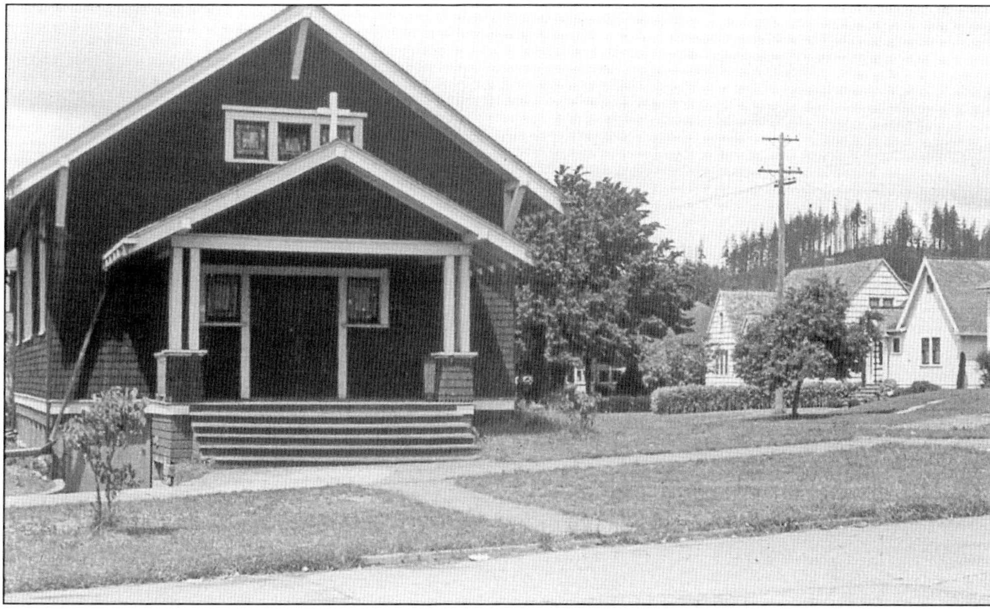

In 1909, the Catholic Church was established when Fathers Dan Curley and F.J. Springer from the Mercy Hospital in North Bend provided services in homes throughout the Coquille Valley. In 1915, the Holy Name Catholic Church building was constructed at the intersection of Third Street and Dean Street under the direction of Fr. Hugh McDevitt of Marshfield, who provided mass once a month. (CVM.)

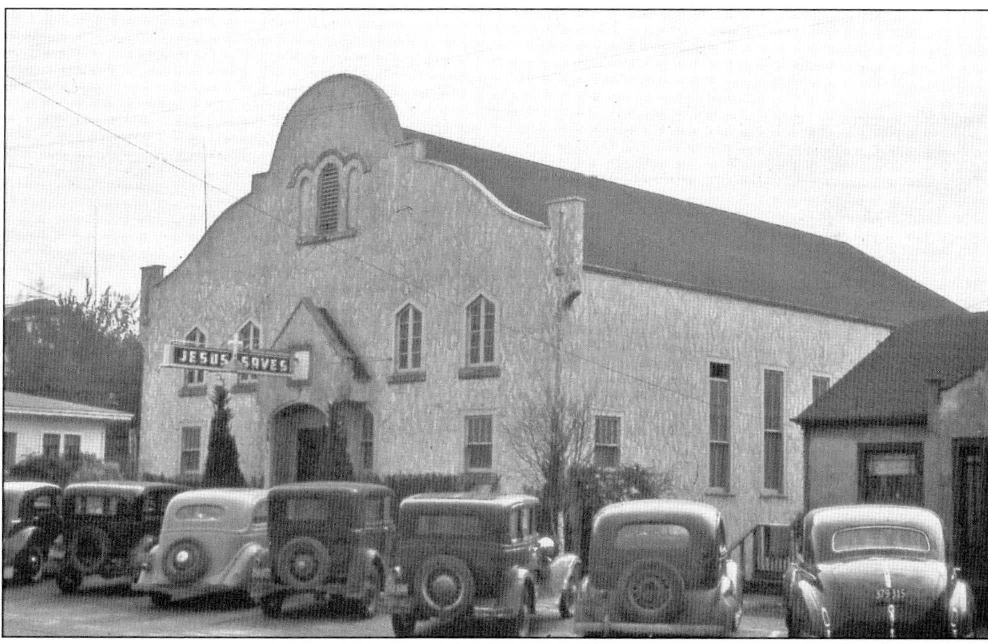

The first praise center of the Foursquare Gospel Church was at the intersection of Second Street and Gould Street. In the spring of 1926, construction began, and the building was dedicated in October 1926. The church had a myrtle wood pulpit constructed by the Oerding brothers. In 1960, a new Foursquare Church was built on North Hemlock Street near Jefferson Elementary School. (CVM.)

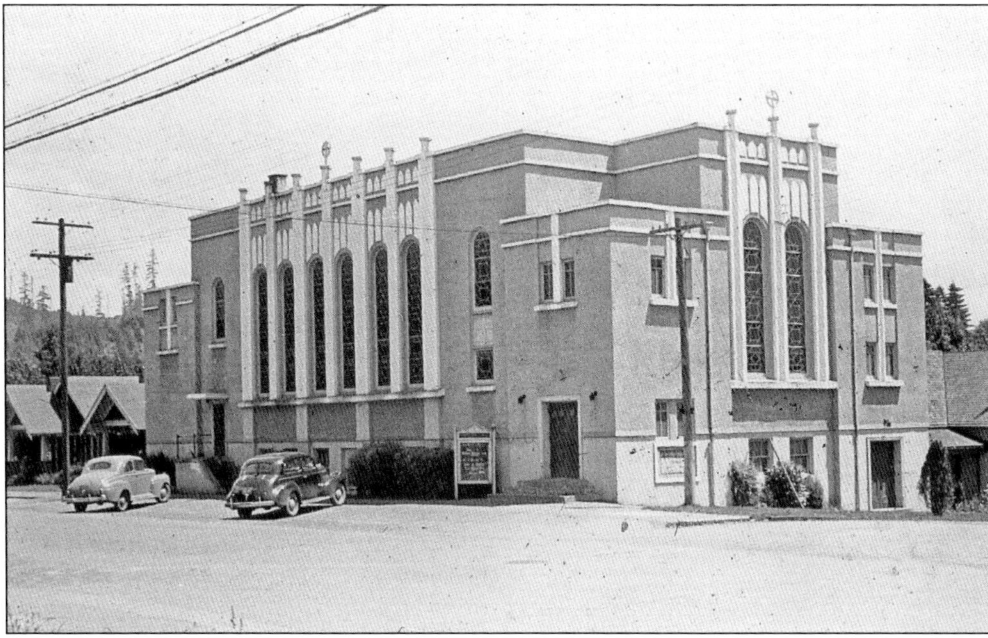

The Pioneer United Methodist Church, at the southeast corner of Baxter and Second Streets, was built in 1928. Prior to this large concrete building, the wood-framed Methodist Episcopal Church South building was in the same location, and the Methodist Episcopal Church North building was one block north. In 1916, the two churches united. (CVM.)

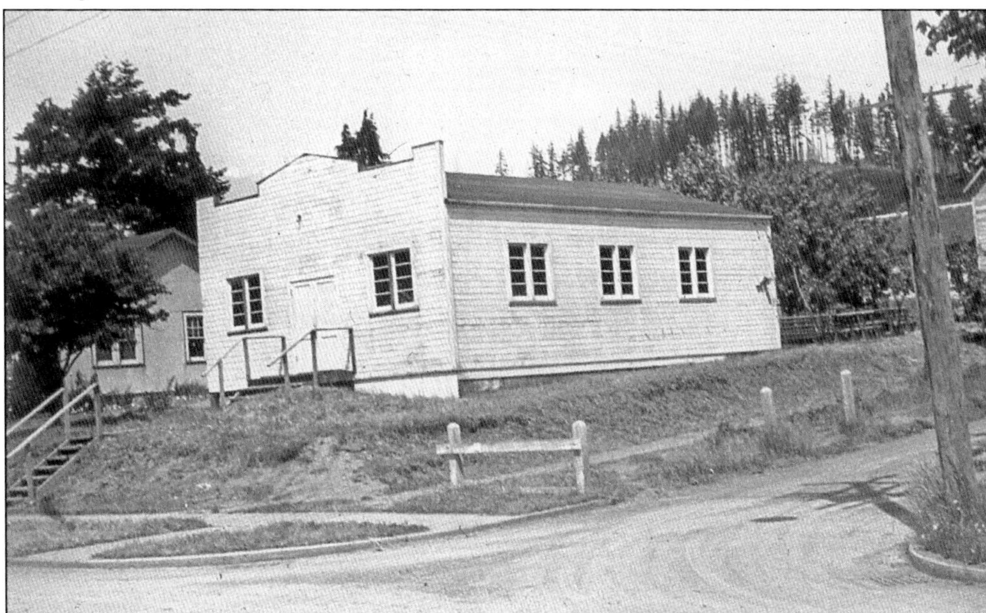

In 1941, the Nazarene Church was organized with 13 charter members who purchased property to build a church the corner of Ninth Street and Elliott Street. The Reverend Miles Short served as first pastor at the new church. The building served the congregation until 1952, when it became too small for the growing membership. (CVM.)

Eight

Activities

Civic activities have always been an important part of the Coquille community. Participants have been members of the various lodges, societies, and other organizations that have existed within the area. During the 1880s, these organizations included the Odd Fellows and Rebekahs; Masons and Eastern Star; the Knights of Labor; Foresters of America; Good Templers; and the Grand Army of the Republic.

Holidays were big events: Memorial Day, Labor Day, Independence Day, Christmas, and others were always a reason to celebrate with a parade that included bands and floats. Grand masquerade balls were held on Christmas Eve. Churches and schools held community picnics and carnivals.

Team sports were always big events, especially baseball. Before the automobile, people would load onto riverboats or trains to play or watch games with teams from other communities. Later, Coquille even boasted a semipro minor-league baseball team.

The city enjoyed indoor roller skating as early as 1888. It was offered in the Masonic Opera Hall, with a dedicated rink established in 1907. This traditional activity was continued in later years at the community building. Billiards was popular, and pool halls were present even during Prohibition. Bowling was first played in a building with a designated bowling alley on Front Street in 1910.

Horseracing was a regular event at the county fair and part of celebrations. Hunting and sport fishing were popular due to an abundance of various species of game and fish catchable from the riverbank. Newspaper reports from the late 1800s describe catches of over 100 fish per person. Swimming was another favorite pastime on the river.

The performing arts were consistent attractions, with numerous bands, acting troupes, films, and performance venues. The early Masonic Opera Hall had a stage on the first floor and hosted many events. Later, theaters included the Dime, Heazlet, Grand, Scenic, Liberty, Roxy, and the Myrtle Lane Drive-In on Rink Creek.

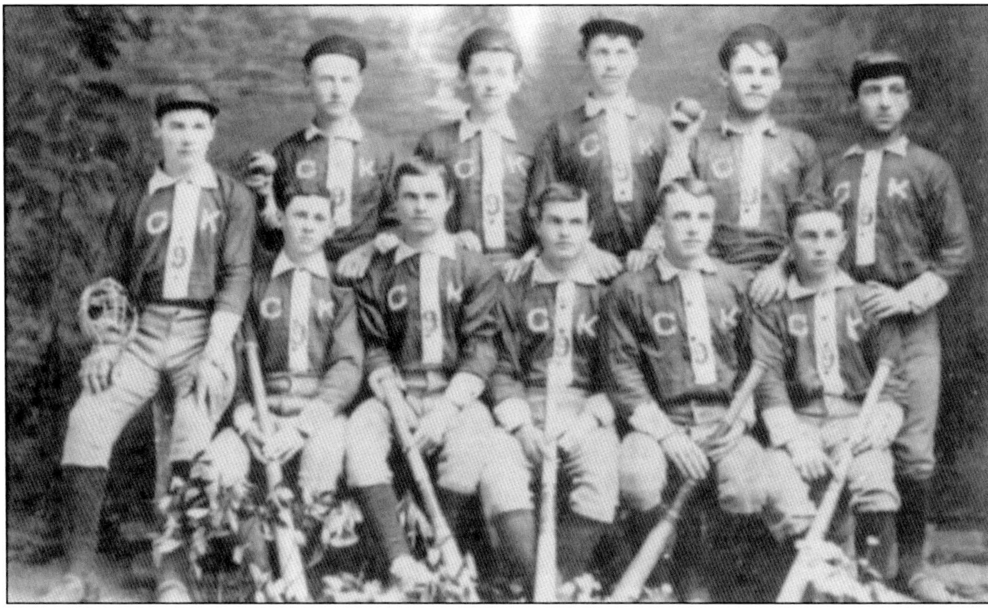

This is the Coquille Kid Nine baseball team around 1891–1892. The Kid Nine was the boys' team, while the Coquille Nine was the men's team. From left to right are (first row) Dave Johnson, Claud Nosler, Sam Norton, Gene Norton, Chas Baxter, and George Lorenz; (second row) Bunk Buzan, George Robinson, Role Anderson, Curtis Price, and Bert McDuffie. (CVM.)

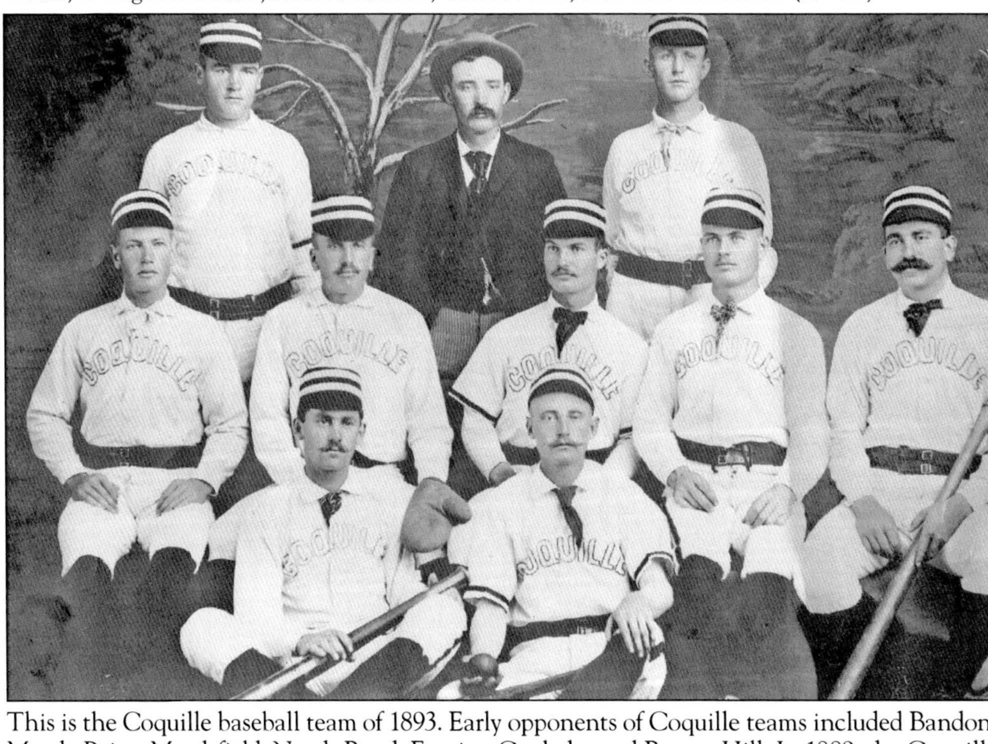

This is the Coquille baseball team of 1893. Early opponents of Coquille teams included Bandon, Myrtle Point, Marshfield, North Bend, Empire, Coaledo, and Beaver Hill. In 1889, the Coquille City Nine was challenged by the Coaledo Nine and won 19-18. In 1895, the *Herald* reported that the Coquille Star Flats defeated the Beaver Hill Nine 20-9. (CVM.)

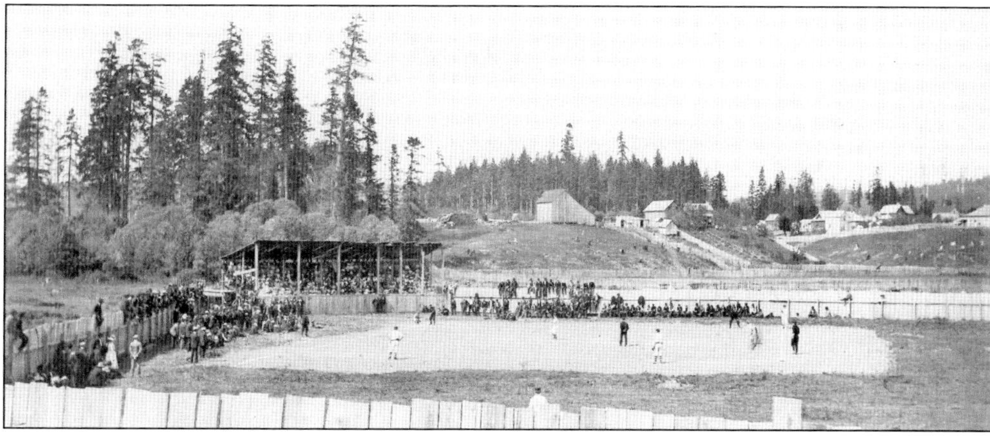

Here are two views of the Kistner Baseball Field, west of downtown in the fields below the Spurgeon Hill or Fourth Street neighborhood. Baseball was the dominant team sport in the early days, with games held between neighboring towns. In 1895, the Coquille Star Flats baseball team provided a fine exhibition of the sport on Valentine's Day. Music was provided by the Misses Woodruff. Tickets for the event were 75¢. The team also sponsored a St. Patrick's Eve masquerade ball to raise funds for balls, bats, and other essentials. T.A. White was the manager, and Bird Nosler was the team captain. (Both, CVM.)

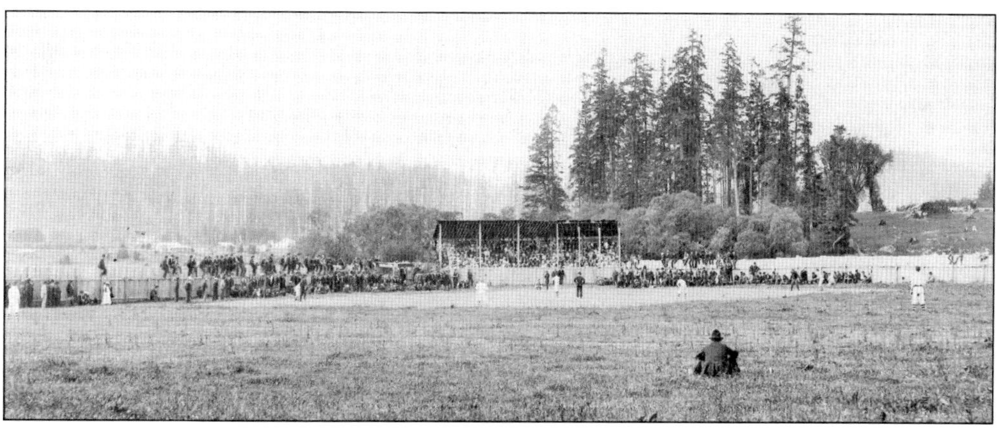

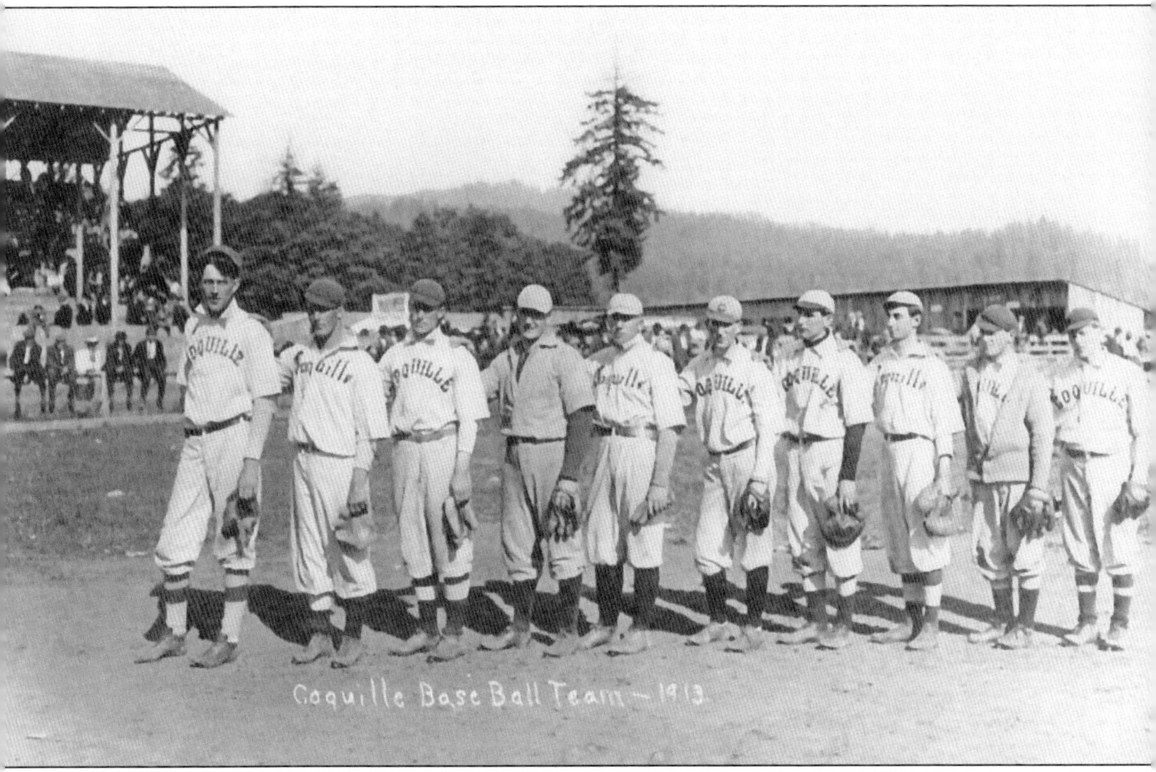

This is a Coquille baseball team in 1913. Civic pride in sports was especially important to the sawmills that sponsored baseball teams. The Coquille Loggers, a semipro minor-league baseball team, existed from the 1890s until the 1950s. The team played against the communities of Marshfield, North Bend, Roseburg, and Medford in the Sawdust League. Vern Alan Baily began as a batboy and eventually played for the team. Well-known Penny Sturdivant was employed by Coos Bay Lumber for many years and was a pitcher on the original Coquille Loggers. Roy Harrington, who earned All-Northwest Conference honors in football and baseball, received Willamette's J.H. Booth Award in 1949–1950. After graduation, he played baseball with the Coquille Loggers. Glenn Dale Murray Sr., a left-handed-batting outfielder and right-handed pitcher, began his career in organized baseball in 1934 with the Coquille Loggers. Baseball scouts noticed Murray's exceptional hitting, and he began his professional career in 1935 with the Tallahassee Capitals. Bill Fortier, "Mr. Baseball," retired as manager of the Coquille Loggers in July 1952 at the age of 65. (CVM.)

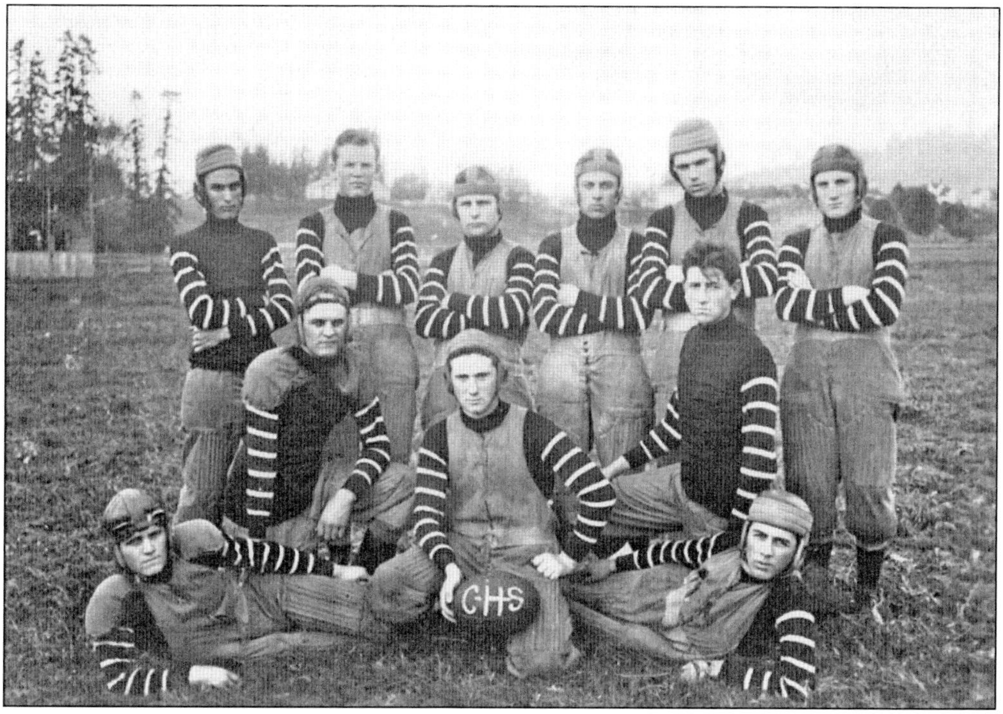

While baseball may have been the primary team sport in the early years, as early as 1901, the Coquille city football team challenged the Marshfield team to play for a purse of $100. An early mention of basketball in the *Herald* in 1908 announced a game on skates at the roller rink. Later, basketball and football became popular sports for the Coquille High School. Pictured are the high school football team of 1913 and the basketball team of 1914. Boys' and girls' sports continued to grow in the schools, and the teams would later be called the Red Devils. (Both, CVM.)

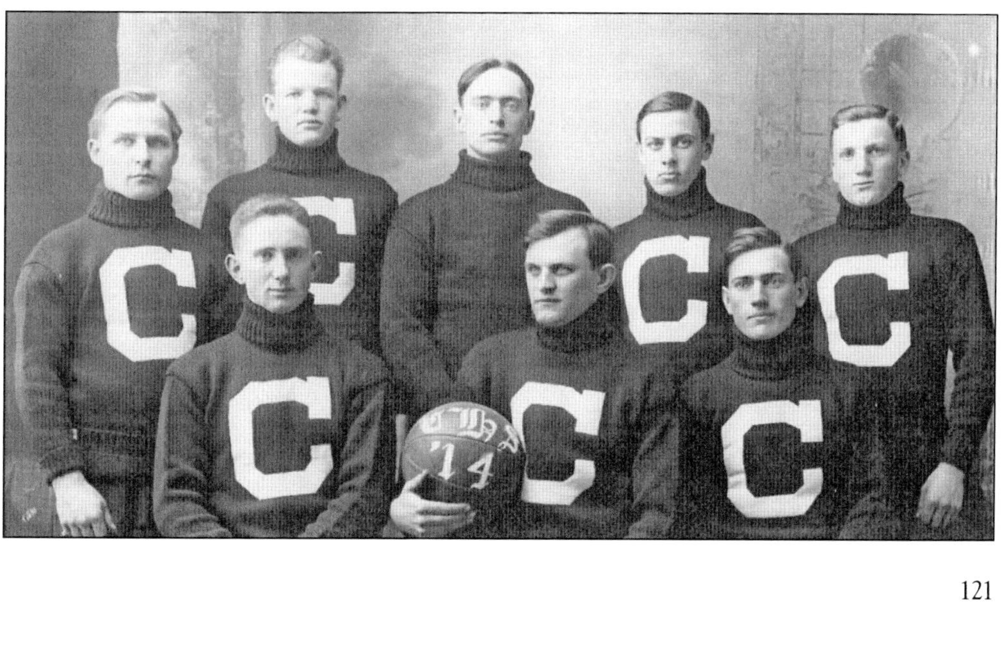

SKATING RINK!

Masonic Hall,

Coquille City,

C. B. STOKES,

MANAGER.

Skating every Tuesday, Thursday and Saturday evenings, excepting the Saturday evenings on or before each full moon and the one immediately after. Skating 25cts.

The first skating rink in Coquille was opened in December 1888 at the Masonic Opera Hall and was managed by C.B. Stokes. In July 1889, the rink was operated by a man named Hunnewell and drew a good crowd. Due to the noise associated with the rink, operations were suspended in August 1890. By 1895, the skating rink was back in operation at an unknown location. On October 1, 1897, Bert Dean and Frank Goodman opened a skating rink in the Odd Fellows hall. Within two weeks, Bud Stone and George Martin purchased the goods and operated the rink. In February 1907, Clyde Gage and I.R. Nosler opened a first-class rink in the Nosler Hall on First Street, later the home of W.C. Laird's Complete Home Furnisher. (Both, CCH.)

SKATING RINK.

Rink Open From 7:30 Until 10:00 P. M.

The winter schedule is as follows: Tuesday, Thursday, Friday and Satuaday nights and Saturday afternoon of each week. Friday nights will be ladies night when all will be required to skate in couples. If you can't skate, learn how. Lessons free afternoons. Admission 10 cts. Use of skates 15 cts. For a good laugh be a spectator.

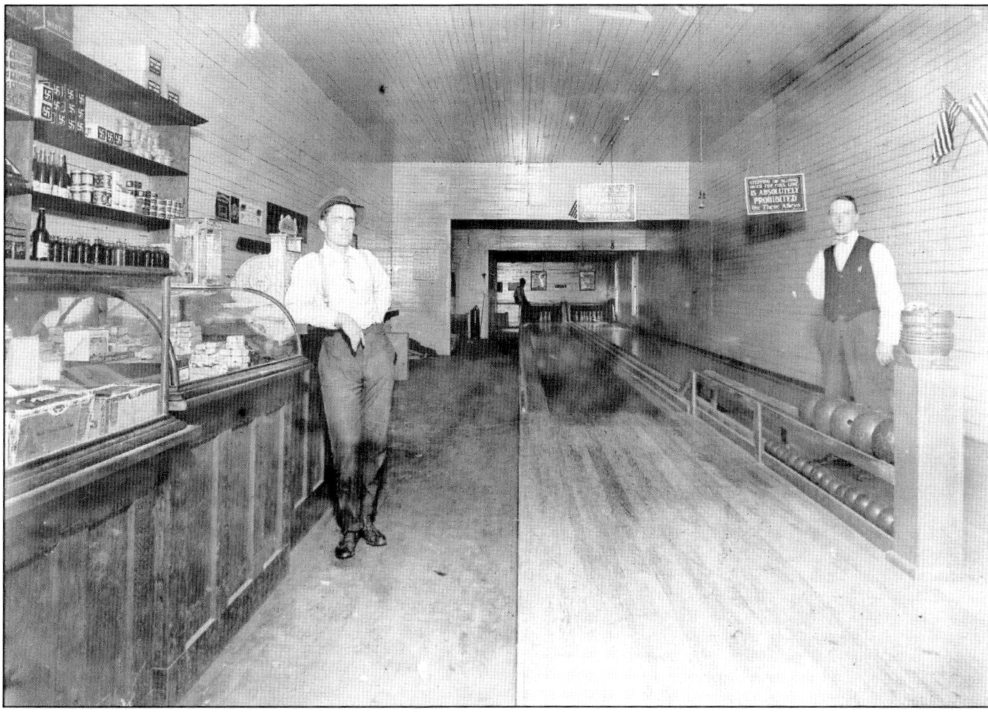

In June 1909, J.H. Oerding established a two-lane bowling alley in the Hermann building in Myrtle Point. The bowling alley, which was strictly high grade and up to date, was shipped in from Michigan. In May 1910, Oerding relocated his bowling alley to Front Street in Coquille. J.H. "Harry" Oerding is pictured on the left. (CVM.)

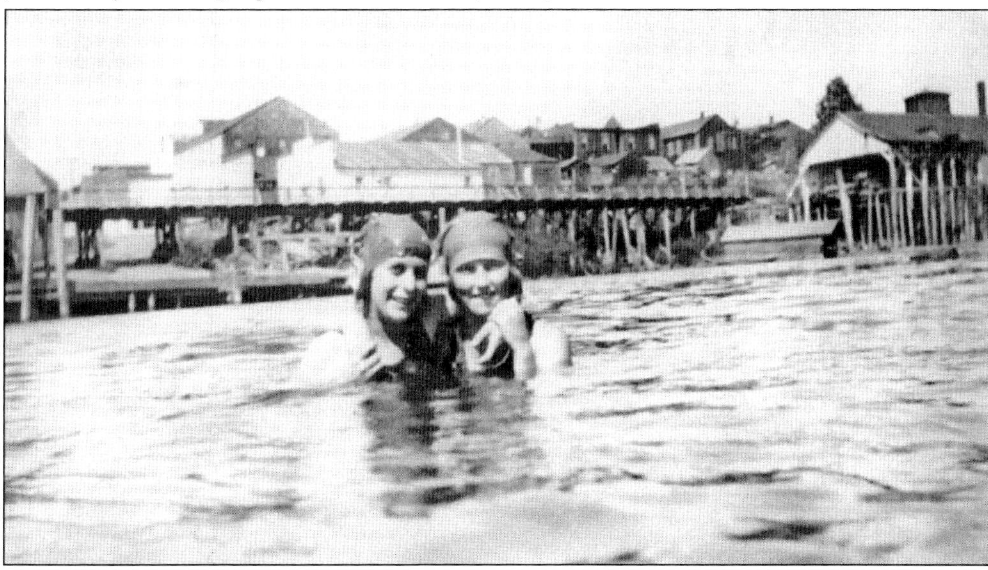

In the summer, swimming in the river was a popular activity for the local children. A humorous side benefit of swimming was reported in the July 29, 1884, issue of the *Coquille Herald*. The article stated, "For the first time in twelve months boys are beginning to have clean faces. They don't wash them. They unavoidability come in contact with clean water while they are swimming." (CVM.)

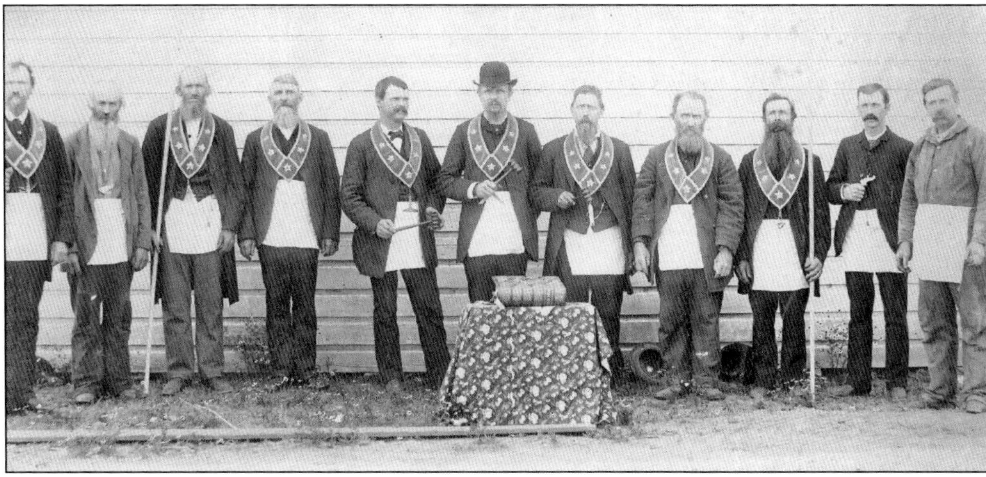

The Chadwick Lodge No. 68 of the Ancient Free & Accepted Masons was established in 1876. Thomas R. Willard served as the worshipful master, Christian Lehnherr as senior warden, and R.N. Rosa as junior warden. The first Masonic hall or opera house was built in 1887 and had a stage on the first floor. It was shared with many other fraternal organizations to host community events and meetings. (CVM.)

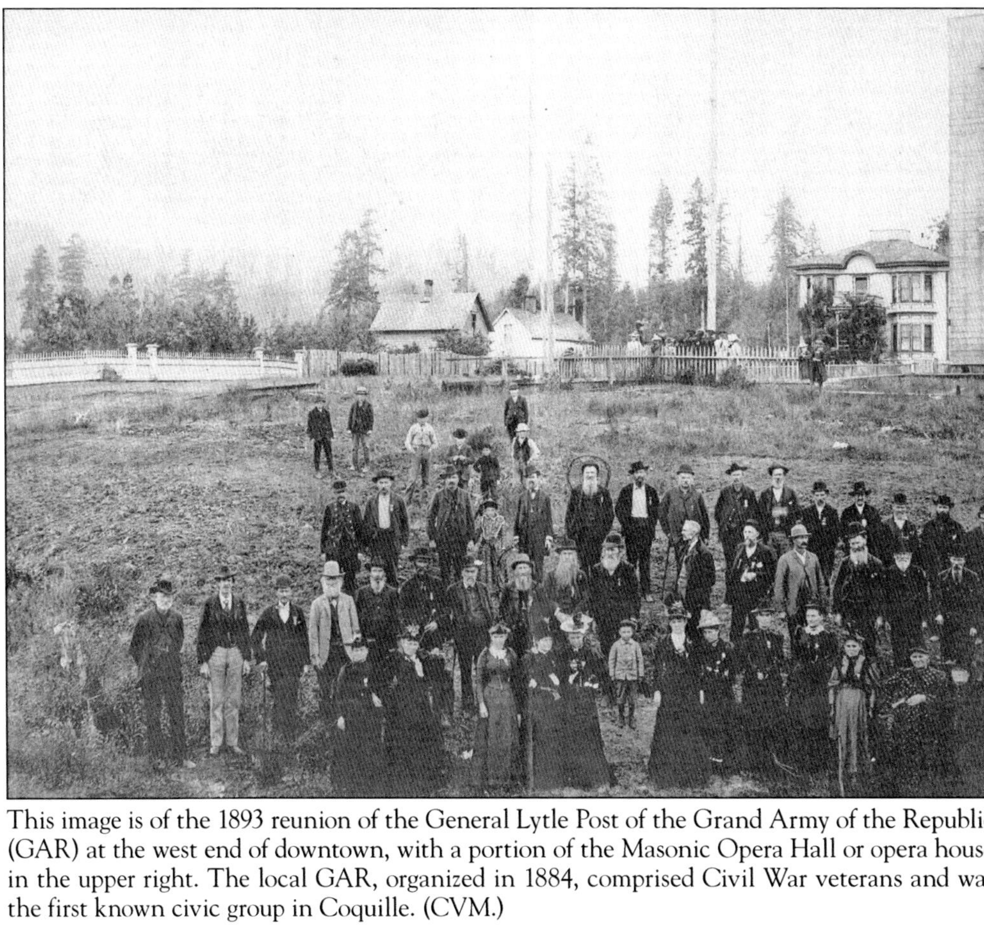

This image is of the 1893 reunion of the General Lytle Post of the Grand Army of the Republic (GAR) at the west end of downtown, with a portion of the Masonic Opera Hall or opera house in the upper right. The local GAR, organized in 1884, comprised Civil War veterans and was the first known civic group in Coquille. (CVM.)

Pictured are the members of the Coquille City Trombone Band. In 1889, the band was formed with George Leach as the leader. Throughout the years, the band performed for private party celebrations, holidays, and parades in Coquille, Marshfield, Myrtle Point, Bandon, and Norway. The band occupied the upper rooms of the Moulton building, which was referred to as "Red Front." (CVM.)

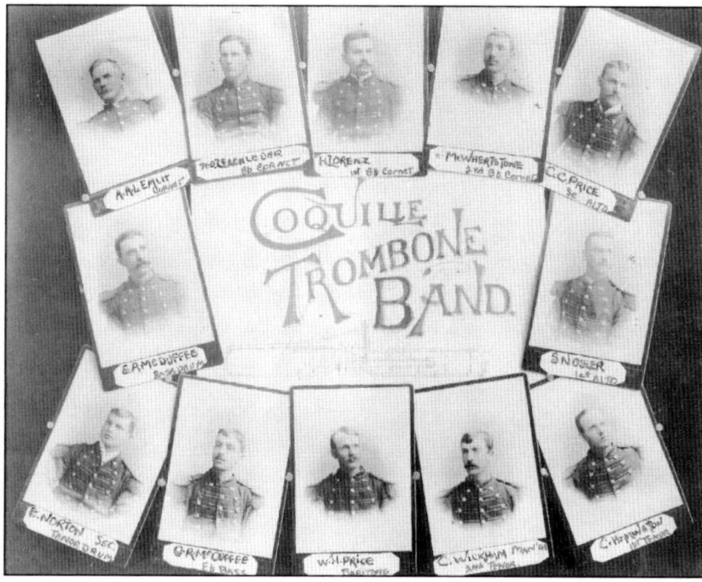

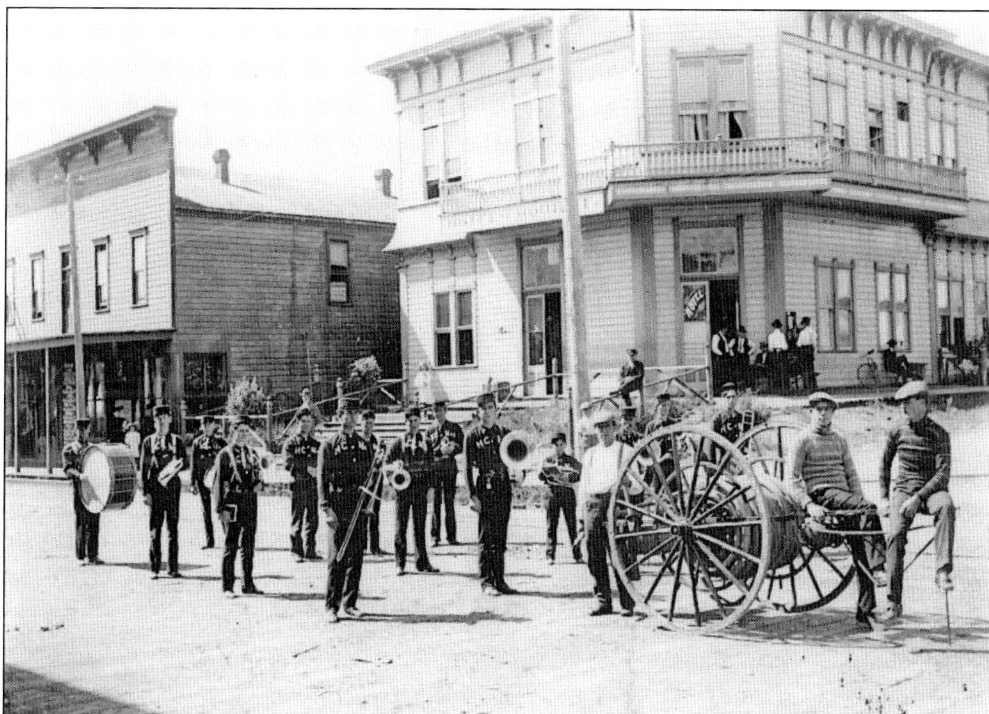

Here is an early band in front of the Hotel Coquille around 1900. To the right of the band is a hose cart utilized for fighting fires. The initials "HC" on their uniforms may mean they were sponsored by the Hotel Coquille. Before the invention of radio, television, and computers, local bands were an important source of music and entertainment. (CVM.)

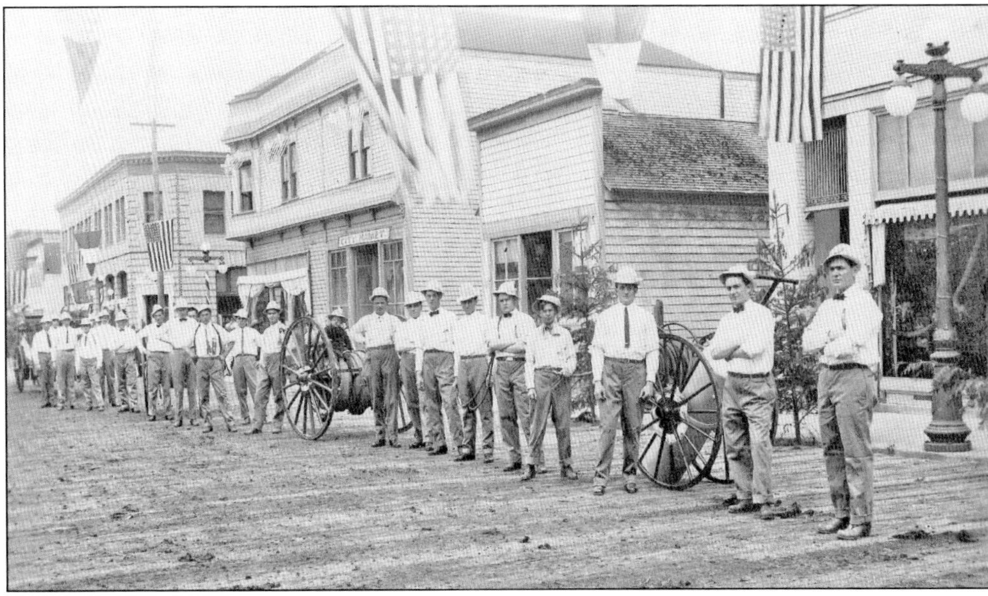

This is a volunteer fire department crew with hose carts on First Street in line to participate in a Fourth of July parade around 1915. Firefighting was taken seriously, as major fires in 1892 and 1918 destroyed much of the downtown. After the railroad was completed in 1893, nearby towns like Myrtle Point and Marshfield could send firefighters to help with serious fires. (CVM.)

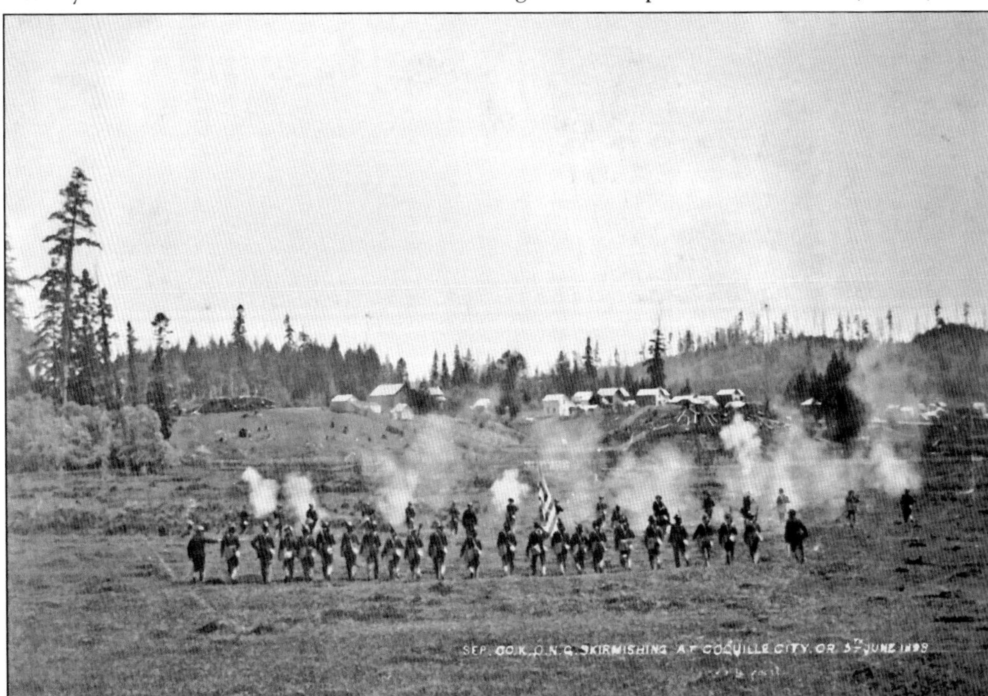

This is the local Company K of the Oregon National Guard skirmishing in 1898. The skirmish is being done in the low ground between downtown and Spurgeon Hill and Fourth Street near the early baseball field. Units were formed throughout the state, and Company K was from Bandon. (BM 29917.)

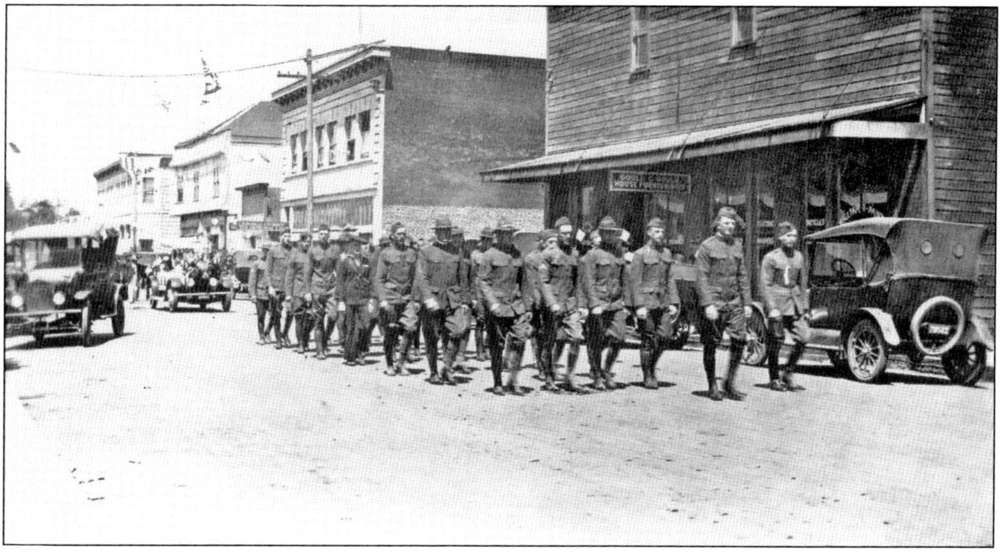

Pictured is an Independence Day parade on First Street around 1918 with soldiers, likely from the Sitka Spruce Mill. The 1900 celebration was attended by 1,200, and activities included speeches, prayers, music performed by bands and choirs, dinners, foot races, horse races, log rolling, and other contests. Dating back to the 1880s, celebrations and parades were grand events for Coquille. The first recorded parade was noted in the August 10, 1886, issue of the *Coquille Herald*, in which Roseburg's Yankee Doddle Band led a parade, marching with military exactness, on the principle streets of the community. Parades would grow to include numerous floats from various civic groups. (Both, CVM.)

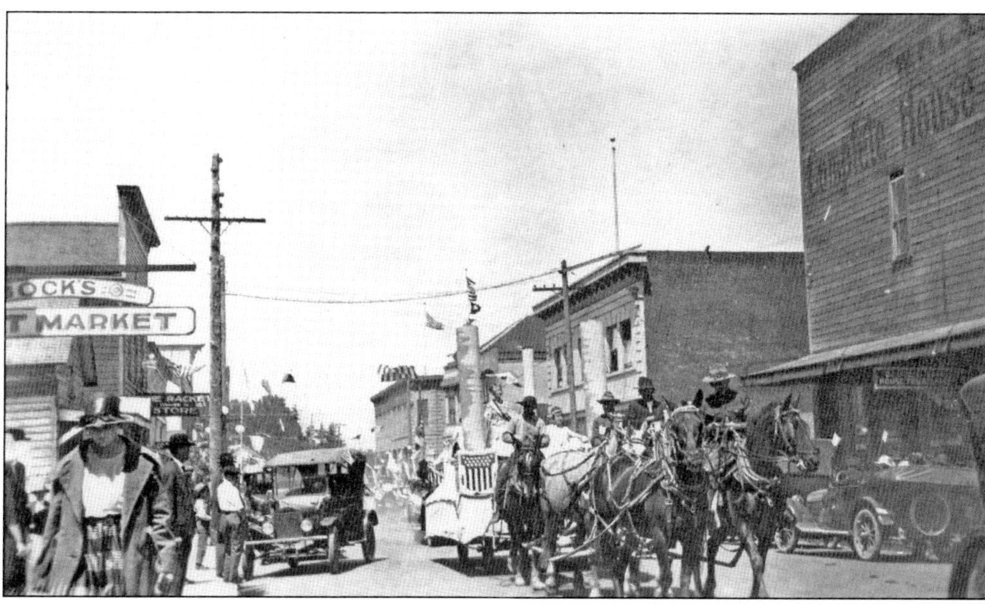